The Death of Hitler

THE DEATH OF HITLER

The Final Word

JEAN-CHRISTOPHE BRISARD
AND LANA PARSHINA

Translated by
SHAUN WHITESIDE

DA CAPO PRESS

Da Capo Press
Hachette Book Group
1290 Avenue of the Americas, New York, NY 10104
dacapopress.com
@DaCapoPress, @DaCapoPR

Printed in the United States of America

Originally published as La Mort d'Hitler in 2018 by Fayard, France

First U.S. Edition: September 2018

Published by Da Capo Press, an imprint of Perseus Books, LLC, a subsidiary of Hachette
Book Group, Inc. The Da Capo Press name and logo is a trademark of the Hachette Book
Group.

The Hachette Speakers Bureau provides a wide range of authors for speaking events. To find
out more, go to www.hachettespeakersbureau.com or call (866) 376-6591.

The publisher is not responsible for websites (or their content) that are not owned by the
publisher.

Library of Congress Cataloging-in-Publication Data has been applied for.

ISBNs: 978-0-306-92258-9 (hardcover); 978-0-306-92259-6 (ebook)

LSC-C

10 9 8 7 6 5 4 3 2 1

CONTENTS

PART I

THE INVESTIGATION (I)

MOSCOW, 6 APRIL 2016

Lana is perplexed.

Her contacts within the senior Russian administration have made no bones about how hard it is going to be for us to achieve our objective. Our meeting for 11:00 has been confirmed, but in Russia that doesn't necessarily mean anything. Our faces are stung by frost as we approach the area around the "State Archives of the Russian Federation." In Russia they're called GARF (Gosudartstennyy Arkhiv Rossyskov Federatsii). A national institution right in the heart of Moscow. It is based around one of the biggest archive collections in the country, with almost 7 million documents from the nineteenth century to the present day. Chiefly paper documents, but also some photographs and secret files. And it's for one of those secret files that we are braving the harsh Muscovite climate as well as the no less rough Russian bureaucracy. Lana Parshina isn't entirely unknown in Russia. A journalist and documentary maker, this young Russian-American woman is regularly invited onto television platforms to talk about what remains her major achievement: the last interview with Lana Peters. Lana Peters was a penniless old woman, forgotten by everyone in a hospice for the poor in the depths of the United States. She hid herself away and refused to talk to journalists. Let alone discuss the memory of her father, one Josef Vissarionovich Djugashvili, otherwise known as Stalin. Lana Peters' name was in fact Svetlana Stalin, and she was the dictator's favourite daughter. At the height of the Cold War in the 1960s, she had fled the country and applied to the US for political asylum. From that moment she became the symbol of those Soviets who were prepared to do anything to escape a tyrannical regime. Lana Parshina had managed to persuade the dictator's shy descendant to grant her a series of filmed interviews. That was in 2008. It was a success that attracted attention all over Russia. Stalin has in fact been coming back into fashion in Moscow for a number of years. Lana Parshina knows the complex gear-wheels of the administrative and bureaucratic Russian machine only too well. She knows how to get access to secret, sensitive, and complex files.

And yet on that morning in April 2016, I sense that she's worried. We have a meeting with the director of GARF, Larisa Alexandrovna Rogovaya. She alone can authorise us to consult File H. "H" for Hitler.

The tone is set as soon as we enter the main hall of GARF. A soldier with a very 1970s moustache, a bit like Freddie Mercury's, demands to see our passports. "Check!" he bellows, as if we were intruders. Lana, with her Russian ID, isn't a problem. My French passport complicates matters. The soldier doesn't seem at ease with the Latin alphabet, and can't decipher my name. In Cyrillic characters, Brisard becomes БРИЗАР. That's how I'm listed in the file of people who have been granted access for the day. After a long check and Lana's life-saving assistance, we are finally allowed through. The office of the director general of the archives? The lowly official was horrified by the mere question. He was already tending to his next customer with the same cordial tone. "Right at the end, after the third building on the right." The young woman who answered our question didn't wait for our thanks before turning her back on us and climbing the dimly lit stairs. GARF looks like a Soviet workers' city. It spreads over several buildings with sinister façades in the most austere Soviet style, a mixture of constructivism and rationalism. We wander from one building to another, trying to avoid the big puddles of muddy snow. "General Director," large letters announce on a plaque above a double door in the distance. A black sedan bars the entrance. We have another twenty or so metres to go when a woman with an imposing build hurries from the building to dive into the vehicle.

"That's the director," Lana murmurs with a note of despair as she watches the car driving away.

It's 10:55, and our 11:00 meeting has just flown away from under our noses.

Welcome to Russia.

The two secretaries of the director of GARF have shared out the roles between them: one nice, the other frankly unpleasant.

"What's it about?"

Even if you don't understand a language, which is my case with Russian, it's easy to sense when someone's being rude to you. So the younger woman – if I wished to be rude I would say the less old of the two – is not our friend.

Lana introduces us, we are the two journalists, she is Russian and I'm French. We're here because we had a meeting with the director, and also to view a rather special object.

"You won't see her!" the hostile secretary cuts in. "She's left for the day. She isn't here." Lana explains that we know that already – the dark car outside, the director forgetting that we're there and evaporating right in front of us. She says all that without shedding an ounce of her enthusiasm. Might waiting be an option? "If it amuses you," the secretary says at last, leaving the room with a stack of files under her arm, to suggest the importance of the time of which we have dared to deprive her. A Swiss cuckoo clock hangs on the wall above her desk. It says 11:10. The other assistant has been listening to her colleague without a word. Her contrite expression hasn't escaped us. Lana walks over to her.

A meeting at the Kremlin, in the president's office. It wasn't in the director's diary. Clearly, when Putin or, more probably, his cabinet rings, you run, the secretary explains, lowering her voice, in short phrases. She seems so sweet and her voice is comforting, in spite of the rather negative nature of the information that she's giving us. And who knows when the director will be back? She doesn't, at any rate. Has she been summoned away at the last minute because of us? "No. Why would it be because of you?"

It's just after 5:00 pm. Our patience has paid off at last. Right in front of our eyes a stiff cardboard box has just been opened. Inside, there it is, very small, delicately preserved in a casket.

"So is that him? Is it really him?"

"Da!"

"Yes, she's saying yes."

"Thank you, Lana. And that's all that's left?"

"Da!"

"You don't need to translate, Lana."

Looking more closely, the casket is very like a box for computer disks. In fact that's exactly what it is. Hitler's skull is preserved in a disk box! To be precise, it's a piece of skull presented by the Russian authorities as being Hitler's. Stalin's trophy! One of the best-guarded secrets in the Soviet Union and then in post-Communist Russia. And for us, the end of a year of waiting and investigation.

You need to imagine the scene to understand the strange feeling that comes over us. A rectangular room big enough to hold about ten people. A table, rectangular too, in dark lacquered wood. On the wall, a series of drawings under glass, with red frames. "Original posters," we are told. They date from the Revolutionary era. The Revolution, the big one, the Russian one, the one organised by Lenin in October or November 1917, depending on whether you follow the Julian or the Gregorian calendar. They show proud workers with concave stomachs. Their powerful arms hold a scarlet banner up to the world. A capitalist, an oppressor of the people, crosses their path. How can you tell he is a capitalist? He is wearing a very smart suit and a top hat and has a big fat paunch. He exudes smugness, the smugness of the powerful in the face of the weak. In the last poster, the man with the hat has lost his pride. He is lying on the ground on his back, his head crushed by the worker's huge hammer.

That perennial symbol. However powerful you might be, you will end up crushed, your head smashed in by the resistance of the Russian people. Had Hitler seen these drawings?

Too bad if he had, because the Russians got him in the end. Or at least they got his skull.

But let us return to the description of the scene.

This little room, this conference room with its hints of revolution, is on the ground floor of GARF, just beside the secretaries' office where we waited patiently for the return of the director, Larisa Alexandrovna Rogovaya. That opulent woman in her fifties doesn't just impress her interlocutors with her imposing physical presence. Her sense of calm and her natural charisma distinguish her from the run of Moscow functionaries. Back from the Kremlin, she had passed through the secretaries' office. Without seeing us. Lana and I had taken our seats in the only two armchairs in the room. An enormous potted plant stood between them, and generously invaded the little space remaining to us. Even if you concentrated very hard, even if you were in a terrible hurry, it was impossible not to notice the presence of two human beings around the giant ficus. It was 4:00 pm at that point. We had leapt to our feet; hope was returning. The telephone had just rung. "In the next room? The conference room? In thirty minutes ..." The nice secretary repeated the orders given to her into the receiver. Lana leaned towards me with a smile. It was for us.

In silence, the director had sat down at the end of the big rectangular table. On either side of her, standing to attention, stood two clerks. On her right, a woman old enough to have laid claim to a well-deserved pension. On her left, a man with a sepulchral appearance straight out of a Bram Stoker novel. The woman's name was Dina Nikolaevna Nokhotovich, and she was in charge of the special collections. The man's name was Nikolai Igorevich Vladimirsev (he prefers Nikolai); he is head of the department of document preservation at GARF.

Nikolai had set a large cardboard box gently in front of the director. Dina helped him lift the lid. Then they stepped back, hands behind their backs, and focused their eyes on us. An attitude intended as a warning by these two sentries, who were ready to intervene if necessary. Larisa, still seated, put her hands on either side of the box as if to protect it, and invited us to look inside.

It was a moment we had stopped hoping would happen. That bit of skull had seemed inaccessible only that morning. After months and months of interminable negotiations, repeated demands formulated by email, by regular mail, by telephone, by fax (well yes, still often used in Russia), in person with stubborn officials, here we were at last looking at this human fragment. The remains of a cranial box, a good quarter of one, to the naked eye, from the back left part (two parietals and a bit of occipital, to be precise). The object of so much greed on the part of historians and journalists from across the world. Is it Hitler's, as the Russian authorities claim? Or does it belong to a woman in her forties, as an American scientist recently asserted? To ask that question within the GARF fortress is to talk politics, to cast doubts on the official word of the Kremlin. An option unimaginable to the director of the archives. Absolutely unimaginable.

Larisa Rogovaya has only been the director of GARF for a few days. She has replaced the former director, Sergei Mironenko. An oh-so political and sensitive position in this Putin-era Russia. In our presence, Larisa Rogovaya weighs each word. She is the only one who answers our questions, the two clerks don't get to say a word. Always concise, two or maybe three words, and that face, in a permanent state of tension. The senior official already seems to regret granting our request. To be precise, she hasn't granted anything at all. The order to let us study this bit of skull comes from someone higher up than her. How high exactly? Hard to guess. From the Kremlin? Most definitely. But who at the Kremlin? Lana is convinced that it all comes straight from the President's office. As in the days of the Soviet Union, the State Archives have once again become an effectively secret place. On 4 April 2016 Vladimir Putin signed a decree stipulating that the management, publication, and declassification of the archives, and access to them, fell directly within the remit of the President of the Russian Federation, meaning Putin himself.

The end of the period of open access to historical documents that began under Boris Yeltsin. Exit the charismatic director of

GARF, Sergei Mironenko, a friend to many foreign historians and advocate of almost free access to hundreds of thousands of historical pieces in his institution. "Fewer commentaries, more documents. The documents must speak for themselves," was the refrain he liked to give by way of reply to his colleagues, surprised by this open-door policy. It's over! Mironenko has gone. His twenty-four years of good and true service as director of GARF changed nothing. With a stroke of the pen, the Kremlin demoted him. He wasn't fired, he wasn't retired (at sixty-five he would have been due to retire anyway), he wasn't moved to a different service – he was demoted. Humiliation was added to disgrace because, of course, the new director is none other than his former subordinate, our dear Larisa Rogovaya. Stalin couldn't have done better.

Putin's decree dates from 4 April 2016. And we are standing in front of the box with that piece of skull on 6 April 2016. The thought that Larisa Rogovaya would give a lot to get rid of us doesn't take away the feeling of paranoia. Her whole body cries out her aversion towards us, her fear of ending up like Mironenko. Then, when we ask if we can take the diskette case from the cardboard box, the tension in the little room immediately goes up a notch. Larisa turns towards her two sentries. A brief confabulation ensues. Nikolai shakes his head disapprovingly. Dina picks up a piece of paper at the bottom of the cardboard box, adjusts her little glasses, which give her a sly look, and walks over to Lana.

At that very moment, the director waves to Nikolai to indicate that she hasn't changed her mind. He is still dubious, and hesitates for a moment. Then, reluctantly, he plunges his thin arms into the box and delicately takes out the diskette case. "You need to sign the visitor log. Put the date, the time and your names." Dina shows us where to fill in the form. Lana carefully does so. I let her get on with it and start inspecting the skull. Nikolai interposes himself. He places himself in front of me and, with an appalled "tsutsut" points out my mistake. "First fill in the visitor log," the director insists. Lana excuses my blunder. The blunder of a Frenchman, a foreigner. He doesn't understand, she tries to explain to them with a smile, embarrassed as if by a fractious child. Why so many precautions, why this tension? Mironenko passes in front of the open door of the little room. I recognise him from having seen him several times in reports when researching the Hitler file.

He's alone in the corridor. With a heavy, bowed body, he drags his carcass around without even so much as glancing at us. He clearly knows what we're doing. Before, he was the one who used to meet journalists. He knows the skull extremely well. It is 5:30 pm, he's already picked up his thick coat, his cap hides his grey hair, his day is over. Larisa's isn't. "Everything has to be done according to the rules. Times change. We must be careful," the director says as Mironenko leaves the building. "The central administration have given us the green light to show you the skull, but we need to give an account of what happened." We say we understand, that's quite normal, obviously, not a problem. Larisa wouldn't hear a word of complaint from us. This skull, or what is left of it, is becoming a source of discord, of controversy between Russia and … a large part of the rest of the world. Is it Hitler's? Is Russia lying? Larisa is waiting for us to ask the essential question, the one about the authenticity of the bones. She gives a two-word answer: "I know!" Dina and Nikolai, her deputies, know too. We don't know. "How can you be so sure?" The precise phrases, prepared in advance, mechanically repeated – Larisa recites them to us perfectly. The years of investigation, of analysis, of cross-checking carried out by the KGB and the Soviet scientists, the best there are …. This skull is him, it's Hitler. "At any rate, officially, it's him." For the first time, the director of GARF modulates her discourse. Her confidence cracks slightly. "Officially." It's not an anodyne term. It isn't scientifi-cally, but "officially" Hitler's skull.

Nikolai melts away as if by magic. The diskette case and the skull are all ours. Our faces approach the plastic lid. A big label, the brand of computer disk, obstructs our vision. Our contortions as we try to see it from the side change nothing. With a gesture of my hand I ask if we might lift the lid. The key, turn the key? My pantomime works. Nikolai returns, takes a small key from his pocket and frees the bolt.

Then he returns to his place just behind us. But he hasn't lifted the lid. So I repeat my gesture. This time I perform the motion of opening, of lifting. I do it twice, slowly. Larisa blinks, Nikolai has understood and, grumbling, opens the box. The skull is really in front of us at last.

Fragment of the top portion of a skull discovered outside the Führerbunker in Berlin in May 1946 stored at GARF in Moscow

So, this is Hitler. The fragment of bone stored in an ordinary diskette case from the 1990s. What irony for someone who wanted to crush part of Europe and enslave millions of human beings! Hitler, who dreaded ending up in a glass case in Moscow, exhibited by his Russian enemy as a vulgar trophy. He doesn't have the right to a display worthy of the importance that he has assumed in contemporary history: that of the absolute incarnation of Evil. The Russians put him away in a forgotten corner of their archives and, deliberately or not, they are treating him with as much respect as the remains of a dog. And if it's so hard to obtain the right to look at it, it isn't because the Russians fear that it might be damaged, or its preservation compromised, but for political reasons. No one must examine it any more and call into question its authenticity. The skull is Hitler's. No conditional tense. At least for the Russians.

To be frank, I feel a certain disappointment. Is this really the most secret item in the Russian archives: a sad little bit of bone stored in a diskette case? Remembering that this may be the last human remains of one of the biggest monsters the planet has ever known adds a feeling of disgust to the disappointment. But we must rally. Return to the investigation and remember why we are here: to lift the veil on Hitler's last hours. To do that, we have to ask the right questions. Where was this skull found? By whom? When? And most of all, how to prove that it really is Hitler's. We want all that. And to start, we have to analyse this skull. "Analyse?" Larisa says in astonishment as she catches the conversation in English between me and Lana. "Yes, tests ... DNA, for example. Bring in a specialist, a medical examiner ..." Lana translates our request in detail into Russian. Politely, the director listens to her without interrupting. "That way there would be no more doubt. None. No more questions about the identity of the skull. Hitler or not. Isn't that important?" And it would put an end to the crazy rumours about the last days of the Nazi tyrant. Hitler in Brazil, Hitler in Japan, at the South Pole ...

BERLIN, MAY 1945

A legendary monster or terrifying ghost, Hitler continues to haunt the imagination. After the fall of Berlin on 2 May 1945 two questions remained: Is he dead? Or has he escaped? According to the survivors of his bunker, he took his own life on 30 April 1945. Then he was burnt so that his corpse would not be found. It is precisely this absence of a body that would inevitably prompt a series of rumours to the effect that he might in fact have survived. On 8 May 1945 Leonid Leonov, an author hailed by the Soviet regime, published a passionate text in *Pravda*: "We demand material proof that this wily corporal has not turned into a werewolf. The little children of the world can sleep peacefully in their cradles. The Soviet armies, like their Western allies, want to see the Führer's corpse 'as large as life.'" The tone was set. While that ultimate "large as life" proof was still missing, Hitler's ghost would linger in people's minds. And an increasing number of people claimed to have seen him. Among the stories, some were based on tangible facts. One of them is like a spy film. It concerns the journey of the U-530 – U for *Unterseeboot*, the German for submarine. In spite of the fall of the Third Reich, this vessel refused to surrender to the Allies and reached the coast of Argentina on 10 July 1945. Perhaps with secret passengers on board.

At the command post of the U-530 was a very young officer, perhaps too young. His name was Otto Wermuth, and he was only twenty-four. This undistinguished Oberleutnant zur See (the equivalent of a British Sub-Lieutenant or an American Lieutenant Junior Grade) was swiftly promoted on 10 January 1945 to commander of this fighting submarine. In this last year of the war, the Kriegsmarine (the German navy) was suffering, like the rest of the armies of the Reich, from an all-too-obvious shortage of battle-hardened officers. Of course, Otto Wermuth wasn't a complete beginner, but he hadn't had time to put himself to the test. He was recruited to the Kriegsmarine with the outbreak of the war against Poland, France, and the United Kingdom, in September 1939. He was nineteen years old at the time, and a long way from the battling figure of the Aryan warrior celebrated by the German regime. Otto Wermuth looked more like an elegant student, with his long face and equally slender, almost skinny, physique. He was quickly appointed to the "U-Boot" division of the Nazi army. Once he had completed his training, he was sent on a mission, in September 1941, as a watch officer.

By the time he found himself in charge of the U-530, an up-to-date submarine with a very long range, in January 1945, Wermuth had never been a commander. The vessel under his command was quite daunting. It was over seventy-six metres long, and could hold a crew of up to fifty-six. With its torpedo and mine launchers, as well as its deck gun, it was a formidable weapon. But the young commander would not really have time to put it to the test.

Sent on a mission off the American coast in April 1945, the U-530 fired nine torpedoes on Allied ships just south of Long Island, near Hudson Bay. These attacks were a complete failure. None of the bombs hit their targets. Wermuth learned of the German capitulation and received the order from his staff to surrender. He refused and decided to flee to Argentina. At the time, that country was a military dictatorship. Even though, under pressure from the United States, the Argentinian rulers had declared war on Germany on 27 March 1945, they continued to feel a certain admiration for the Nazi model. On 10 July 1945, after a two-month voyage, the U-530 arrived 400 kilometres south of Buenos Aires, at the city of Mar del Plata. Wermuth was taken prisoner along with his vessel and its crew. The news spread very quickly. And with it, the suspicion of the presence of Adolf Hitler and his wife Eva Braun on board the submarine. As well as being drawn towards fascism, Argentina had a German community clustered together in Bavarian-style villages in Patagonia. Perfect ingredients for the scenario of Hitler taking refuge in South America.

As soon as he had disembarked, Wermuth was interrogated by both the Argentinian and US navies. The German officer was suspected of berthing in other small towns a few hours before his surrender on 10 July. Had he taken advantage of those stops to unload passengers or documents? On 14 July 1945, a memo was sent to Washington by the American naval attaché based in Buenos Aires. He reported the arrival of a submarine that had unloaded two unidentified passengers.

The Argentinian press also picked up the adventure of the U-530 and published article after article about Hitler still being alive. One of those reports, published in the magazine *Critica* on 18 July, claimed that the German dictator had found refuge at the South Pole, in an area where the temperature was bearable. The Argentinian Foreign Minister, César Ameghino, was obliged to intervene officially, to put a stop to these rumours. On the day of the publication of the article, he issued a formal denial. Hitler had not been set down on the Argentinian coast by a German submarine.

Still, the FBI investigated the South American trail. Not least because the American secret service had also received some surprising reports. In particular, one about Robert Dillon, a mediocre Hollywood actor. On 14 August 1945, he contacted the FBI to tell them he had met an Argentinian who had been involved in taking Hitler into his country. The story of the submarine again! Dillon went further in his details. The Führer had disembarked with two women, a doctor, and about fifty men. They had hidden in the hills of the Southern Andes. Hitler was suffering from asthma and ulcers. He had also shaved off his moustache. After being checked by the American special services, Dillon's "scoop" melted away.

Over the years, reports of this kind piled up on the desks of the FBI. They concern Hitler, but also the presence of other Nazis in Brazil, Chile, Bolivia and, of course, Argentina. Not all of these rumours were wildly far-fetched. There really were systems of escape routes for Nazi criminals. One of the best-known of these was the Odessa network. Over the years, it would allow officials from the Third Reich to escape from Europe. It is also true that Argentina offered asylum to numerous Nazi torturers. Among the most notorious of these, Josef Mengele (a doctor in the Auschwitz concentration camp, guilty of barbarous medical experiments on the inmates there), Adolf Eichmann (an active organiser of the "Final Solution'), and Klaus Barbie (head of the Gestapo in the French city of Lyon). But not a trace of Adolf Hitler.

Ten years after the Nazi capitulation, in July 1955, the German legal system decided to close the file on Hitler once and for all. The court in Berchtesgaden, the little town in Bavaria with 7,000 inhabitants, was appointed to lead the investigation. A purely symbolic choice: the German dictator had liked to withdraw to the town for some peace and quiet. He had built his personal residence there, the Berghof. So it was this provincial court that would rule on the Führer's legal status: dead or alive. The timing was no coincidence. It coincided with the return of Nazi prisoners held by the Soviets. These included key witnesses of the last hours in the Führerbunker, the air-raid shelter where the dictator ended his days. Close to Hitler, they had been captured by the Red Army and immediately imprisoned secretly in the Soviet Union. Their statements had never been made public or transmitted to the Western allies. And certainly not to the German courts. But in 1955 Moscow agreed to free the last Nazi war criminals who were still rotting away in its jails. A political gesture that would have a cost for West Germany; in exchange, the country committed itself to establishing diplomatic and economic relations with the USSR. As soon as they returned, the German courts interrogated these senior dignitaries of the Third Reich. Thanks to their testimonies, it was possible to conclude that Adolf Hitler and his wife, Eva Braun, had taken their own lives on 30 April 1945. On 25 October 1956, Hitler and his wife were officially declared dead by the court in Berchtesgaden. From that moment, the death of the master of the Third Reich could be officially written down and published in history books around the world. The FBI also called off its investigations. For a decade, the American secret services had been carrying out investigations all over the world. With a certain relief Washington accepted the evidence of Hitler's suicide in his bunker. But the essential factor was still missing: the body. At the time, there was still no physical proof of his death. Until the skull appeared.

Early 2000. The USSR had ceased to exist eight years previously, since its dissolution on 25 December 1991, to be precise. A new Russia tried to rebuild itself amid the ruins of a Communist regime that had been dying for years. Its status as a superpower had disappeared at the same time as the hammer and sickle on its flag. The liberal shock treatment applied by Boris Yeltsin turned the already precarious social and economic balance of the country into a train-ride to hell. In the eyes of the world, the red peril with its enormous nuclear arsenal had disappeared for good. The Russians felt humiliated. But in the year 2000, hope revived in the Kremlin. A new president had taken control of the reins. Admittedly he was young and a little bit shy, but he brought a welcome gravity and temperance to Russia after the Yeltsin years. His name was Vladimir Putin, and he was only forty-seven. This lieutenant colonel in the KGB had only one idea in mind: to restore his country's glory, and put it back at the centre of the global political chessboard. By way of introduction, he reminded the world that Russia was a great military power. And that it was Russia that had won the war against Hitler.

On 27 April 2000, the eve of the fifty-fifth anniversary of the victory over Nazi Germany, Moscow opened a major exhibition of its secret archives. Its title left no doubt about the Russian President's intentions: "Agony of the Third Reich – the Punishment." This was unheard-of. In all, a hundred and thirty-five previously unpublished documents were revealed to the public; documents that the historians of the Second World War had dreamed of consulting for half a century. Soviet secret service reports classified as "top secret," photographs, objects ... everything that lifted the veil on the last minutes of Hitler in his bunker. The diary of Martin Bormann, the Führer's secretary and confidant, was also on show: "Saturday 28 April: our Reich Chancellery is now nothing but a pile of ruins. The world is hanging on by a thread. [. . .] Sunday 29: fire storm over Berlin. Hitler and Eva Braun got married." Photographs of the Goebbels children, the correspondence of Nazi officials such as the architect of the regime and its arms minister, Albert Speer: "Hitler is decomposing before our eyes. He has turned into a bundle of nerves and completely ceased to control himself." But the key exhibit was elsewhere, in a special room. An article from Le Monde describes the scene: "In the middle of a room hung with red velvet, a charred fragment of skull, punctured by a bullet-hole, has pride of place in a glass case."*

The exhibition was an international success. The Western media flocked to see it. The Russian authorities had won their bet. Or almost. Doubts concerning the authenticity of the skull arose very quickly. The organisers were embarrassed by the questions of the press. These included the director of the State Archives, the famous Sergei Mironenko – the same Mironenko whose shadow we have spotted in the long corridors of GARF. In 2000, he wasn't yet hugging the walls, and still held his head high. He reigned over the Russian archives like a tsar. Journalists and historians wooed him with glasses of increasingly strong vodka in a bid to get into his good graces. And more importantly, to get closer to that bit of skull exhumed from the secret store-rooms. In the full glare of publicity, Western doubts put proud Mironenko in a delicate situation. How could he assert that this human fragment was really a part of Hitler? The director of the archives heard these remarks constantly. While he replied that there was no doubt about its authenticity, he felt that it wasn't enough. Even Alexei Litvin, one of the curators of the exhibition in 2000, had to acknowledge: "It's true that we haven't subjected it to a DNA analysis, but all statements conclude that this is Hitler."† Statements? Not

*Le Monde, 2 May 2000, Agathe Duparc.
†Libération, 2 May 2000, Hélène Despic-Popovic.

indisputable scientific analyses? It was at that moment that Mironenko became aware of the risk of losing control of the situation and seeing a revival of the controversy over Hitler's death.

Rather than taking a step back, he went into action and dared to go a step further. A new forensic analysis? Carried out by foreign scientists? No problem! The director of the archives was quite proud of himself. Except that he couldn't close the Pandora's box that he had just opened.

Of course the Russian authorities wouldn't grant authorisation for those analyses. However, Mironenko's offer got people's hopes up and, with or without authorisation, became one of the last mysteries of the Second World War.

★　　★　　★

Larisa Rogovaya had been Mironenko's deputy. Today, the new director of GARF is using the same methods as her illustrious predecessor. Never confronting journalists head on. Around the big rectangular table there are four of us, standing up, looking at the skull. Lana, the two archivists Dina and Nikolai, and me, my eyes fixed on this brownish bone. Apart from Larisa, who is still sitting in her black leather armchair. She seems to be amused at the sight of us, impressed and keen to take things further. She expected that we would want to subject it to forensic analysis. Like Mironenko sixteen years earlier, she too confirms that analyses of the skull are entirely feasible. She even adds that she has dreamed of such analyses. "It would be a lovely opportunity for us," she claims, giving us her first smile since we arrived. "Yes, that would be perfect. We will support you in this project, you can count on us." Dina and Nikolai cry in chorus. "That would give us a chance to establish the truth. And to put an end to this disastrous controversy. The one sparked a few years ago by that so-called American researcher."

Larisa grimaces suddenly as she struggles to conceal her profound revulsion. Her two colleagues freeze as if someone has poured a bucket of icy water over their heads. They try very hard to put on a bold front. Why this unease? Is the director of GARF alluding to the work carried out by a team of American investigators in 2009? The case caused a considerable stir at the time. Nick Bellantoni, an archaeology professor at Connecticut University, claimed to have taken a sample of the skull. That bone sample had then been analysed in his university's genetics laboratory. And the result was broadcast in a television documentary on the History Channel. "The bone seemed to be very thin," the American archaeologist says. "Male bone tends to be more robust, and the sutures where the skull plates come together seem to correspond to someone under forty." Bellantoni was undermining the story put forward by the Russian authorities. Basing his analysis on a DNA test, he also claimed that the skull preserved in Moscow was that of a woman. Nothing to do with Hitler. Doubts resurfaced. The theories of the Führer's plot and escape gained currency with the American revelations.

Bellantoni's scoop was immediately repeated in the world's press. The information was summed up as follows: for years, the Russians have been lying! For Moscow, the insult was both painful and humiliating. Even today it's a bitter pill to swallow. All the more so in that the director of GARF claims never to have seen that American archaeologist within her walls. Or have authorised the taking of a sample.

Dina picks up the visitors' log that Lana has filled in. There are several names in the columns above our own. Only a very few visitors have had the privilege of seeing the skull. No more than ten in over twenty years. "All the teams of journalists and researchers who have seen this skull have signed this document. Look, that American's name doesn't appear there. He never came here." Curiously, his visit to GARF has never been recorded in the registers. Unlike our visit. Nick Bellantoni doesn't deny this administrative oddity. When we asked him the question by email, he replied simply that "all procedures for my work in the Russian archives were managed by the producers of the History Channel. So it is no surprise that my name does not appear on this list. It must have been recorded under the name of the History Channel or the producers." An argument refuted by the director of the Archives. To be clear, she wrote us an official letter: "I wish to inform you that GARF did not sign any agreements with any television channel, Mr. Bellantoni or anyone else to carry out a DNA examination based on the fragment of Hitler's skull."

Might the American archaeologist have acted without permission? The Russian media were categorical. The case became a national scandal. The scholar from Connecticut found himself at the heart of an almost ideological controversy: West vs East, the capitalist bloc against the former Communist bloc. On the Russian national television channel NTV (close to Russian power), in 2010, a whole programme was devoted to Bellantoni's "scoop." In the presence of Russian Second World War historians and other popular personalities old enough to remember the war, the American tried to reassure everyone. Above all, he was keen not to come across as a looter of archives. First, he assured everyone that his work had been completely legal. "We received official authorisation from the Russian Archives, with whom we signed a contract to carry out our work." A claim refuted by GARF, as we have already seen.

But let us return to the thread of the interview with Nick Bellantoni on NTV. The presenter quizzes him about the analyses that he has carried out on the skull:

Bellantoni: "No. We didn't do that! [...] You know, there are a lot of difficulties involved in working on burnt remains. For geneticists, exploring this subject is a real nightmare. It's extremely difficult to extract markers from this matter that capture the sex of the subject. But we can conclude that the skull in your collection belonged to a woman. Perhaps it was Eva Braun, but we can't be sure."

On the stage of the programme, among the guests, an elderly lady comes forward. Her name is Rimma Markova. This actress, famous for acting in Soviet films, embodies the nostalgia for the Stalinist regimes. Even though she is eighty-five, she is still furious: "How did he manage to take those samples? He is telling the world that he's a thief! He needs to go to prison for what he did."

Bellantoni: "I'm just a scientist who was invited to examine this skull."

Rimma Markova: "Tell us who gave you those samples. The Archive staff or the representatives of your television channel?"

It's always the same line of questioning. Bellantoni is cornered. Is he going to crack on live TV?

Bellantoni: "We've been authorised to examine and take samples. It's part of the contract. I must stress once again that I'm working on this project as a scientist. If you want more details, ask the people in charge of the channel."

Seven years have passed since then. We also asked Nick Bellantoni to explain to us how he had managed to get hold of those fragments of skull. He replied very promptly: "Our team was authorised to take some small pieces of burnt bone that had become detached from the skull. We didn't damage or take samples from the skull itself [. . .] I didn't take those pieces to the United States. They were sent to us by the producers when we came back to the university to carry out the analyses. I imagine that these pieces were given to us by officials. You can check that with the History Channel."

And that's what we did.

Joanna Forscher produced Nick Bellantoni's documentary on Hitler's skull. Her reply to our questions has the merit of concision: "I have often been asked that question, and unfortunately I cannot reveal any details about how we had this access to the skull." And she concludes with a mysterious remark: "The circumstances of our access can no longer be reproduced in any way."

Seven years after the visit by Bellantoni and the History Channel team, the mystery remains unsolved. And GARF is still deeply traumatised.

Larisa grits her teeth. Her fury isn't directed at us. She narrows her eyes at Dina and Nikolai. Has some corruption taken place? Has money been passed to an archivist to leave the American researcher alone with "Stalin's trophy" for a few moments. "We don't know what happened," the director says, rising to her feet. "We know that this was all illegal, and we deny the results of these analyses."

Our meeting is about to be cut short. We have to find a way of extending it, to give us time to convince the director of our good intentions. We too want to do tests on the skull. Who can grant us that authorisation? Lana asks the essential question, the only one worth asking, just as Larisa is leaving the room. No answer. Undaunted, she follows the director into the corridor, refusing to let go. They are now in the secretaries' office – only a few more metres and Larisa will have reached her office. Russian protocol will prevent us from going in uninvited. "What must we do?" Lana asks as politely as possible. "Is it just you? The President's office ...?" Appalled, Larisa turns round. "Certainly not me," she begins. Then continues, "Sort it out with the Bureau of Investigation! This is nothing more or less than a criminal investigation, into a corpse, part of a corpse. It is the Department of Justice that can reopen this inquiry." The grey of the walls around us has never seemed as depressing to me as it does now. The trap is closing in. Russian bureaucracy, that hideous child born of seventy years of Soviet control, is waiting to crush us. "I know, it can take months, but I'm going to support your request." Larisa senses how overwhelmed we are. She seems almost sorry. "Don't worry," she says to us at last. "*Spasiba, spasiba,*" Lana thanks her, and gestures to me to do the same. Once again the director's face relaxes. "So who would come to carry out these analyses? Find someone scientifically irreproach-able, and not an American. Anyone but an American."

MOSCOW, OCTOBER 2016

The war in Syria, the conflict in Ukraine with the annexation of Crimea, possible interference in the American elections … So many crises are linked to Russia, so many reasons why the Putin regime turns in on itself to complicate our investigation in the National Archives.

"It is an inopportune moment," we are told by the different services of the sprawling Russian administration. Next month conditions will be better, after the holidays, the summer holidays, then All Saints … Six months have passed like that. Three more stays in the city of Ivan the Terrible, three return trips between Paris and Moscow, and for what? For nothing? Larisa Rogovaya is still director of GARF, but she's stopped answering us. Her secretaries have skilfully erected a barrier between her and us. My colleague Lana grew up in this country at a time when it was still called the Soviet Union. She understands the reaction of the Russian authorities. "In the eyes of my compatriots, the West wants to hurt us, it rejects us," she explains. "Our investigation into Hitler is far from anodyne. The story of the skull is a powerful symbol in Russia; it is the symbol of our suffering during the Second World War, of our resistance and our victory. Since this skull was displayed to the public, its authenticity has frequently been called into question. Part of the glorious past of the Soviet Union is being stolen in this way." When one of these challenges comes from an American supported by an American university within the context of a television documentary … for the Russians, the fact that the channel is American cannot be a coincidence. It must be an attempt at destabilisation on the part of the former American ally. For the American documentary team, they have no intention of destabilising the

Russians. So, over seventy years after May 1945, Washington and Moscow are still disputing the paternity of the final victory over Hitler. And that makes any investigation into the Hitler file so sensitive in Russia. Above all, so complicated. "The human factor." But Lana won't let go. She repeats those words out loud like a protecting mantra, a Cabalistic formula. "In my country," she insists, "you mustn't act rationally, you must be guided by your instinct and stake everything on the shortcomings of our interlocutors."

So, the human factor. Since our many official requests have got us nowhere, we're going to bet everything on luck. Kholzunova Avenue, a smart part of town nestling in a loop of the Moskova, the base of GARF, the State Archives of the Russian Federation. By visiting at regular intervals, we have become intimately acquainted with the weekly guard roster. Tuesday is our favourite. On that day, the checks at reception are carried out by a pleasant soldier. Nothing like the severe and rather limited man with the moustache on Monday, or the big-nosed simpleton on Friday. Petite and always cheerful behind her counter, the guard on Tuesdays always activates the turnstile and lets us through without a problem. On this damp Tuesday in autumn, she doesn't change her good habits. She suspects the reason for our visit. "It's still Hitler, isn't it?" Who doesn't know about that within GARF? "Which service are you visiting today?" she asks, checking our names in her register. "Ah, Dina, you're going to see Dina Nikolaevna Nokhotovich? I expect you know where to find her ... Straight on, last building at the end of the courtyard ..." Lana finishes the phrase for her: "... middle door, fourth floor, first left." She's trying to sound relaxed. But she isn't, and neither am I. We're staking a lot on this visit. Dina Nokhotovich was there when we studied the skull six months ago with the director of GARF. She had witnessed the scene with one of her colleagues, pale Nikolai. Dina is ageless. Time has ceased its assault on this tiny, energetic woman. Do the gloomy halls of the Russian State Archives conceal some sort of magical power, a bubble in time? Why not. The mere fact of walking all the way up to her office makes us feel as if we are plunging into some bygone era, the past of the totalitarian Soviet utopia. Each step we take sends us ten years backwards. As we climb, the dilapidated state both of the steps and of the walls becomes increasingly apparent. Once we reach the fourth-floor landing, we have gone back forty years. Here we are in the middle of the 1970s. The Brezhnev era. The one in which the head of GARF's special collection, Dina Nokhotovich, still lives and will live forever. The idea of a face-to-face meeting with this eminent functionary of GARF didn't immediately occur to us. Our first encounter last April lacked a certain warmth. Discreet, if not entirely silent, passive and then almost hostile in her treatment of us, Dina at first displayed no major interest in our investigation. At least that was how it seemed to us. Her secret had not yet been revealed to us. That only happened very recently, the day after our meeting in late October. We were consulting archived documents at GARF once again. The young archivist was surprised to see us so often. Although she was very shy, she finally plucked up the courage to ask why we were there. Hitler's skull, his death, the investigation … And the hope of an analysis of the human remains. "The bones? But Dina's the one who found them." The skull? Our reaction was so immediate that we startled the young archivist. We didn't care. We absolutely had to know more. So Dina had found the skull. But how? When? Where?

"You'll have to ask her," our informant said, still on the defensive. "Here she is now, you can ask her directly." The head of the special collection, our new friend Dina, was about to finish a day that had started so early that she was exhausted already. While the elderly archivist closed a thick armoured door – one of the many doors leading to the shelves of the archives – Lana put into practice her theory of the "human factor." A failure. Dina resisted. What did we want from her now? She didn't have time. She didn't want to. Lana lost her footing; she couldn't find the slightest angle, the slightest foothold to cling to. What about vanity? That might work. "Isn't it strange that you're never mentioned in all those articles about Hitler's skull?" I asked Lana to translate word for word. She was acquitting herself to perfection. I continued without letting Dina reply: "We've just been told that the skull was rediscovered thanks to you! Your discovery is historical, ground-breaking. The public needs to know." "Da, da." Dina replied with several "da's." She was coming round. The corridor in which we were talking was tiny and narrow. It connected three doors and a lift. The opposite of the ideal place to receive a confession. "A tea; would you like to come and join us for tea, in a tea room or a restaurant? It would be quieter and easier to talk." A rookie's tactlessness, a misunderstanding of Russian culture, Lana would tell me later, explaining my mistake. A man can't invite a woman for a drink, even if she's as old as his grandmother. A meeting in her office, yes, that was possible. Tomorrow? "Why not, tomorrow. If you like. But I don't think it will be terribly interesting," Dina simpered like a schoolgirl.

If the level of seniority of a state employee must be judged by the size of her office, then Dina could lay claim to the post of "toilet lady." It was far from that of the head of the special collection of the big State Archives of the Russian Federation. What mistake could this woman have committed, to find herself in such a small and uncomfortable room? Low-ceilinged, with a window so narrow that a child would have had trouble getting its head through it, her office was so small that if more than three people had been in there they would hardly have been able to breathe. It was accessed directly by the stairs, which, on the other floors, normally lead to the toilets. Hence "toilet lady." A thick silvery mane about ten centimetres long rocks back and forth above a formica table in front of us. Dina is sitting working in semi-darkness. Our arrival doesn't disturb her activity. Her baroque hairdo resists the laws of gravity and remains powerfully attached to her skull. No stray strand comes away from the capillary mass. Is it a wig? Without even looking up, Dina addresses Lana. She reminds her how precious her time is. In return we assure her that we are perfectly aware of that, and we apologise for interrupting her very important work ... Lana is never one to hold back. Dina listens to her not without displeasure [is this what is meant?] and then decides to look at us. "I'd forgotten about our meeting. As I told you yesterday, I don't know if I can help you, and I still have lots of documents to file." The transformation is striking. Moving. Dina is dressed up as if for a dance. Colour on her cheeks and on her lips. Pink, unless it's mauve; at any rate, it's very much apparent. No, Dina hasn't forgotten about us. She was waiting for us. For the first time in ages, Lana and I relax. The conversation should go well.

The Viet Cong had won after two decades of war. In that year, 1975, the Communist doctrine triumphed and spread over all the continents. The Soviet Union carried more weight in the world than ever before, and treated the United States as an equal. In Moscow, food shortages had been a thing of the past for a long time, and political purges had become less frequent. The future for the Soviets seemed radiant at last. Leonid Brezhnev had been in charge of the country for eleven years. He had the jowly face of an *apparatchik*; not brilliant, perhaps, but less terrifying than Stalin. It was in this almost peaceful Soviet Union that Dina Nikolaevna Nokhotovich, at the age of thirty-five, saw her life collapsing from one day to the next. GARF has ceased to exist. The whole of the state administration (a perfect pleonasm, since in the Soviet Union the private sector didn't exist) was identified in Soviet-compatible terms. The administration for which Dina worked didn't escape this process, and was soberly entitled "Central State Archives of the October Revolution and the Edification of Socialism." That was forty-one years ago. In a different era, in a different country, under a different regime.

Dina can't help pursing her lips between each of her phrases. Her eyes are staring at an imaginary point that removes her from the present moment, from her tiny office at GARF and this neo-capitalist twenty-first-century Moscow. For a long time she says nothing. Then her story begins. "I had just been put in charge of the 'secret' department of the archives. That was in 1975. The post was like no other, because it dealt with the confidential documents of the history of our country, the Soviet Union. At that time, the state worked perfectly, and we weren't short of qualified staff. Custom decreed that my predecessor came to give me the basic information, the information that was supposed to allow me to accomplish my mission as well as possible. Strangely, that never happened." The former head of the secret department had simply disappeared. Gone, flown away, not a trace. As if he had never existed. And today, Dina can't remember his name. What happened to him? A sudden transfer to another administration? An accident? A serious illness? Dina never knew and never asked. A Stalinist habit – some people might call it the survival instinct – reigned in this people's "paradise." In the Soviet Union, those who disappeared could hope for no help from those who stayed behind. Their memory was erased from the collective memory. In the mid-1970s, Dina didn't feel like playing at being the heroine; her predecessor was nowhere to be found. Too bad. She would get by without him.

"I was impatient to discover what kinds of documents I was responsible for. I remember, when I went into my new office, I found several safes. Security gave me the keys and I was able to open them." Even today, these huge safes, tall as sideboards, wide as fridges, stand in most of the rooms in GARF. What do they hide? All of our questions went unanswered. Perhaps they're just empty. They would be too heavy to move. In 1975, Dina's safes were really used. "There were documents inside, but also objects. The most surprising thing is that none of those objects had been inventoried. No code, no register, no classification. They quite simply didn't exist." A lot of people, in those days, would simply have put everything back in the safe and been particularly careful to forget their existence. Not Dina. "I was curious to know, I wasn't afraid. Why would I have been afraid? I wasn't doing anything forbidden. I asked a colleague to join me, and we both started going through this treasure trove. There were objects wrapped in cloth. Some were bigger than others. When I opened the smallest one, I'd have to say that we were quite frightened. It was a piece of human skull."

The story is interrupted by a strange metallic click. The sound comes closer to Dina's office. It's Nikolai. He comes in, pushing a supermarket trolley. The same pale Nikolai Vladimirsev who had been so horrified about the manhandling of the skull. Now we just need the director of GARF and we'd have the full team. Dina isn't surprised. She gets up and asks us to follow her. The rest of the conversation will take place in the room where we were able to study the skull six months before, on the ground floor of the building. Without taking the trouble to reply to our greetings, or even to apologise for interrupting our discussion, Nikolai follows us with his ridiculous little trolley. The clatter of the wheels on the tiles echoes down the sleepy corridors like some infernal machine. Reaching the room with the rectangular table, Dina takes a seat and asks us to do the same. Nikolai parks his trolley in a corner and takes out some battered files and a thick cotton sheet. The scene is played out in silence. Dina guides her colleague with a wave of the hand and shows him where to set it all down. Files at the end of the table, the worn sheet just in front of us. "There … Everything that I've found is here." Just as Dina says this, her colleague unfolds the sheet with a wide and graceful gesture to reveal … some table legs. "Step forward. You're allowed to do that." Nikolai has regained the gift of speech, and seems almost chatty. "Here's the other proof of Adolf Hitler's certain death: traces of blood on the legs of his sofa."

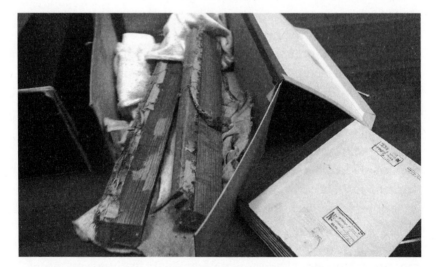

Parts of the sofa taken from the Führerbunker in Berlin in May 1946 (GARF)

Does Larisa Rogovaya, the director of GARF, know that we're in here with these historical pieces of forensic evidence? Has she organised this little show? It would be amazing if not. Nothing can be decided without her agreement. Certainly not after the dubious episode with the American archaeologist. I don't let Lana get in her phrase about the "human factor" again, and pick up the thread of our questions with our new best friends, Dina and Nikolai. "Apart from the skull, there were these bits of wood," she confirms. "At first, when we took the boxes out of the safe, we had no idea what they could be. When we did some searching, we found a piece of paper. It said: 'This is a piece of Adolf Hitler's skull. It must be transferred to the State Archives.' Without intending to, we had shed light on one of the biggest mysteries since 1945."

The cult of secrecy, the endless care with which information was hidden away, and punishments for neglecting to obey these two rules: Dina's professional life, over a long time, is simply summarised here. Of course the archivist wasn't part of the KGB, but she still had to behave like a spy. Not out of pleasure, but out of obligation. The staff of the Soviet State Archives, depending on their seniority and level of accreditation, were all subject to the same paranoid surveillance by the authorities. Quite simply because they had access to the heart of the matrix of the regime: its deepest, darkest secrets. The Katyn massacre, those thousands of Polish officers executed in a Russian forest on Stalin's orders during the Second World War, the little arrangements made with the leader of nationalist China, the right-winger Chiang Kai-shek, against Mao the Communist, or internecine battles within the Red Army. Whoever controls the archives can rewrite official history and, with a click of the fingers, destroy the legends that have shaped it. Why should we be surprised that, unlike many states, Russia continues to keep its past locked away? Today, the conditions for consulting the archives remain basic: on the one hand there are open documents, and on the other those that might damage the higher interests of the state. The latter fall under the category "sensitive," and can only be consulted with express authorisation from the very highest levels of the regime. Which is to say, hardly ever. The problem with Russian documents is that they can all fall under the heading of "sensitive."

Dina, with her simple post as an archivist, had to accept the life of a pariah without even the frisson of adventure. At least until the fall of the regime, late in 1991. "The USSR was a different time, with different rules," she acknowledges with a pout. Is it a pout of disapproval or nostalgia? "In 1975 life wasn't the way it is today. I'm talking about mentalities, material comforts, everything … We had instructions that had to be respected. And so many things were related to 'defence secrets' …" One of the most important of those instructions was to be suspicious of everyone. Of your colleagues, your neighbours, your own family. And to report the smallest subversive action to your superiors. Finding Hitler's skull hidden in a box at the back of a safe in the archives – was that subversive? Potentially yes.

After its discovery, there was no going back for Dina. She had to report it to her superiors. Very quickly, it appeared that nobody in her service had ever heard of this human fragment. "I think only my predecessor knew it was there. But since he had disappeared, I never got to the bottom of this affair." Is that all? Dina finds Hitler's skull and the story stops there? Wasn't she rewarded? A promotion, a bigger apartment in a part of the city for deserving citizens? "None of any of that. The director of the archives asked me never to talk about it. You can't understand, you're both too young. You, Lana – you're Russian, aren't you? You've known the Soviet system?" Lana has forgotten nothing. She often speaks emotionally about the USSR, the way one remembers distant childhood memories. Brezhnev had got fat and old and he was still in charge of the country when Lana was born. That was in 1978. Only a few years after Dina's adventure. "The atmosphere was very special at that time," the old archivist continued. "Very special. Any information like the business about the skull could end the life of someone who couldn't hold their tongue. Hitler and his bones were still classified as 'top secret.' For all those years, I never broke my vow of silence."

Nikolai has set down a photo album in front of us. He probably knows the ins and outs of his colleague's history so much by heart that he doesn't need to pay attention to it. The album contains a series of black-and-white photographs neatly glued in and surrounded by a frame drawn in black ink. Each of the photographs has a caption, long or short, handwritten with great care.

Photos of the New Reich Chancellery and entrance of the bunker taken in May 1946 (GARF)

Lana translates them for me. "Entrance of the New Reich Chancellery ... Gardens of the Chancellery ... Entrance of the bunker ..." We are holding in our hands the photographic record of the investigation into the death of Hitler. It's dated May 1946. It contains everything, the external views of the bunker, the inside too, and particularly the scene of the crime, or at least the suicide. But no body. The sofa on which Hitler was supposed to have died was photographed from every angle. Front, side, underneath – nothing is omitted. The back rests in particular held the attention of the investigators. And rightly, since the dark drips appear clearly on the right-hand side of the sofa. On the following page, there are more photographs of the back rests, but this time they have been removed from the rest of the sofa. The precise caption: "Pieces of the sofa with traces of blood. These pieces have been removed to be used as evidence." Their shapes and sizes correspond feature for feature with the pieces of wood that Nikolai has brought us. "They're the same," Dina confirms. "The Soviet secret services removed them from the sofa to bring them to Moscow. They hoped to analyse these traces of blood and check that they were Hitler's." Nikolai picks up one of these pieces of wood and shows us the section of the back rest from which the Soviet scientists took their samples in May 1946. Obviously the archivist doesn't wear sterile gloves. Does he know that he might be destroying any potential traces of DNA? He doesn't understand when we point this out. What was the result of the samples taken in 1946? "It was blood type A," Dina goes on. A very widespread blood group in the German population (almost 40 per cent), and more importantly one which, according to Nazi doctrine, proved membership of the "Aryan race." Of course, it was Hitler's blood group. The last few pages of the album linger on the skull. The one believed to be Hitler's, the one we had been able to see for a few moments in that very room. In one of the photographs, an arrow drawn in red points to a hole in the skull.

The Soviet secret services suggest that it looks like the entry wound of a projectile. If the skull is indeed that of the Nazi dictator, it means that he received a bullet directly to the head. A sacriligious hypothesis in 1975. And very dangerous for Dina. Until the fall of the Soviet Union, Moscow wouldn't let go. Hitler killed himself with poison, the weapon of cowards in the eyes of the Soviet rulers. This version, validated by Josef Stalin, failed to stand up if the skull with the bullet wound was made public.

Dina would have to live with that secret for decades. She wouldn't be able to travel abroad, she would be under the surveillance of the authorities and wouldn't be able to change jobs. As a result she spent forty years in the same service, wasting away amid dusty documents that no one could consult. "Our department was called

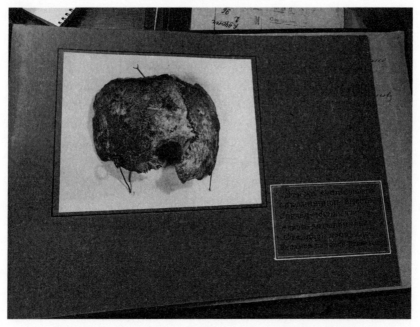

Photo of the skull believed to be Hitler's in a photo album at GARF.

the 'Department of the Secret Collection,'" she goes on. "The only things kept here were confidential files. And there was no question of declassifying anything. None of the staff of this department were able to talk about anything they did. Even among ourselves, we didn't talk about the documents of which we were in charge. There was no communication between one floor and another."

The dashing septuagenarian pursues her mission just as diligently as always. Dina no longer really understands the new rules of her country. Declassified, reclassified – which documents are accessible? She's a bit lost. "The last time I was able to speak openly about that skull was in the early 1990s. My superiors suddenly opened up all our doors to researchers. There were historians, and then, very quickly, journalists turned up. A lot of journalists. And that's where everything got complicated." An article published in the Russian daily *Izvestia* on 19 February 1993 marked the start of a crisis. "I'm holding in my hands the remains of Hitler's skull," the journalist

Ella Maximova wrote. "They are preserved amidst conditions of the greatest secrecy in a cardboard box labelled 'blue ink for fountain pen,' along with some blood-stained fragments of a sofa that was in the bunker." She was the first to reveal the scoop. The news was immediately picked up all over the world. For many years, there were rumours claiming that the KGB had not destroyed the Führer's body, but had kept it hidden somewhere in Moscow.

And then a national newspaper confirmed that the legend was partly true. But wasn't the skull a fake? Mightn't it be one of those manipulations of which the Russians were so fond? Western historians immediately declared their fury. They stated categorically that all of this was impossible. Hitler's skull? What nonsense. Meanwhile the foreign press got very excited. They wanted to see. In this Russia recently freed from its Communist trappings, money dictated the rules. Anything could be bought, anything could be sold, everything had a price. Including Hitler's skull? Some people said yes. Tension mounted when the correspondent of the German magazine *Der Spiegel* said he had been offered access to the bones and five interrogation files from eyewitnesses of the last days of Hitler for a large sum of money. And not in roubles. The Russians had been too greedy, and *Der Spiegel* preferred to withdraw from the auction. "We wouldn't have given half of what they were demanding,"* the magazine's Moscow correspondent explained at the time.

"Those articles harmed us a lot," Dina says. "The journalists ... saying that we didn't want to show the skull, that we were asking for money, that's all false. It was in order to prove it that our authorities decided to organise a big exhibition about the end of the war and display Hitler's final remains." With the success that we know about. New scandals about the identification of the skull, and then the decision by the Russian authorities to put the object back in its safe and not let the journalists get anywhere near it. "Of course everyone wants to know if it is really Hitler." Nikolai can't conceal the faintly irritated expression that never leaves his

*The *Independent*, 20 February 1993, Helen Womack.

face. "You want to study the skull, analyse it, why not? I know it's his. I know how Hitler killed himself. I've read all the dossiers from the investigation. From 1945, when the inquiry began, it's all there. But if you want to start again, go ahead." Is that the answer, at last, to all our questions? Is this strange archivist conveying his director's decision to us? "Can we carry out tests on the skull? Is that it?" Dina and Nikolai look at one another. They are both reluctant to speak. "Our task is to keep the archives in the best possible condition so that future generations can consult them. We don't have to carry out scientific experiments." Nikolai doesn't give a clear answer. Lana points this out as politely as possible. He replies in the same monotonous, reedy voice. "None of these questions concerns us." A smile. Hold that smile, even if it's starting to look a little tense. Given her age and her long history in this post, it's Dina we should be concentrating on if we want to get that important reply. "I imagine that's possible, yes," she says at last. When? How? Through whom? So many parameters to be determined, so many points to be illuminated. We can come back very quickly with an important specialist. We've chosen him. He knows all about it. "His name?" Nikolai asks. "You know him, we've told you all about him in our emails. His name is Philippe Charlier. A Frenchman. He is a qualified medical examiner. Very well known in France. You must know him. The identification of the skull of Henry IV: that was him."

We've made an agreement. Lana talks to the two archivists to confirm once and for all what they have just told us. In the meantime I avidly consult the files that Nikolai has taken the trouble to bring with him. They are the reports by the Soviet secret services into the disappearance of Hitler. Unusually, I am given permission to take photographs of them. "All of them?" I ask. Nikolai says yes. I don't hold back. I take pictures of everything. Dina looks at me out of the corner of her eye. I can see that she's uneasy. She's not happy about a foreigner freely taking pictures of her precious documents. She hovers around me, murmuring a few words in Russian. I don't understand a word and that suits me fine.

She goes on repeating the same words. I go on. All of a sudden she loses her temper and calls Lana, who is still talking to Nikolai. She talks agitatedly to my colleague, pointing at me with her finger. Lana turns towards me, slightly panic-stricken: "You've got to stop. You're only allowed to take ten photographs. No more than that!" I pretend not to hear her and go on. Now Dina is really shouting at Lana. Why ten? I try to gain some time and pretend to be surprised. Nikolai said I could take as many as I liked. "That's just how it is," Lana replies. "She thinks ten is enough." How can I be cross with dear Dina? She has spent her whole professional life guarding these secret documents. Forty years protecting them from prying eyes, and you can't just delete something like that. I imagine the shock she must feel seeing me, a Frenchman, a capitalist, pillaging the treasure trove of her professional life right in front of her eyes. She reacted too late; I've finished. I've got photographs of everything. The Hitler files are now in the memory of my smartphone. Several hundred pages to translate and digest. A painstaking job.

PARIS, OCTOBER–NOVEMBER 2016

The first translations of the documents photographed in the offices of GARF came in quite quickly. Lana has worked wonders. She prefers to send them to me in the evening, after her day's work. Apart from this investigation into Hitler, she is still freelancing for the Russian media. For my part, I've gone back to France. I'm classifying the translated texts by subject and date. Some remain quite obscure. So many unknown names and obscure acronyms clogging up the administrative phrases. The Russian investigators hadn't much time for poetry. Their work was dictated by efficiency and precision. Here's one of the first documents I've been given:

Top Secret
To Comrade Stalin
To Comrade Molotov

On 16 June 1945, the NKVD of the USSR, under Number 702/b, presented to you and Comrade Stalin the copies received from Berlin via Comrade Serov of the records of the interrogations of certain members of the entourage of Hitler and Goebbels concerning the last days of Hitler and Goebbels' time in Berlin as well as copies of the description and the files of the medico-legal examination of what are presumed to be the corpses of Hitler and Goebbels and their wives.

Nothing's missing: not the big historic names of Stalin, Hitler, and Goebbels, nor the abbreviations NKVD and USSR. And this was only the beginning. Other names and other equally resonant abbreviations would haunt Lana and me during the months of this investigation like so many ghosts emerging from an accursed past. On the German side: Himmler, the SS, Göring, the Third Reich ... On the Soviet side: Beria, Molotov, the Red Army, Zhukov ...

As well as these reports, we have collected a series of captioned photographs and some drawings, including diagrams of Hitler's bunker. They are drawn in pencil on paper by prisoners, SS men, all members of the Führer's inner circle. They had been ordered to draw them by the Russian special services. The aim was to understand how life was organised in their enemy's air-raid shelter. Everything is precisely annotated: the apartments of the Nazi dictator, Eva Braun's bedroom, her bathroom, the conference room, the toilets ...

Diagrams of the Führerbunker (GARF)

The mass of documents in the GARF collection includes several dozen pages in German. Some interrogations of Nazi prisoners have been transcribed directly in their language and by hand as most of the Red Army typewriters used Cyrillic characters. Luckily, the handwriting of the Soviet interpreters is still quite legible. Except in one particular case, in which the letters look like the scrawls of a spider, not to mention the many crossings-out. These barely decipherable texts wore out the eyes of two of my German-French translators. The first ended up throwing in the towel. As for the second, he asked me not to rely on him in the future if the situation came up again. Their determination was not in vain: thanks to them, I was able to place this document within the great historical puzzle formed by the Russian archives of the Hitler file. These spidery squiggles record the interrogation of a man by the name of Erich Rings, one of the radiographers in Hitler's bunker. In particular, Rings gives an account of the moment when his superiors asked him to pass on a message about the Führer's death: "The last telegram of this kind that we have communicated dates from 30 April, at around 5:15 pm in the afternoon. The officer who brought the message told me, so that we would also be informed immediately, that the first phrase of the message was as follows: 'Führer deceased!'"

If Rings is telling the truth, this information implies that the German dictator's death occurred before 5:15 pm on 30 April 1945. But might the Nazi radiographer have been lying to the Soviet investigators? They assume that he might. Suspicion is the essence of any good spy. It is a great asset in all circumstances, and allows them to climb through the ranks of their hierarchy with confidence. Suspecting the enemy, his declarations, including those made under torture. Still, this systematic attitude does obstruct the progress of the inquiry. And my own work, too. The texts that I have in front of me concern a period of almost twelve month, leading up to the middle of 1946. So, almost six months after the fall of Berlin on 2 May 1945, the officers in charge of the Hitler file still hadn't completed their investigation. They asked the USSR Ministry of Internal Affairs to grant an additional delay. As well as the transfer of certain German prisoners from Russian prisons to Berlin. The aim was to reconstruct Hitler's last hours.

10 April 1946 Top Secret
To the Ministry of Internal Affairs of the Union of Soviet Socialist
Republics, Comrade S.N. Kruglov.

Within the context of the investigation into the circumstances of
the disappearance of Hitler on 30 April 1945, the following are
currently held in Butyrka Prison [in Moscow]: ...

This is followed by a long list of Nazi prisoners; then the document
resumes:

In the course of the investigations into these individuals, apart
from the contradictions causing doubts about the plausibility of
the version of Hitler's suicide already given to us, certain additional facts have been revealed, which must be examined on the
spot.

In this respect, we think that the following arrangements
should be put in place:

All individuals arrested in this case must be sent to Berlin.

[. . .]

Give the task force the job of investigating, within a month, all
the circumstances of the disappearance of Hitler and to deliver a
report on the subject to the Ministry of Internal Affairs of the
USSR.

Give Lieutenant General Bochkov the task of organising the
accompaniment of prisoners under escort, and to allocate to that
end a special wagon for the inmates to the city of Brest [in
present-day Belarus]. The accompaniment of the prisoners under
escort from Brest to Berlin will be undertaken by the Berlin task
force.

For the study of pieces of evidence and the scene of the inci-
dent, send to Berlin the qualified criminal investigator of the
General Directorate of the Militia of the Ministry of Internal
Affairs of the USSR, General Ossipov.

The letter is signed by two Soviet generals based in Berlin.

April 1946. Why did the investigation into Hitler take so long? What happened in the bunker? The Russians devoted such energy to investigating that truth that escaped them. And yes, more than any other Allied army (the Americans, the British and the French), Soviet troops had taken hundreds of eyewitnesses of the fall of Berlin and the Führer prisoner. Witnesses who were put severely to the test by their jailers. I can see that determination to solve this mystery just below the surface of many of the reports and interrogations. The same questions keep returning, the same threats. Why not simply accept the evidence? Why can't Stalin and his men admit that the prisoners are telling the truth? I would have made a very bad member of the Soviet secret police. The proof lies in this confrontation between two SS prisoners who were close to Hitler.

The first is called Höfbeck and is a sergeant, the other is called Günsche and is an SS officer.

Question to Höfbeck: Where were you and what did you do on 30 April 1945? The day when, according to your statement, Hitler took his life?
Höfbeck's reply: On 30 April 1945 I was posted to the emergency exit of the bunker by my departmental head, State Councillor [Regierungsrat Högl, head of a group of nine men].
Question to Höfbeck: What did you see there?
Höfbeck's reply: At 2:00 pm, or perhaps a little later, as I approached, I saw several people [. . .]. They were carrying something heavy wrapped in a blanket. I immediately thought that Adolf Hitler must have committed suicide, because I could see a black pair of trousers and black shoes hanging out on one side of the blanket. [. . .] Then Günsche shouted: "Everyone out! They're staying here!" I can't say for definite that it was Günsche who was carrying the second body. The three other comrades immediately ran off, I stayed near the door. I saw two bodies between one and two metres from the emergency exit. Of one body, I was able to see the black trousers and the black shoes, of the other

43

(the one on the right) the blue dress, the brown socks and shoes, but I can't say with any certainty. [. . .] Günsche sprinkled petrol over the bodies, and someone brought him a light near the emergency exit. The farewells didn't take long, five to ten minutes at most, because then there was some very heavy artillery fire. [. . .]

Question to Günsche: What can you say about Höfbeck's witness statement?

Günsche's reply: It wasn't at about 2:00 pm, but shortly after 4:00 pm that the bodies left the bunker by the emergency exit. [. . .] I didn't help to carry Adolf Hitler's body, but a little while later I passed through the emergency exit with Frau Hitler's body. Adolf Hitler's body was carried by people I've already mentioned in previous interrogations. [. . .]

Question to Höfbeck: Do you have any objections about Günsche's testimony that you have just heard?

Höfbeck's reply: I have no objection to Günsche's testimony that I have just heard. [. . .] I have to say that my previous statement may contain some inaccuracies, given that these unexpected events have unsettled me very much.

The inaccuracies in the witness statements drive the investigators mad. Are the prisoners doing it on purpose? There are strong reasons for thinking they are. Let us not forget that for the Nazis, the Communists embody absolute evil (according to Hitler's doctrine, just after the Jews). Resisting, lying, or distorting reality may seem natural to men inspired by Nazi fanaticism that is still very much alive. Be that as it may, their contradictory answers complicate the precise establishment of the events that preceded the fall of Hitler's bunker.

Lana and I thought we were sufficiently prepared for this plunge into one of the last mysteries of the Second World War. Big mistake. Even in our most pessimistic scenarios, we couldn't have imagined the level of complexity of an investigation such as this. We would soon discover that the collection of documents in the GARF stores wouldn't be the hardest part. Our confidence and optimism were quickly dampened. It was Dina, the head of GARF's special collection, who alerted us.

Let's return to our meeting during autumn break 2016 within the walls of the Russian State Archives. Lana and I were busy thanking Dina and Nikolai for their patience. They had already filled the shopping trolley with the pieces of wood from the sofa and the files about Hitler. The interview ended cordially. "We succeeded, we have all the documents about the disappearance of the Führer, it's a first!" Lana was getting carried away and I let her. Dina didn't share her enthusiasm. Nikolai had already left without saying a word. We could hear him pulling his trolley along the corridors with the same delightful racket as before. "You haven't got everything," Dina suddenly announced, almost sorry to spoil our pleasure. Not everything? "There are still bits of Hitler elsewhere in Russia?" I asked without really believing it myself. "It's possible …" Dina had trouble answering frankly. "In fact, yes," she acknowledged at last. "But you won't be able to see them." Our house of cards was collapsing. Still biting her lips and avoiding our eyes, Dina felt uneasy. Lana started talking to her as gently as possible to reassure her. To tell her that it wasn't very serious, but she had to explain everything.

Good news and bad news. Where did I want to start? Lana let me choose. We had left the GARF offices and caught a taxi to get back to our hotel. Let's start with the bad news. "Not all the Soviet reports on Hitler's death are kept at GARF. Some of them are stored in the archives of the FSB." Silence … Was there more bad news? Not for certain. The three initials mean "Federalnaya Sluzhba Bezopasnosti" (Federal Security Service), the Russian secret service. The FSB was set up in 1995. In a way, this was the successor to the KGB, which had been dissolved on 11 October 1991, following an attempted coup d'état against Mikhail Gorbachev in August 1991. The FSB's methods haven't fundamentally changed from those of its illustrious elder sibling. Methods based on manipulation and, if necessary, violence. If access to GARF had seemed difficult, how hard would it be to get into the archives of the FSB (the TsA FSB, short for Tsentral'ny Arkhiv FSB)? Lana was almost laughing, our quest had taken such a desperate turn. "There's something else you need to know," she continued with a nervous hiccough. "Dina also told me that we would certainly have to dig in the military archives. On the other hand, she was very clear, we can't expect any help from GARF. The FSB, the military archives, and GARF all hate each other. We're going to have to manage on our own."

The taximeter was ticking off the roubles that our route was going to cost. It all seemed so easy for the driver. Two customers, an address, a good GPS, and he was all set. The exact opposite of our investigation. "You don't want to know the good news? The positive thing that Dina wanted to tell us?" Lana sensed that I was growing weary. Over a year of Sisyphean research was beginning to dent my enthusiasm. "Dina assured me that she liked us, and that she'd support us in our bid to carry out scientific examinations on the skull." Did Dina have the slightest power over the examination of the skull? Lana started thinking, and then shook her head. Moscow was playing with us, with its fine drizzle. Other people had tried to investigate Hitler. If they'd all failed, was it a coincidence?

A fierce and almost desperate combat? Perfect! Lana doesn't give up, quite the contrary. She promised me she would obtain all the permissions before the end of the year, the ones that we needed to access the FSB archives and those opening the doors of the Russian State Military Archives (RGVA). "No one resists me for long. I will wear them down," she assured me with her swaggering air in the departure hall of Sheremetyevo Airport in Moscow. That was less than a month ago. Since then, not a day goes by when I don't talk to her on the telephone, when we don't give each other encouragement. I've been working on the documents, she's been working on the Russian authorities. "I'm nearly there, another few days and I'll have my answer. Stay alert, we're going to need to react quickly." Lana doesn't let go, and she can't imagine a second failure. Are her connections with Russian power really so solid? How would she convince administrations that were usually so impervious to this kind of request? "Since my work on Svetlana Stalin, I can count on good relations with people of influence, and they know me, they know I'm like a pit bull. I never let go of my prey. And believe me, dictators know me …"

PART II

THE LAST DAYS
OF HITLER

As of March 1945, Hitler decided to take refuge in his bunker beneath the new Reich Chancellery, in the heart of Berlin. The big final Allied offensive was launched a few weeks earlier. In the East, the Red Army, after a first failed attempt in October 1944 (Operation Gumbinnen), entered Eastern Prussia on 20 January; the Western Allies (in this instance the troops of the 1st American Army) had also entered German territory on 12 September 1944, near Aachen. The city would fall on 21 October. As the threat became more clearly apparent, Hitler left his refuge less and less often. He spent the last days of his life 8.5 metres underground. All of the details of the Führer's last moments are supplied by the survivors of the bunker. Those men and women were mostly military personnel, as well as a few civilians (particularly secretaries). Their witness statements need to be treated with caution. Let us not forget that they were all members of the Nazi Party and, to varying degrees, admired Hitler.

These statements come from two different sources: the interrogations carried out by the Soviets and/or the Allies after the arrest of the witnesses, and the witnesses' memoirs which they published after being freed, as well as a number of interviews. In the first instance, the information was taken by fair means or foul, not intended to be published and revealed to the wider public; in the other, it came freely from the individuals themselves. It allowed them to justify their own actions to the whole world and, most often, distance themselves from the Nazi regime.

In either case, the stories are far from neutral. But a comparison of the two sources does allow us to establish a fairly credible picture of the twelve last known days in the life of the German dictator. At least until the afternoon of 30 April 1945.

19 APRIL 1945

"Where are the Russians? Is the front holding?
What's the Führer doing? When is he leaving Berlin?"
(*Senior Nazi officials in the Führerbunker in Berlin*)

In the Führerbunker, they were finally getting their smiles back. The order to flee should be coming soon! Escaping the bombing, and the Berliners who were becoming increasingly hostile to the Nazi regime. They were scheduled to leave the next day, 20 April, Hitler's birthday. What better present could they hope for than an escape to the fortress of Berchtesgaden in the Bavarian mountains? That way he would be able to celebrate his fifty-sixth birthday under the milky sky of the German Alps that he loved so much. And most importantly, he would be leaving his bunker, that reinforced concrete mausoleum buried beneath the gardens of the new Reich Chancellery. Since mid-March, Hitler had transferred his quarters to this air-raid shelter right in the middle of the German capital.

The whole of the dictator's entourage dreamed of that escape. From the Wehrmacht officers to the men who had been in the SS from the beginning, via the senior officials in the state apparatus, they were only waiting for a sign from Hitler to pack up all their belongings. Of course their haste to leave the front was officially dictated only by the need to preserve the physical health of the master of Germany and continue the fight. Few confessed their fear and wish to save their skin. How many people had taken refuge in the Chancellery? About fifty? Sixty? Hard to say. Every day, new people turned up at 77 Wilhelmstrasse and requested a place, a bed, in a dormitory or even a corridor. Technically speaking, the whole of the Führerbunker could hold two hundred people. More than that and they risked running out of oxygen in spite of the powerful ventilation system. The Führerbunker consisted of two underground shelters. First of all there was the Vorbunker, or "upper bunker," buried 6 metres beneath the big hall of the New Chancellery. It was built in 1936 and extended over almost 300 square metres. It consisted of fourteen rooms with an area of 10 square metres each on either side of a 12-metre corridor. Created to resist the air attacks, its ceiling was 1.6 metres thick and its walls were 1.2 metres deep. Or exactly twice as thick as the shelter beneath the Aviation Ministry in Berlin. But it still wasn't enough.

Hitler, after the first British bombing raids on Berlin in January 1943, ordered the construction of an even more solid bunker, the Hauptbunker, or "main bunker." It was 2.5 metres deeper than the Vorbunker, or 8.5 metres underground. The two bunkers were connected by a staircase at right angles framed by airtight armoured doors capable of resisting a gas attack. The security norms in the Hauptbunker swept away all previous records. The walls were 4 metres thick. It was protected by a 3.5-metre layer of concrete and measured just under 20 metres wide by 15.6 metres long, a total of 312 square metres.* The partition walls of the rooms were designed to resist large-scale bombing attacks. They were 50 centimetres thick. Creature comforts were few. No parquet on the floor, no carpet, and only the barest minimum in terms of furniture. Damp was a constant presence at this depth. The pumps with the task of removing any water that seeped in did not prevent the sensation of damp and cold. The walls were painted grey or left bare. Because of the thickness of these partitions, the rooms were even smaller than in the Vorbunker. Even the ones attributed to Hitler

*Sven Felix Kellerhoff, *The Führer Bunker: Hitler's Last Refuge*, Berlin, Berlin-Story-Verlag, 2004, p. 50.

were no more than 10 square metres in area and 3 metres high. There were six tiny rooms for the military personnel opposite his apartments. The only luxuries for the Führer were a personal bathroom, an office, and a bedroom. These rooms, unlike the rest of the shelter, were thoughtfully furnished.

"Hitler had his own bunker with only a few rooms for himself, his doctor, his manservant and the staff absolutely necessary for his team,"* his personal pilot, Hans Baur, remembered in his memoirs. The men that Hitler didn't want to be separated from included: his personal doctor, Dr. Theodor Morell; his secretary, Martin Bormann; his aide-de-camp, Otto Günsche; and his valet, Heinz Linge. There was also Blondi, the Führer's dog. She was sometimes locked up in the room where the daily strategic meetings were held. Eva Braun returned to the shelter of the New Chancellery early in April. Hitler didn't know whether to be furious or delighted that his companion had the audacity to venture into the heart of battle. Be that as it may, he accepted her presence near him and ordered a bedroom to be assigned to her next to his own. She would be in safety there, he thought.

At least for now. Because the two bunkers soon risked being turned from refuges into a death trap if the order to flee the capital was not given quickly. The military situation was catastrophic. Since 16 April, Russian troops led by Marshals Georgy Zhukov and Ivan Konev launched their big offensive on Berlin. For now, they were still some way away fighting about a hundred kilometres east of the Reich capital, on the River Oder. But all the German officers knew that the city would be difficult to defend. Vast in area, with a large urban conglomeration, Berlin required too much effort in terms of men and materials to be protected. Hitler couldn't ignore it. And yet he didn't order the evacuation of the civilian population. By the time the fighting extended as far as the central district around the Brandenburg Gate, Berlin was still refuge to 2.5 million inhabitants.

*Hans Baur, *I was Hitler's Pilot*, London, Muller, 1958, p. 180.

At first, with resolute speeches and slogans, Nazi propaganda tried to transform the Oder into the last natural bulwark against the vengeful invasion of the Soviet soldiers. Muddy water against the wave of Russian steel – an image that might carry a certain panache in a Wagner opera, but in the spring of 1945 it looked like collective suicide.

The idea of suicide wasn't displeasing to Hitler. Not his own, but that of his people. Suicide as the ultimate sacrifice to his murderous ideology.

To persuade public opinion to go on fighting, the Nazi dictator joined in personally. In early March he went to the front line at the Oder. It would be his last official outing into the combat zone. The intention was to show the Germans that their Führer was in control of the situation. The slogans proclaimed in the papers and cinema newsreels sought to be sober and martial: "The Führer in person is on the front line of the Oder!" and "The defence of Berlin is being carried out on the Oder." But it had been a month since then … and another era, the era of hope.

If war is a matter of will, sacrifice, and, sometimes, tactical genius, most often it is based around the simplest mathematics. Stalin knew that all too well. And he didn't stint on the forces deployed. Against a million German soldiers, the master of the Kremlin assembled over twice as many men, 2.1 million. Most importantly, the Russians were better equipped: 41,600 pieces of artillery, 6,250 tanks, and 7,500 fighter planes against 10,400 pieces of artillery, 1,500 tanks, and 3,300 fighter planes on the Nazi side.

Hitler's generals were well aware of this. If the Red Army crossed the Oder, Berlin would only hold out for a few days. But that wasn't serious because provision had been made for everything in the Nazi camp. The battle would be fought in the "Alpine redoubt" towards Bavaria and Austria, in a mountainous triangle between Salzburg, Bad Reichenhall, and Berchtesgaden. Since mid-March, the Führer's secretariat had given orders to transfer the Nazi state apparatus there. A network of bunkers was built, specially connected by telephone lines. Even the Chancellery's fleet of cars had been sent there.

Years later, during their detention in Russian prisons, Heinz Linge and Otto Günsche, Hitler's valet and personal aide-de-camp, revealed this planned withdrawal.

During the first days of April 1945, Hitler summoned three Austrian Gauleiters [regional Party leaders]: Hofer from Innsbruck, Uiberreither from Klagenfurt and Eigruber from Linz. He talked to them in the presence of Bormann [Hitler's secretary and adviser]. The discussion concerned the construction of an "alpine fortress" in the high Austrian mountains, a fortress that would be the "last bastion" allowing the further pursuit of the war.*

After the fall of the Reich, the British secret service would interrogate Hitler's close colleagues, whom they had taken prisoner. Their testimony corroborated the planned escape on 20 April. Here is an extract of the secret report issued on 1 November 1945 by the British Brigadier Edward John Foord, who was in charge of military information at Supreme Headquarters Allied Expeditionary Force (SHAEF). This report was meant for his counterparts in the American, Soviet, and French secret services based in Berlin. "Hitler's original intention was to flee for Berchtesgaden on 20 April 1945, the date of his birthday, and orders had been given to his servants to prepare for his arrival on that date."† But Hitler would suddenly change his mind. On the afternoon of 19 April, General Hans Krebs, the new chief of staff of the land army, informed him that Russian tanks had managed to pierce the line, and that they were only 30 kilometres north of Berlin. The situation in that territory was becoming untenable. Hitler raged at his officers. He thought each was more incompetent than the other, and concluded that he would have to take charge of operations himself.

*Heinz Linge and Otto Günsche, *Le Dossier Hitler*, trad. par Danièle Darneau, Paris, Presses de la Cité, [2005] 2006, p. 281.190
†GARF 9401/2/552, f.114

Consequently, he had to stay at the heart of the battle and put off the withdrawal to Berchtesgaden.

The Führer's decision soon circulated along the corridors of the two bunkers. His entourage were stunned by the news, and saw it as a tragedy. For the inhabitants of the Chancellery shelters, but also for any officials still in the capital – it was impossible to leave if Hitler didn't wish to. Would he change his mind? Heinz Linge witnessed this anxious dance among the biggest figures in Nazism: "Ley, Funk, the Minister of the Economy, Rosenberg, Speer, Axmann, Ribbentrop and others who were still in Berlin were constantly making phone-calls. Their questions were always the same: 'What's happening at the front? Where are the Russians? Is the front holding? What's the Führer doing? When is he leaving Berlin?'"* Otto Günsche systematically gave them the same reply: "The front at the Oder is holding. The Russians will not reach Berlin. The Führer sees no reason to leave Berlin."

*Ibid., p. 299.

20 APRIL 1945

"Führer's birthday. Sadly no one is in the mood for a party."
(Martin Bormann's private diary)

The orders were precise. Hitler didn't want a party for his birthday. It would have been both ridiculous and inappropriate. The day before, he informed his valet, Heinz Linge, of this, and immediately demanded that his will be respected by everyone in the bunker. But no one paid any heed. The Führergeburtstag (Führer's birthday) remained a holy date in the calendar in Nazi Germany, almost the equivalent of 25 December. So how could the most fervent zealots of the regime be prevented from celebrating their hero? It was the custom in the dictator's closest circle to wish him a happy birthday at midnight. Hundreds of thousands of Soviet soldiers advancing on Berlin wouldn't change that. Like good school pupils anxious to attract the favour of their teachers, seven Nazis crammed into the dictator's tiny antechamber. Their uniforms perfectly ironed and their medals on display, chins held high, nothing in their attitude revealed their ardent desire to flee Berlin. Linge remembered that those present were General Hermann Fegelein (Eva Braun's brother-in-law), General Wilhelm Burgdorf, SS officer Otto Günsche, the diplomat Walther Hewel (Ribbentrop's liaison agent, Reich Minister of Foreign Affairs), Werner Lorenz (representative of the Reich's head of press), Julius Schaub (Hitler's personal aide-de-camp), and Alwin-Broder Albrecht (Hitler's naval aide-de-camp).

They were all bustling about around Linge, the dilettante SS officer who had only ever seen the front from an open-topped car beside his master. Linge, who wore the epaulettes of a lieutenant colonel even though he was only a valet. But this was no longer a time for contempt. Linge was the last person in the bunker who was in permanent contact with Hitler. All of those proud officers, those Nazi Party officials, came to him to persuade the Führer to accept their best wishes. "After informing Hitler of this," Linge recalled, "he gave me a tired and depressed look. I had to tell the arrivals that the Führer had no time to receive them."* But that didn't take into account Fegelein's determination. This young and scheming thirty-eight-year-old general had felt almost untouchable since marrying Gretl, Eva Braun's sister, on 3 June 1944. Hitler couldn't refuse to receive them if it came from Eva, Fegelein said to himself. And he was right! He asked his sister-in-law to persuade Hitler. Reluctantly, the Führer came out and quickly shook the hands extended to him. His men barely had time to wish him "happy birthday," before he returned to his study, his back bent. Fegelein was proud. He thought he had made his point. That could always be useful when the right time came.

During the rest of that day, other personalities from the Reich came to the Chancellery that stood above the bunkers. Hitler left his shelter and came up into the fresh air to meet them in the halls of the imperial building. One by one the *apparatchiks* saluted the Führer like serfs saluting a feudal lord, more out of obligation than devotion. The Gestapo kept a close eye on everyone's attitudes, and no one was immune to the possibility of a death sentence for treason. Not even the generals and the ministers. Top-ranking visitors included the Nazis most fully implicated in the regime: Heinrich Himmler, the head of the SS; Hermann Göring, Reich Vice-Chancellor; Admiral Karl Dönitz; Marshal Wilhelm Keitel; and Joachim von Ribbentrop, the Minister of Foreign Affairs.

With an arm outstretched in attempts at a fascist salute, they were engaging in an act of pretence. Pretence that the man in front

---

*Heinz Linge, *With Hitler to the End: The Memoirs of Adolf Hitler's Valet*, trans. Geoffrey Brooks, Barnsley, Frontline Books, 2013, p. 187.

of them was still capable of saving Berlin, let alone the country. Hitler was officially fifty-six, but he looked more like a cursed phantom. A phantom haunting the damp soil of the capital of his Reich.

What had become of the man who had galvanised millions of Germans only twelve years before? An old man with Parkinson's disease, barely capable of ruling over a reinforced concrete air-raid shelter. Here is what Erwin Giesing, one of his personal doctors, wrote of the Führer after examining him in February 1945:

> He seemed to have aged, and to be more bent-backed than ever. His face was pale and there were great rings around his eyes. His voice was clear but faint. I noticed that the trembling in his left arm was getting worse if he didn't hold it with his hand. That was why Hitler kept his arm resting on the table or on the headrest of an armchair. [. . .] I had a sense of a man who was completely exhausted and absent.*

Erich Kempka, his personal chauffeur, was present on that occasion. "On the Führer's fifty-sixth birthday, 20 April 1945, I reflected on past years when the German people celebrated this day and held great celebrations and parades."† Gone were the grand parades! Gone the military bands with their bombastic music in the square of the Technische Hochschule in Berlin. The cohorts of admirers lined up by the side of the road clutching little black swastika flags lay crushed by the Allied bombs. As to the hundreds of diplomats who had come from all over the world to offer their allegiance to the strong man of a conquering Germany, where were they now?

There is an astonishing document that sums up this fall of the Nazi regime. It is in the Russian State Military Archives in Moscow. When the Red Army entered the Reich Chancellery on 1 May 1945, they laid hands on a curious book. It is a large book bound in red

---

*Ibid., p. 174.
†Erich Kempka, *I was Hitler's Chauffeur: The Memoirs of Erich Kempka*, Barnsley, Frontline Books, 2012, p. 57.

leather, emblazoned with an eagle holding a laurel wreath with a swastika in the middle. This document is nothing other than a visitor's book. Foreign diplomats invited to major ceremonies had to write their names in it. The feasts celebrated included New Year's Eve, the national German day of celebration, and, of course, the Führer's birthday. Every guest signed, gave their function and sometimes declared their fervent admiration of the Nazi regime.

On 20 April 1939, Hitler celebrated his fiftieth birthday. He had already been in power for six years, he had annexed Austria, the Sudetenland, and then Bohemia-Moravia, he had openly persecuted the German Jews, and he had caused ever greater alarm to the European democracies. But no matter. The dictator was no less available to the sixty or so diplomats who had come to pay him tribute. Their decoratively written signatures are lined up over six pages of the visitors' book. They include representatives from France and the United Kingdom. For them, it would be the last opportunity to wish Hitler a happy birthday, because in less than five months, on 1 September, war would be declared between those two countries and Germany.

Let us turn the pages. Here we are in 1942. Hitler is celebrating his fifty-third birthday. He's stopped making the western democracies nervous; he terrifies them now when he isn't actually destroying them. The list of victims is long: France, Belgium, the Netherlands, Denmark, Norway, Poland ... The Führer is at the height of his power, and that is apparent from the number of diplomats attending his birthday party. Over a hundred signatures over twelve pages. Admittedly there are no French people now, no British names, and even fewer Americans, but there are still Italians, Japanese, Spaniards. And one loyal guest at the Nazi celebrations, the apostolic nuncio of Pope Pius XII.

20 April 1945. The last date in this imposing collection of signatures. No more block capitals at the top of the chapter. One imagines that the Führer's personal secretariat were short of time. In its place, a simple date hastily scribbled in the margin: 20.4.45. And five signatures from diplomats. Five. Who are they? Their names are barely legible, the writing seems so nervous. The ones that can be

deciphered are the following: an Afghan ambassador, a Thai, one from China. Where are the other ambassadors? The ones who were honoured to attend the regime's celebrations? They have disappeared. Even the representative of the Vatican no longer added his signature to this now cursed book. But the apostolic nuncio hadn't missed a single Nazi ceremony since 1939. He was still there for the New Year's celebration on 1 January 1945. His conscientious handwriting on these villainous pages attests to diplomatic connections that many would prefer to keep under wraps.

On 20 April 1945, everyone is fleeing Hitler. All those who can, or who dare. Even among the Nazis, not least in the first circle of senior leaders, including one of the most emblematic of the regime: Marshal Göring.

Hermann Göring certainly did come to Berlin. In line with his outrageous temperament, he enthusiastically swore his profound attachment, his eternal loyalty and his certainty of imminent victory. Then he fled as quickly as possible for the mountains of Obersalzberg. Not for fear of the fighting in Berlin but, he claimed, to prepare the counter-offensive in the Bavarian Alps. The hasty departure of the spirited marshal did not go unnoticed in the bunker. "After a surprisingly short time, Göring left Hitler's office and the Führerbunker," wrote the Führer's personal chauffeur, Erich Kempka. "The same day he fled Berlin and never came back."[*] Göring's escape shocked the other inhabitants of the bunker, but more than that, it terrified them. Would they have time to wait for Hitler's decision to leave Berlin? Adjutant Rochus Misch was a telephone operator in the Führerbunker. He bears witness to the danger that lay in wait: "On 20 April, the day of Hitler's fifty-sixth birthday, Soviet tanks had reached the outskirts of the capital. The city was practically encircled. That day or the day before, someone went down to the bunker to announce that the roar of artillery fire could be heard."[†]

*Erich Kempka, *I was Hitler's Chauffeur*, op. cit., p. 58.
†Rochus Misch, *J'étais garde du corps d'Hitler* (1940–1945), Paris, Le Cherche Midi, 2006, p. 193.

For the Russian troops, 20 April 1945 was an extremely worrying date. What if the rumours of a Nazi special weapon, a weapon that could turn the war around, were true? According to German propaganda, that weapon was due to be unveiled on the day of Hitler's birthday. "Some people had seen tarpaulin-covered vehicles transporting the secret weapon in question," said Elena Rzhevskaya, a German interpreter with the Red Army. "We fantasised, trying to imagine its destructive force. We waited for the announcement on the radio."[*] But nothing came. That new weapon was the atom bomb. Nazi engineers had been working on it for years. The Allied air raids on German industrial sites over several months considerably hampered Hitler's mad project. The Armaments Minister, Albert Speer, speculated in his memoirs that "with extreme concentration of all our resources, we could have had a German atom bomb by 1947, but certainly we could not beat the Americans, whose bomb was ready by August 1945."[†]

---

[*]Elena Rzhevskaya, *Carnets de l'interprète de guerre*, Paris, Christian Bourgois Éditeur, 2011, p. 287.
[†]Albert Speer, *Inside the Third Reich*, London, Orion, 1970, p. 229.

21 APRIL 1945

"This is the final act."
(Erich Kempka, Hitler's personal chauffeur)

The Russian tanks were now no more than a few kilometres from Berlin. The Soviets threatened the capital on three fronts: to the north, the east, and the south. To the west, on the other hand, the city was still spared. The Anglo-American offensive had slowed down, and their first troops were 500 kilometres away from the outskirts of Berlin. Hitler took advantage of the fact to transfer his units from the western front towards the Russians.

That didn't make the situation any less catastrophic. The Soviet shells were now reaching the Chancellery gardens. The exploding bombs blew in the windows of Hitler's palace, dug furrows in the marble walls as if they were made of cardboard, and the noise echoed all the way down to the underground shelters. Once more, the Führer's entourage begged him to flee. There was still time. Gatow Airport, south-west of Berlin, was accessible. Hans Baur, Hitler's personal pilot, had moved to the bunker some weeks previously to be ready to evacuate the Führer at any moment. Several aeroplanes had been specially prepared, and were only waiting for a green light to take off. Bormann, the most trusted member of Hitler's inner circle, was also urging an immediate departure. The previous day he had even taken the initiative of accelerating the transfer of Berlin General Headquarters to Obersalzberg.

Hope faded again with Hitler's decision to launch a counter-attack. In order to carry it out, he was counting on SS General Felix Steiner, a military man with a strong character and a complexion tanned by two years on the Russian front. He was given the difficult task of preventing the fatal encircling of Berlin. Steiner had certain points in his favour in this respect. Hitler had assembled thousands of well-equipped and battle-hardened men for him, in a new army that he called "Armeeabteilung Steiner" (Steiner Army Detachment). It was clear to the Führer that these shock troops would smash the assault from the Red Army. As in 1940, during the battle for France, Hitler would show these gentlemen of the Wehrmacht how to wage a war. But things had changed in five years. The German units, by virtue of having been killed, now existed only in Hitler's auto-cratic ravings. The troops who were supposed to join Steiner's army were virtual. They had disappeared in the noise of combat, or were obstructed by Soviet troops and unable to move towards Steiner.

Hitler refused to see that. And his entourage didn't dare to put him right. Whatever the situation, the Führer decided to stay as close as possible to the fighting, in his bunker. There was no ques-tion of him leaving Berlin at the height of battle. However, he did agree to his personal belongings and the military archives being transferred to safety in the "alpine fortress." At the same time he indicated that anyone who wanted to leave was free to do so. The news immediately spread through the two bunkers and at first set off a panic. The candidates for evacuation knew that the few four-propeller Condors and three-engine Junkers still in service wouldn't be able to take everyone. A list of the lucky elect was drawn up. People were practically fighting to appear on it. "Everyone wanted to leave. New people were constantly turning up who absolutely had to get to Obersalzberg on the pretext that their families were in Bavaria, that they came from the region, that they wanted to defend it on the spot, etc. In fact they only wanted to get away from Berlin as quickly as possible."*

*Heinz Linge and Otto Günsche, *Le Dossier Hitler*, op. cit., p. 306.

All the planes would reach their destination. All but one. The one containing Hitler's personal documents was shot down by the American Air Force.

The chief Nazi's luck had deserted him once and for all.

22 APRIL 1945

"The war is lost!"
(*Adolf Hitler*)

In the morning, the Russian artillery fire resumed its murderous rain of shells on the Chancellery. Even about ten metres underground, the bombing echoed dully, and finally woke Hitler at about 10 o'clock in the morning. The Führer complained about the noise. Who was daring to disturb his sleep like that? Everyone in the Führerbunker knew that he didn't usually wake until 1 pm.

For several months Hitler had suffered from insomnia, and didn't go to bed until about four or five in the morning. Everyone around him quickly had to adapt to the new sleep cycle of the master of Germany. Because he couldn't get to sleep, he decided to take advantage of his wakeful nights. So it was quite natural for him to organise military meetings at between two and three in the morning. The secretaries weren't spared, because they were regularly summoned to drink tea with him. And that always happened in the middle of the night. An exhausting rhythm of life.

Hitler couldn't bear to be woken at ten in the morning. He complained to his valet, SS officer Linge. "What is that noise?" he asked. "Was the Chancellery district being bombed?"

Linge reassured him that it was only the German anti-aircraft defence, and a few Russian long-range guns.

The reality was quite different. The defences around Berlin were cracking under pressure from the Russians. To the south, they had opened a breach, and were making their way towards the outskirts.

To the north and east, the Red Army tanks were crushing everything in their path.

But that would soon stop because Steiner and his army must by now have started attacking the assailing forces. A matter of time, Hitler imagined. At four o'clock in the afternoon, during a situation conference, his general staff dared to tell him the terrible truth: for want of men and materials, the Steiner offensive had not taken place. And more importantly, it never would.

According to witnesses, the dictator's reaction was terrifying. Nicolaus von Below, the Führer's Luftwaffe armaments officer, was there. "Hitler became very irate. He ordered everybody from the room with the exception of Keitel, Jodl, Krebs, and Burgdorf and then unleashed a furious tirade against the Army commanders and their 'long-term-treachery.' I was sitting near the door in the annexe and heard almost every word. It was a terrible half-hour."* The dictator was so furious that the Wehrmacht and SS generals present in the room reacted like terrified schoolboys. They lowered their heads and avoided their master's eye. Trusty Linge, an intimate of the Führer's, wasn't spared his fury. "There you have it, Linge. Even the SS goes behind my back and deceives me wherever they can. Now I shall remain in Berlin and die here."†

Die here! The idea that the Führer might die chilled everyone in the room. Josef Goebbels was informed, and hurried back to the bunker. At first he tried to bring him back to reason. Seeing that that was impossible, he did an about-turn. As usual, he aped his master and announced to anyone willing to listen that he too would stay in Berlin whatever the cost. He even managed to find the idea of the ultimate sacrifice absolute genius. Among those in the room, discouragement did battle with disgust. The officers couldn't understand Goebbels' morbid complacency. Suicide

---

*Nicolaus von Below, *At Hitler's Side: The Memoirs of Hitler's Luftwaffe Adjutant*, trans. Geoffrey Brooks, London, Greenhill, 2001, p. 236.
†Heinz Linge, *With Hitler to the End*, op. cit., p. 189.

meant abandoning the German people. That was an impossible option! Not with the enemy at the gates of the capital. "What are your orders?" the generals asked, almost begged Hitler. They had become so accustomed to blind obedience over many years that taking initiatives seemed impossible, inconceivable.

Just after the war, in June 1945, one of the officers present in the conference room, General Alfred Jodl, later captured by the British, would communicate some details about the crisis of 22 April. "I have no orders to give you, Hitler replied. If you want a boss, turn to Göring. He's the one who will give you orders." Göring? Jodl, like the other officers in the general staff, refused to be ordered about by one of the most corrupt and incompetent men in the Reich. "No soldier will agree to fight for him!" they cried. "But who's talking about going on fighting? It's no longer a question of fighting, Hitler continued seriously. We need to negotiate ... and Göring is better than me at that game."*

Like a good Bavarian officer, Jodl clicked his heels and transmitted the information to General Karl Koller, Göring's representative in the bunker. Koller left immediately afterwards for Obersalzberg to warn them about Hitler's decision.

Goebbels witnessed the scene. There was no question of letting his mortal enemy, fat Göring, take power. If Hitler died, the new Führer would be automatically Göring. To Goebbels, it was obvious that he had to persuade the Führer to keep the war going. It had to remain a hope, a military option. Goebbels went to see Jodl. He asked him if it was still possible to prevent the fall of Berlin. "I told him it was possible only if we disengaged our troops from the Elbe to relaunch them in the defence of Berlin."† Goebbels immediately informed Hitler. That hope exists, he said. So it wouldn't be Steiner's army that would deliver the Reich, but the army of another general, Walther Wenck, at the head of the 12th army. This was made up of about fifteen divisions consisting of almost 70,000 men, most of

*Elena Rzhevskaya, *Carnets*, op. cit., p. 289.
†Ibid.

them trainee officers and cadets, badly trained and badly equipped.

Hitler agreed to believe in this new chimera.

Goebbels had won against Göring.

23 APRIL 1945

"I know Göring is rotten."
(Adolf Hitler)

The previous day's crisis had left its traces deep in the two bunkers. Some of the generals and senior officers in the Nazi apparatus had left the shelter as one leaves an area contaminated by a deadly virus. The intimate circle shrank a little more. The only ones remaining were the last stalwart supporters, the crazed devotees of the Reich, including Goebbels, who had gone to the Führerbunker the previous day with his wife and children, the loyal Eva Braun, and the servile Martin Bormann.

Since making the decision to stay in Berlin to the bitter end, Hitler seemed calmer, almost resigned. Of course, his physical health remained fragile, his left hand trembled more and more, and he regularly complained of pain in his right eye. Every day, Linge had to give him an eye ointment containing 1 per cent cocaine. Despite this, according to the testimony of the bunker's inhabitants his mental health was unaffected.

However, a radio telegram shook Hitler's fragile serenity to the core. The message arrived from Obersalzberg late in the afternoon, and was signed by Göring. The commander-in-chief of the Luftwaffe had been informed of Hitler's decision to give him the chance of negotiating in his name. This was quite unthinkable in normal circumstances, so accustomed was Hitler to make all his decisions himself. The regime's heir apparent drew the conclusion that his master was no longer at liberty to move or even to act. Was he already in the hands of the Russians? Or technically incapable of communicating his orders to the various general staffs of the German Army? However that might have been, from the depths of his command post in the Bavarian Alps, Göring surmised that Hitler was no longer in a position to rule the Reich, and that he had to take his place. He prudently informed his master of his intention, and gave him the opportunity to reassure him and therefore stop everything. Here is an excerpt from the radio telegram: "[. . .] I feel obliged to consider, if no reply reaches me before 22 hours, that you have lost your freedom to act. I should then apply the conditions of your decree and take the necessary decisions for the good of our Nation and our Fatherland."

No sooner had the message reached the bunker than Bormann intercepted it. The Führer's secretary was delighted. At last he was going to be able to get rid of Göring, that man whom he had considered incompetent and corrupt for years. He presented himself before Hitler clutching the radio telegram and shouting about a coup d'état, an ultimatum, treason. And he suggested leaving immediately for Obersalzberg to restore order to the Reich and throw Göring in irons.

Bormann had discovered that on this day, 23 April, south-west Berlin was still free, and they would be able to find an escape route. Albert Speer, the Armaments Minister and architect of the Reich, witnessed the scene. At first Bormann's ranting had no effect on Hitler. But then a second radio telegram from Göring arrived:

Important business! To be passed on only by officers! Radio telegram no. 1899. Robinson to Prince Elector, 23-4, 17.59. To Reich Minister von Ribbentrop. I have asked the Führer to provide me with instructions by 10 PM on 23 April. If by that time it is apparent that the Führer has been deprived of his freedom of action to conduct the affairs of the Reich, his decree of 29 June 1941 will come into effect. From that moment, in line with the decree, I will assume all his offices as his deputy. If by midnight 23 April 1945 you hear nothing either directly from the Führer or from me, you are to come and join me immediately by air. Signed: Göring, Reich Marshall

Bormann was delighted, here was confirmation of Göring's duplicity. "It is an act of treason," he told a shocked Hitler. "He is already sending telegrams to the members of the government to tell them he is going to assume your functions tonight at 24.00." Speer remembered the Führer's reaction: "With flushed face and staring eyes, Hitler seemed to have forgotten the presence of his entourage. 'I've known it all along. I know that Göring is lazy. He let the air force go to pot. He was corrupt. His example made corruption possible in our state. Besides, he has been a drug addict for years. I've known it all along.'"* Göring would not have the opportunity to plead his case. Bormann assumed the task of writing the telegram to his enemy:

> To Hermann Göring, Obersalzberg. Through your actions, you have made yourself guilty of high treason against the Führer and National Socialism. Treason is punishable by death. Still, because of the services you have performed for the Party, the Führer will not inflict this supreme punishment on you, as long as you renounce all your offices for reasons of health. Reply yes or no.

At the same time, the commander of the SS units of Obersalzberg received another message from Bormann. It stated that Göring has been guilty of treason, that he must be arrested immediately and that if Berlin were to fall over the coming days, Göring would have to be executed.

Half an hour later, Göring's reply reached the Chancellery bunker. Officially, he stepped down from all his functions because of a serious heart condition.

---

*Albert Speer, *Inside the Third Reich*, op. cit., pp. 482–3.

24 APRIL 1945

"Soldiers, wounded men, all of you to arms!"

(Goebbels' appeal to the Berlin press)

Berlin was almost entirely encircled. Schönefeld Airport on the city outskirts had fallen. Zhukov and Konev were making rapid progress. The two Soviet marshals were staking their careers on this battle. Whoever caused the fall of Berlin and caught Hitler would emerge victorious.

Every hour, thousands of Germans were perishing under the Russian bombs. Most of them were civilians, women and children, all trapped in the capital. In the German army, the legal age limits for bearing arms had been considerably enlarged. Teenagers and pensioners were being requisitioned and thrown onto this apocalyptic battlefield.

Refusal to fight, trying to surrender to the Russians to bring an end to a war that was lost in advance, would lead to an equally tragic end. Groups of Nazi fanatics scoured the streets of Berlin day and night in search of "traitors," who they publicly shot or hanged.

Hidden away in his little room in the Führerbunker, Goebbels was bursting with energy. The Reich capital was about to fall, while the Propaganda Minister sent out more and more delirious and threatening communiqués. He called on all Berliners, healthy or wounded, to come and swell the groups of Nazi fighters. Vacillators were "sons of bitches." At the same time, German radio unstintingly broadcast messages like: "The Führer is thinking for you, you have only to carry out orders!" or "The Führer is Germany."

The Nazi daily *Panzerbär* ("The Armoured Bear," in reference to the historically emblematic bear of Berlin), published on its front page on 24 April 1945 what would be Hitler's last declaration:

> Remember:
> Anyone who supports or merely approves of the instructions that weaken our perseverance is a traitor! He must immediately be condemned to be shot or hanged.

Nearly ten metres underground, Hitler and his last faithful followers could not imagine the hell that Berliners were living through above ground. And for good reason – they didn't dare to emerge into the open air. Only the SS men responsible for the safety of the air-raid shelter and its occupants went in and out of the building. But their opinion concerning the situation was never sought and, besides, they didn't think for a moment of giving an account of events to the Führer. As for the idea of trying to leave the shelter, even battle-hardened soldiers shivered at the very idea. Martial law had been imposed on the whole of Berlin since 20 April. Rochus Misch, the bunker's telephone operator, did not escape that anxiety: "Wandering through the ruins, the Gestapo would soon pick me up. [. . .] Hentschel [his colleague on the bunker telephone switchboard] and I were convinced that the secret police would kill us if they ever caught us."*

With every passing hour the Führerbunker was turning into a tomb for its occupants.

Still, life was becoming gradually more organised between the thick concrete walls. The daily reports of bad news were flooding in monotonously. The final act of Hitler's tragedy was playing itself out most dramatically. There were barely a few dozen players, but they played their part with absurd perfection. In this microcosm of a Third Reich in its death throes, a small group of animals were

*Rochus Misch, *Hitler's Last Witness: The Memoirs of Hitler's Bodyguard*, pp. 158–9.

desperately trying to survive. There were military men convinced that blind obedience to their boss would absolve them of all responsibility, politicians united in mutual hatred, and a young generation of Germans Nazified from their school days onwards and devoted unto death. Hitler alone was still able to unite men and women whose nerves were in shreds, and keep them from killing each other.

If some people were beginning to doubt, most were still totally devoted to the cult of the Führer. He had calculated, predicted, organised everything, they thought. All those repeated defeats could only be a trap that would inevitably close on the Russians. The proof was that Hitler seemed so relaxed. He played with his Alsatian Blondi, who had just had puppies. They ran yapping around the corridors filled with boots and helmets. Besides, the whole bunker had become a nursery since Goebbels had asked his wife, the proud blonde Magda, to come and join him with their six children. Room was found for them in the Vorbunker. Four rooms were requisitioned just for them and their mother. Joseph Goebbels himself lived in the holy of holies, the Hauptbunker. He was only a few metres away from his beloved little ones. There was Helga, twelve, Hildegard, eleven, Helmut, nine, Holdine, eight, Hedwig, seven, and Heidrun, who was only four. They all had names beginning with the letter H, H for Hitler. That was the least the Goebbels could do for their Führer.

How could children aged between four and twelve spend their time in a bunker under heavy bombing day and night? They played. They squabbled. They ran shouting from one room to another. Sometimes the soldiers were obliged to tell them off and chase them out of the military operation rooms. Others took the time to teach them a song, inevitably a song to the glory of the one they affectionately called "Uncle Führer." The children didn't seem worried. They very quickly got accustomed to the din of the bombs, the trembling concrete foundations. Even more than adults like Hitler's personal physician, Dr. Morell. This obese charlatan with questionable hygiene and a grim expression was literally dying of fear. Unable to go on, he begged for and was granted the right to leave, since his heart, he claimed, could no longer bear the constant hammering of the Russian artillery. The little Goebbels children were almost amused by the severe and worried expressions of the SS men around them. Naively, they couldn't imagine their "Uncle Führer" lying to them. Hadn't he said that nice soldiers would turn up soon and send the wicked Russians packing back home? And that tomorrow they would have permission to go and play in the garden, in the fresh air?

Magda Goebbels tried to keep herself occupied too. That almost Wagnerian figure of the Nazi wife used every means she could think of not to crack. She was forty-three, and had long ago ceased to believe in the fantastical tales that her husband told her. By now she was only pretending to believe in certain victory and the prescience of the Führer. She had understood perfectly well that the bunker would be her and her children's grave. She quickly found an activity to keep herself from losing her mind, an obsession with housekeeping that might have seemed absurd in such dramatic moments, but which brought her back towards the world of the living: keeping her children's clothes clean and tidy. Like the Valkyries so dear to the Nazi imagination, she accepted the tragic end that was about to engulf her family. She was convinced that if the Third Reich had to perish, then she preferred to perish with it and preserve her children from life in a world without Nazism. Only one fear paralysed her – that of being killed too soon. Too soon to be able to take her beloved children's lives herself. Or worse, to lack the courage at the last moment, and not find the strength for the six-fold infanticide that she had to commit. Then, regularly, with an almost crazed look in her eye, she asked around in the bunker for help, for support. Help to kill her children when the moment came.

25 APRIL 1945

"Poor, poor Adolf, abandoned by everyone,
betrayed by everyone!"

(Eva Braun)

The offensive by the Wenck army produced nothing. The spirited general was stopped at Potsdam, half an hour south-west of the capital. The centre of Berlin now offered itself up to the Soviet shock troops. The New Chancellery, that massive building designed and built by the regime's architect, Albert Speer, was standing up surprisingly well to the deluge of the Russian guns. And yet the artillery of the Red Army was concentrating its fire on the Führer's lair. For their part, the Americans were carrying out a heavy bombing raid on Obersalzberg. The Nazi leaders' main option of retreat had just disappeared.

In the corridors of the Führerbunker, discipline, normally so strict, had made way for an end-of-an-era atmosphere. Men smoked and drank alcohol, both normally unthinkable, so opposed was Hitler to both. The Führer's secretaries, Gerda Christian and Traudl Junge, had nothing to do (the two other secretaries, Christa Schroeder and Johanna Wolf, had left the bunker on 22 April), and talked with the Führer's personal dietician, Constanze Manziarly, often joined by Eva Braun, around a cup of tea. Magda Goebbels kept to herself. Everyone avoided her, so close did she seem to madness, and liable to burst into tears every time she mentioned her children.

Eva Braun, on the other hand, was quite at her ease in the bunker. The young thirty-three-year-old was as radiant as ever. She passionately savoured those historical moments. After all, the Führer's mistress was able to live life to the full. Hitler was too enfeebled not to need her. The elegant Bavarian never shed her smile, and loved receiving high-ranking visitors at the bunker. Obviously, comfort was sparse, and she apologised in advance. So when Speer dropped in to say goodbye to the Führer, Eva Braun invited him to have a drink. For the occasion, she even managed to lay her hands on some chilled champagne – some Moët et Chandon. Instead of the Promethean reception rooms of the Chancellery, they had to make do with a little room with bare walls and the sharp smell of concrete. "It was pleasantly furnished; she had had some of the expensive furniture which I had designed for her years ago brought from her two rooms in the upper floors of the Chancellery," Albert Speer recalled. "She was the only prominent candidate for death in this bunker who displayed an admirable and superior composure. While all the others were abnormal – exaltedly heroic like Goebbels, bent on saving his skin like Bormann, exhausted like Hitler, or in total collapse like Frau Goebbels – Eva Braun radiated an almost gay serenity."* And with good cause – the young woman was about to get what Hitler, her lover, had been refusing her for so long: marriage! While she waited for her wedding night, she spent her time making herself up, adjusting her clothes, serving tea to her unfortunate neighbours, and regretting the fact that the war was so murderous for the Germans. As to her own death, it wasn't a problem, she was ready for it. But how to die with dignity? "I want to be a pretty corpse," she confided in Traudl Junge. So she couldn't very well fire a bullet into her mouth and blow her pretty face apart like an over-ripe melon. That would be terribly ugly, and besides, how would anyone recognise her? she argued. She was in no doubt that her body would be photographed by the winners and presented to the whole world and then in the history books. The only solution, she concluded, was poison. Cyanide. Apparently all the officers in the bunker had some in capsules. Even Hitler.

---

*Albert Speer, *Inside the Third Reich*, op. cit., p. 484.

26 APRIL 1945

"Stay alive, my Führer, it's the will of every German!"
(Hanna Reitsch, German flying ace)

All Hitler's generals were abandoning him. Hitler woke up in a bad mood. The Wehrmacht officers, the SS officers, he loathed them all. In his eyes they were incompetent at best, at worst they were traitors and cowards. The bunker was surrounded. Now it was the time for Tempelhof Airport to fall into Russian hands. All that remained was the runways in Gatow, in the south-west of the city. For how long would they hold out? The Russians had doubled their attacks. But a small two-seater aeroplane, a Fieseler-Storch, managed to land. Its pilot was the air force general Ritter von Greim. He travelled with Hanna Reitsch, his companion, twenty years his junior, who acted as his navigator. She had just celebrated her thirty-third birthday and didn't want to miss the opportunity to see Hitler again for anything in the world. And as a plus, as a civilian German flying ace, she wasn't afraid of slaloming between the shells of the Soviet anti-aircraft fire. Von Greim and Reitsch had been in Rechlin, a Nazi base 150 kilometres to the north, when, two days earlier, they had received a clear order from the Reich general staff: "Come to Berlin straight away! The Führer wants to see you."

Having arrived in Gatow, von Greim interrogated the Nazi officers: why was he risking his life to come to Berlin? Secret defence, they told him. "But does the order still apply?" the general said irritably. "More than ever." the officer replied. "Go to the bunker whatever the cost."

Gatow Airport was only about thirty kilometres from the Führerbunker, but the routes were almost entirely blocked by enemy checks. The only way of reaching the Führer was by air. So they had to take off again in their little aeroplane. The pair did their best to dodge the Soviet shells that pierced the Berlin sky. After a few minutes, the hedgehopping plane was hit by machine-gun fire. "I'm wounded," von Greim shouted, before fainting. A bullet had passed through the cabin and struck him in the foot. Hanna Reitsch, sitting behind him, reached over his shoulder and grabbed the joystick. She knew Berlin like the back of her hand, having flown over it many times. But she had never piloted a plane under fire from the most powerful artillery in the world. In Gatow, the Nazi officer had assured her that a makeshift runway had been cleared so that they could land near the bunker, beside the Brandenburg Gate. Hans Baur had seen to everything. The lamp-posts had been removed over several hundred metres to keep the plane from breaking its wings on landing. An ingenious idea. Reitsch just about managed to land in the middle of the street, but a little further away from the place Baur had prepared. The propeller was still turning when the Soviet soldiers arrived, but a Nazi vehicle arrived at great speed to pick up the pilot and her wounded companion.

They reached the bunker at about 6:00 pm, safe and almost sound. The first to welcome them was Magda Goebbels. In the middle of a fit of hysterics, she burst into tears when she saw them. Did she think they had come to take them all away? Von Greim paid no attention; he had regained consciousness but was bleeding copiously from his foot. He was immediately taken to a little operating theatre. Hitler soon joined him there. At last a man of courage, he rejoiced. The rest of the dialogue between von Greim and Hitler was reported by Hanna Reitsch to the American secret services in October 1945, after she was taken prisoner:

Hitler: Do you know why I asked you to come?

Von Greim: No, my Führer.

Hitler: Because Hermann Göring betrayed and abandoned me and the Fatherland. He made contact with the enemy behind my back. His action was a mark of cowardice. And contrary to my orders, he fled to Berchtesgaden. From there he sent me a disrespectful telegram. He said I had appointed him as my successor one day and that now, since I was no longer capable of ruling the Reich from Berlin, he was ready to do it from Berchtesgaden in my place. He concluded the telegram by saying that if he had had no reply from me by 9:30 pm [in Göring's version it says 10:00 pm] on the date of the telegram, he would conclude that my reply was in the affirmative.

Hanna Reitsch, who admired the Führer without ever having been a member of the Nazi Party, described the scene as "dramatically poignant." According to her, Hitler had tears in his eyes when he spoke of Göring's betrayal. He seemed deeply hurt, almost like a child. Then, as so often, his mood switched in a flash. His eyes sprang back to life, a frown appeared on his brow and his lips pursed nervously. "An ultimatum!" he began shrieking like a lunatic. "An ultimatum!! I am spared nothing. No allegiance is respected, there is no honour, there are no disappointments I have not had, no betrayals that I have not experienced, and now this on top of everything. Nothing is left. Every wrong has been done to me!"

Von Greim and Reitsch didn't dare to interrupt him. They were petrified by this outpouring of hatred from the man for whom they had just risked their lives.

They knew nothing about the "betrayal." Von Greim was a Luftwaffe general and, as such, depended directly on the "traitor" Göring, who remained the all-powerful German Aviation Minister until 23 April. "I immediately had Göring arrested for treason to the Reich," Hitler continued calmly. "I stripped him of all his functions and drummed him out of all our organisations. That was why I summoned you to me."

Von Greim sat up painfully in his makeshift bed, his foot causing him terrible pain. He concealed a rictus of pain.

"I hereby appoint you Göring's successor as *Oberbefehlshaber* [commander-in-chief] of the Luftwaffe."

So that was why Hitler had asked von Greim to come to the bunker! Such an appointment could have been made perfectly well at a distance. But Hitler had absolutely no idea about the situation outside his shelter, and he was still utterly unconcerned about the lives of his compatriots, even when they were the last generals still loyal to him.

Now that the announcement had been made officially, von Greim had nothing to do but head back towards Rechlin. Not a moment to lose, the Führer told him. And the wound in his foot? An unfortunate incident, but one that was endurable in wartime! "Go away and lead the counter-offensive from the air," Hitler ordered. Except that the sky over Berlin was now Russian-speaking. Making an emergency landing on a bombed street was one thing, taking off again quite another. Hitler couldn't have cared less. His orders were more important than reality on the ground. So Rechlin airbase had sent its best pilots, its very last, to bring the brand-new head of the Luftwaffe to Berlin. One by one, the German planes were being shot down by the Russians. Von Greim and Reitsch would have to extend their stay in the bunker. A prospect that enchanted them, since the prospect of dying by their Führer's side seemed like the ultimate privilege.

Later that evening, Hitler summoned the young woman pilot. She was the same age as Eva Braun, but very different in character. Hanna Reitsch liked nothing more than adventure and risk and the excitement that went with them. A test pilot for the Luftwaffe, she was used in the regime's propaganda to illustrate the valour and courage of the Third Reich. As a result she was the only woman in the Nazi empire to receive the Iron Cross, the country's highest military decoration, and from the hands of Hitler himself. That was at a different time, when Nazi Germany terrified the whole of Europe and defeated all opposing armies one by one. In those days

Hitler had subjugated men and women with his vengeful words. It was said that his eyes penetrated you like a blade of the finest steel. On 26 April, did Hanna Reitsch recognise the man who had charmed her so? The man, or rather the ghost in front of her – was it really Hitler? Here is what she said to the American secret services about that conversation: "In a very small voice, he said to me, 'Hanna, you are one of those who will die with me. Each of us has a capsule of poison like this one.' He gave me a little bottle." For the intrepid pilot it was the *coup de grâce*. She slumped on a chair and burst into tears. For the first time she realised that the situation was desperate. "My Führer, why are you staying?" she asked him. "Why are you depriving Germany of your life? When the newspapers announced that you were going to stay in Berlin until the end, the people were petrified with horror. 'The Führer must live, so that Germany can live,' that's what the people said. Stay alive, my Führer, it's the will of every German!"

How did Hitler react to such a declaration of love, such an act of devotion? There were no witnesses to the scene, and only Hanna Reitsch related it. Did she want to present Hitler as a man of good sense, a head of state concerned about the future of his people, a humanist? Certainly. She attributed sympathetic words to him, words that no other member of his intimate circle had ever reported on other occasions. But let us go on experiencing that episode in Hanna Reitsch's version.

With great calm and profundity, the Nazi dictator told the young woman that he could not escape his destiny, that he had chosen to stay in Berlin the better to defend the three million or so Berliners trapped by the Soviet attacks. "By staying, I thought all the troops of the country would follow my example and come to the aid of the city. I hoped they would make superhuman efforts to save me and thus save my three million compatriots." Hitler sacrificing himself for the good of his people? Until now he had never cared about the fate of the Berliners. Quite the contrary. Though his advisers had begged him to leave his bunker to take refuge in the Bavarian Alps, thus sparing Berlin a long destructive siege, he had always refused.

Traudl Junge, one of the Führer's personal secretaries still present in the bunker, remembered Hanna Reitsch being fascinated by Hitler. "She must have been one of those who adored Hitler unconditionally, without reservations. [. . .] She sparkled with her fanatical, obsessive readiness to die for the Führer and his ideals."*

Hanna Reitsch incapable of the slightest objectivity where Hitler was concerned? What is certain is that she left the Führer with a capsule of poison in her hand and went back to see von Greim with his wounded foot. She told him the war had been lost.

*Traudl Junge, *Until the Final Hour: Hitler's Last Secretary*, trans. Anthea Bell, Hachette, 2012.

27 APRIL 1945

"Eva, you must leave the Führer ..."
(Hermann Fegelein, SS General
and Eva Braun's brother-in-law)

It was impossible to sleep. In spite of the thickness of the ceilings and the walls, the Führerbunker was shaking to its foundations. The inferno of the Russian artillery continued all night. Hitler understood that a counter-attack by Wenck had been blocked, and that his general needed fresh troops. But where were they to be found?

For their part, the inhabitants of the shelter were losing hope and cracking one after another. The ones who didn't drown their sorrows wondered out loud about the best way to put an end to it once and for all. Others locked themselves away in their room to weep, away from other people's eyes. Hitler sensed that he was losing control. Rather than delivering yet another military briefing, he decided to organise a quite extraordinary meeting. He called it simply a "suicide meeting." Calmly, before a thunderstruck entourage, he set out his plans so that no one would miss his suicide when the time came. In plain language, as soon as the Russian soldiers set foot in the garden of the Chancellery, they were all to take their own lives. None of those close to him were to be taken alive. To preserve themselves from such a disaster, those who hesitated could count on the zeal of loyal SS men or members of the Gestapo to help them. The meeting ended with the usual Nazi salutes and noisy pledges to keep their promises until the end.

Once that had been sorted out, Hitler was appalled. A loud noise rang out through the bunker. Not bombs this time, but something else. Linge, his valet, told him that the ventilation in the shelter was barely working. The Führer grew worried. Without it, it was impossible to breathe. An enormous fire was raging outside, just above the bunker. It was the flames that had caused the ventilation system to jam. Hitler listened to his valet's explanations with anxious perplexity. A fire in the gardens of the Chancellery? Could it be? For the first time since 20 April and the little improvised birthday party ceremony improvised in the great hall of the New Chancellery, the Führer asked to leave his shelter. He wanted to see what was happening with his own eyes. He struggled towards the stairs leading to the surface and climbed them one step at a time, clutching the metal rail. Linge was just behind him to keep him from falling. The thick armoured door leading to the garden was closed. Linge was hurrying to open it when a shell crashed only a few metres away. The explosion was deafening. When the valet turned around to check that the Führer was all right, he had disappeared, he had already returned to his lair. He wouldn't leave it again.

SS General Fegelein had left the bunker and had no plans to come back. The absence of Himmler's official representative went unnoticed until the evening, at a meeting of the general staff. The Führer entered in a frosty rage; he knew that Fegelein wasn't joining in with his decision to commit collective suicide. The inveterate gambler and skirt-chaser was only thirty-eight, and an ardent desire to live had led him to do the unthinkable and flee. Hitler took it personally. He wanted Fegelein to be found immediately. Erich Kempka, the Führer's personal chauffeur and also responsible for the bunker's fleet of cars, knew where he was hiding. He revealed that Fegelein, at about five o'clock, had asked him to put at his disposal the two last vehicles that were still fit to drive. "For military reasons," he explained. Thirty minutes later, the vehicles and their drivers came back to the bunker but without the SS general. After a quick enquiry, it turned out that Fegelein had taken refuge in his private apartment in Berlin. Hitler and Bormann cried treason. Soldiers were dispatched as a matter of urgency to Fegelein's address. They found him in bed with a woman. It certainly wasn't his wife Gretl, Eva Braun's sister. In the room, the soldiers laid hands on suitcases prepared for a long journey, but also bags filled with gold, banknotes, and jewels. Fegelein didn't defend himself. He was blind drunk and barely capable of walking.

But so what. As Eva Braun's brother-in-law, wasn't he practically part of the Führer's family? He had married Gretl Braun in June 1944, with the sole objective of protecting himself from the Führer's immediate circle, the Bormanns, Goebbels, and consorts, who hated him so much. They quickly worked out that he had never believed either in Nazism or in the cult of the superman, that Aryan German so dear to Hitler. Fegelein was too fond of women, life, and money to take pleasure in a doctrine as severe as it was deadly.

And besides, wasn't he one of Hitler's favourites? Hadn't he been the first to wish him happy birthday on 20 April? All would be forgiven. This demonstrated a fatal lack of knowledge of the Führer. If at first it seemed that Fegelein would be punished by being made part of a combat unit right in the middle of Berlin, Hitler finally changed his mind. He would be judged by an improvised courtmartial for desertion. The sentence would be death.

Eva Braun didn't want to do anything in defence of her brother-in-law. She even told Hitler that he had called on the phone the previous evening. He wanted to persuade her to flee Berlin with him. This is what he was supposed to have said to her: "Eva, you have to leave the Führer if you can't persuade him to get out of Berlin. Don't be stupid – it's a matter of life and death now!"*

That was all it took to seal the SS general's fate once and for all. But the idea of putting a drunk man on trial was out of the question. Fegelein was put under close guard in a cell. He would have to sober up before his examination.

*Traudl Junge, *Until the Final Hour*, op. cit., p. 178.

28 APRIL 1945

"Himmler's Opening Gambit To End European War"
(*Reuters new agency headline*)

The day got off to a bad start. At about nine o'clock an SS officer from a combat unit came to deliver his report to Hitler. He told him that the first Russian commando squads were approaching Wilhelmstrasse, just over a kilometre from the Chancellery. And Wenck still hadn't arrived. The question was no longer whether the bunker would fall, but when that fall would take place. As soon as the news spread, everyone in the shelter asked for their little cyanide capsule. There weren't enough for everyone, and only a small elite had the honour. The soldiers who formed the last guard around the Führer would have to commit suicide with their service weapons. As to alerting anyone outside who might have been able to bring help, that was a waste of time because the last telephone lines had been cut. To find out about enemy troop movements, the bunker telephone operators listened to wireless radio broadcasts, particularly those of the BBC. Thanks to the British station the Führer learned of a new betrayal. A betrayal yet more painful than Göring's. Although the sound was barely audible, the news being repeated on an endless loop on the BBC left no room for doubt: Himmler had proposed that the Third Reich capitulate to the Allies. The BBC quoted a dispatch from the British Reuters news agency, saying that the supreme head of the SS, Heinrich Himmler, was offering a separate peace to the Anglo-Americans. The Reuters article is headlined "Himmler's Opening Gambit To End European War" and reads:

"Himmler's reported overture of surrender to Britain and America alone, excluding Russia, which provided the sensation of the weekend, is regarded as the opening gambit of moves which will bring the war in Europe to an end." The deal was as follows: Hitler would be deposed, Himmler would take his place, the Third Reich would be maintained, and the German army would join the Allies to fight the Bolsheviks. In the bunker, that was too much. While Göring's attitude hadn't really surprised anybody, the position of Himmler, the man of the "final solution to the Jewish question," the most trusted and true of Hitler's followers, destroyed the last certainties of the Nazi regime.

Hitler reacted like a madman. Hanna Reitsch remembered: "From pink, his face turned crimson and really unrecognisable. [. . .] After that very long fit, Hitler finally sank into a kind of stupor, and the bunker fell entirely silent." As he had done with Göring, Hitler immediately dismissed Himmler and excluded him from the Party.

Fegelein would pay for his betrayal of the head of the SS. Since he was officially Himmler's representative to Hitler, his death sentence was authorised on the spot. For the Führer, Eva Braun's brother-in-law must have been aware of Himmler's plans to take power and negotiate with the enemy. His attempt at flight was proof of that in Hitler's eyes. "An RSD [Reichsicherheitsdienst, Reich Security Service] colleague [. . .] shot Fegelein from behind with a machine pistol in the cellar corridor."*

Following these multiple betrayals, a feeling of paranoia spread throughout the bunker. Who would be next? Everyone was keeping an eye on everyone else, wary of the slightest hint of flight, of any criticism of the supreme commander. Meanwhile, outside, above ground, the centre of Berlin was a field of ruins. The fury of the Russians continued to rain down on the Reich capital. The powerful Soviet tanks were eviscerating the buildings on Potsdamer Platz, very close to the bunker. The German resistance consisting of a few soldiers and, above all, a civilian militia, the Deutscher Volkssturm

*Rochus Misch, *Hitler's Last Witness*, op. cit., p. 197.

("German People's Storm") could only slow down the inexorable defeat by a few days.

The Volkssturm was created in autumn 1944 on the basis of an idea of Himmler's. The whole people had to take part in the war. At first the mass enlistment involved all healthy men between the ages of sixteen and sixty. Then, particularly in Berlin, even the wounded, younger children, and old men were called in to swell troops destined to be cannon fodder. Poorly equipped both in arms and uniforms, the Volkssturm militiamen were seen as mavericks by the Soviets, and as such they did not benefit from the protective frameworks of the international conventions in case of war. In plain language, even if they surrendered they were shot.

For the last time, the inhabitants of the bunker begged Hitler to escape. Artur Axmann, the head of the Hitler Youth, wanted to save the day. He claimed that he could get the Führer out. Thanks to a commando unit of hand-picked men ready to die for him, flight was still possible. There was still one aeroplane fit to fly to Gatow Airport. The improvised runway just beside the Chancellery remained under German control. Hans Baur confirmed that it was dangerous, perilous, but possible. A word, a gesture on the part of the Führer, and the escape would get under way.

Hitler doubted, and listened, but he was tired. With his sick body and his fragile nerves, would he even survive the shock of leaving? For Hanna Reitsch, that fifty-six-year-old man was now no more than an old man at the end of his life. "If a safe passage had existed, allowing him to leave the shelter, he wouldn't have had the strength to take it," she believed. His ultimate hope of leaving the bunker was to win the battle of Berlin.

29 APRIL 1945

"In the presence of witnesses, I ask you, my Führer Adolf Hitler,
if you wish to join Frau Eva Braun in matrimony?"
(*Walter Wagner, officer in the Nazi general staff*)

It was midnight. Hitler was very agitated. He thought he had found
the solution to escaping the clutches of the Soviets. Axmann's offer
to flee beneath the bombs wasn't the one that he chose. He strode
resolutely to the room where his new head of the Luftwaffe, von
Greim, and Hanna Reitsch were resting. The young woman's statement concerning this episode is classified as "confidential" by the
American authorities. Here is what it contains:

"Von Greim was thunderstruck when he heard Hitler giving
him the order to leave the bunker that same evening," she reports.
While the Führer's new air force marshal was still wounded and
trapped in Berlin, he found himself entrusted with the crazed
mission of reversing the course of history and countering, or at
least slowing down, the Russian offensive. To achieve this, first of
all he had to reach Rechlin airbase, ninety miles to the north,
then, from there, he would run the German air raids on the Soviet
forces around Berlin. Hitler was so confident of the success of his
plan that he took advantage of the situation to confer another
task on von Greim, one that was more personal, even very
personal. "The second reason behind your departure for Rechlin
is that Himmler must be stopped." As he uttered the name of the
Reichsführer SS, Hitler's voice began to tremble, his lips and his

hands were almost gripped by convulsions. But he insisted. Von Greim had to warn Grand Admiral Dönitz in his headquarters in Plön, near the Danish border, that Himmler had to be stopped. "A traitor will never succeed me as Führer. You have to leave here to ensure this!"

The whole of Berlin was deluged with Red Army soldiers. On the ground, there were now over two million of them, reducing the Nazi capital to ashes, and the sky was criss-crossed by almost a thousand red-starred fighter planes. Von Greim and Hanna Reitsch tried to bring Hitler to his senses. If he made them leave, he was signing their death warrant. "As soldiers of the Reich," Hitler raged, "it is your sacred duty to try every possibility, however small. It's our last chance. It is your duty and mine to grasp it." The debate was closed. He commanded and his soldiers obeyed. But Hanna Reitsch wasn't a soldier. The young woman was a civilian with a strong character. "No! No!" she shouted. In her eyes it was all pure madness. "Everything's lost, to try and change that now is insane." Contrary to all expectations, von Greim interrupted her. The new marshal didn't want to go down in history as the man who hesitated to help the Führer. Even if there was only a one-in-a-hundred chance of success, he had to take it, he declared, looking his young colleague straight in the eyes.

The preparations for departure took only a few minutes. Von Below, the Luftwaffe representative in the bunker, encouraged his new boss. "You must succeed. It all depends on you: the truth must be revealed to our people, saving the honour of the Luftwaffe and Germany in the face of the world." The inhabitants of the shelter had been warned of Hitler's plan. They all envied the potential leavers. Some gave them hastily handwritten letters for their families. Hanna Reitsch would later tell the Allied officers who interrogated her that she had destroyed them all – including the one written by Eva Braun for her sister Gretl – so that they didn't fall into the hands of the enemy. All but two. Two letters from Joseph and Magda Goebbels for Harald Quandt, Magda's oldest son from her first marriage. Harald was twenty-four at the time, and the only one not to have gone to the bunker. And for good reason, since he had been taken prisoner by the Allies in Italy in 1944. Magda Goebbels gave not only this letter to Hanna Reitsch. She also gave her a diamond-studded ring as a souvenir.

Just thirty minutes had passed since Hitler's order. Von Greim and Reitsch were ready. They went up to the surface and jumped into a light armoured vehicle placed at their disposal. They were only about half a mile from the Brandenburg Gate, where a small plane, an Arado 96, was waiting for them under a camouflaged tarpaulin. The Russian mortar fire rang out in the streets with a crazy jagged rhythm, the sky above the capital echoed with the crackle of hundreds of blazing buildings. The ashes that filled the air blackened people's faces and tickled their throats. In the car slaloming along the streets, which were piled high with corpses, Hanna Reitsch was thrown from one door to the other. She was concentrating so hard that she barely pulled a face. She knew this was the simplest part of their escape.

In a few seconds, she would take the controls of the plane that she could see in the distance. It stood right in the middle of the boulevard, on an east–west axis, beside Berlin's most famous monument, the Brandenburg Gate.

The Arado 96 wasn't a warplane; the Luftwaffe used it chiefly for training its student pilots. It wasn't very fast, only 200 mph, whereas the Messerschmitt 109 fighter plane went at over 400 mph. But it demonstrated impressive manoeuvrability. Hanna Reitsch knew the model well; she had felt capable of all her daredevil exploits in just such an aircraft. But she first had to take off from a road covered with debris. On the plus side, the makeshift runway wasn't pitted with holes like a Swiss cheese by shell-fire. The downside was that it was only a quarter of a mile long. Hanna Reitsch sat down at the controls and barely gave von Greim time to sit down behind her. She only had one chance. The Russians, as soon as they heard the roar of the Arado's 465 horsepower engine, would soon understand the situation. Perhaps Hitler was escaping! Like demons, dozens of them climbed the flaming ruins and ran towards the plane. But it was too late. It was already leaving the ground and rising almost vertically to escape the machine-gun fire. Once they were above the buildings, another danger arose. Giant spotlights from the Soviet anti-aircraft defence darted around the sky. Then came the barrage fire, a wave of metal trying to halt their incredible escape. By some miracle, the plane took only a few harmless hits. At an altitude of 20,000 feet it couldn't be touched. The feat was unimaginable. More than that, it was pointless. Fifty minutes later, at about two o'clock in the morning, von Greim and Reitsch reached Rechlin airbase. As he had been ordered by the Führer, the new Luftwaffe commander-in-chief launched all available planes for Berlin. Obviously there wouldn't be enough of them to change the course of the war.

Von Greim didn't wait in Rechlin to check. His only thought was to fulfil his second mission: that of stopping Himmler. With this in mind, he and Reitsch flew to Grand Admiral Dönitz's headquarters in Plön, almost 200 miles north-west of Rechlin. Dönitz, one of Hitler's last stalwarts, had not been informed of Himmler's betrayal. There were other fish to fry beyond arresting the head of the SS. That was what he explained to von Greim, whose failure was now complete.

At last, on 2 May, Himmler found himself face to face with Hitler's emissaries in Plön. The SS chief had come to take part in a military briefing with Dönitz. Hanna Reitsch intercepted him before he could get to the meeting.

"Just a moment, Herr Reichsführer, this is extremely important, excuse me."

Himmler seemed almost jovial as he said, "Of course."

"Is it true, Herr Reichsführer, that you contacted the Allies with proposals of peace without orders to do so from Hitler?"

"But, of course."

"You betrayed your Führer and your people in the very darkest hour? Such a thing is high treason, Herr Reichsführer. You did that when your place was actually in the bunker with Hitler?"

"High treason? No! You'll see, history will weigh it differently.

Hitler wanted to continue the fight. He was mad with his pride and his 'honour.' He wanted to shed more German blood when there was none left to flow. Hitler was insane. It should have been stopped long ago."

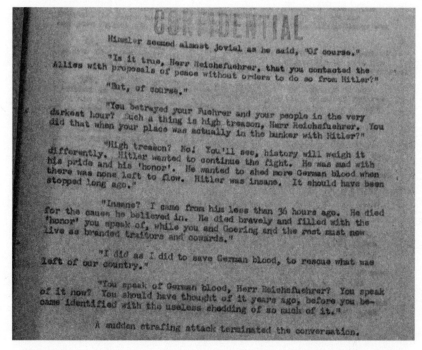

Hanna Reitsch's statement to the American secret services (copy preserved at GARF)

Reitsch assured the American secret services that she had stood up to the head of the SS, and that their conversation was stopped only by an Allied attack on Dönitz's headquarters.

Did Himmler say these things? It is possible. He repeated them several times to other senior Nazi dignitaries. That sudden lucidity about Hitler's destructive madness wouldn't allow him to get away. Hunted by the Allies, he would be captured on 22 May 1945 while attempting to escape to Bavaria. He would commit suicide the following day with a cyanide capsule. The same as the one he had given to Hitler.

★   ★   ★

Let's get back to Berlin on 29 April. Hitler didn't suspect that his order to liquidate Himmler would never be respected. He had just learned of the success of his Luftwaffe commander's crazy escape with Hanna Reitsch. There at last was a sign that the situation was changing, and that all was not lost.

Now he could devote himself calmly to the ceremony that was preparing itself in front of his eyes.

For a few minutes, soldiers had been busying themselves feverishly in the little room where Hitler normally held his military meetings. Beneath Linge's eye, they sorted chairs and changed the position of the furniture with considerable haste. Did this mean they were leaving at last?

A stranger in a Nazi uniform appeared in the corridor. His name was Walter Wagner, and he had just arrived from outside. He was escorted by two severe-looking men. The residents of the shelter wondered what was going on. Who is he? Does he have something to do with Himmler's betrayal? Adjutant Rochus Misch asked one of his comrades who it was.

"That's the registrar."

"The who?" I thought I must have misheard, but Hentschel repeated "The registrar!" He was the Stadtrat (city councillor) and Gauamtsleiter (NDSAP regional office leader) Walter Wagner [. . .]. "The boss is getting married today," the technician informed me.*

Eva Braun was delighted. For several days, she had been begging her lover to marry her. She couldn't resign herself to the idea of dying without officially bearing the name of the man she loved. The man she had met in Munich in 1929. At the time, she had only been seventeen years old, working in the studio of Hitler's official photographer, Heinrich Hoffmann. The couple formed very quickly. She talked to him about marriage. He replied that he wasn't free, that he

*Rochus Misch, *Hitler's Last Witness*, op. cit., p. 197.

already had a bride, her name was Germany. Today, Germany no longer satisfied him. As if she were a mistress unworthy of his love, he decided to break his vows, and since then he had felt free to unite with Eva Braun.

The choice of witnesses for the marriage was limited by circumstances: they would be Joseph Goebbels and Martin Bormann. No female witnesses. Eva Braun raised no objections, and like it or not she accepted the presence of Bormann, whom she so hated. They had contended for Hitler's affections for years. They were jealous of each other's influence over the master. Bormann, like many close to Hitler, was severe in his judgement of the young woman. She lacked depth, she was too trivial, more concerned with the colour of her nail varnish than with politics. Hanna Reitsch, perhaps because she was secretly in love with Hitler herself, even presented Eva as a selfish and infantile simpleton.

At about one o'clock in the morning, the future bride and groom entered the reception room. Hitler had the waxy complexion of those who have not seen sunlight for several days. He wore his usual waistcoat, crumpled by hours spent lying on his bed. In one concession to smart dressing, he had pinned to it the gold party insignia, his Iron Cross first class and his medal for the war-wounded from the First World War. Eva Braun was smiling, wearing a dark blue silk dress. Over it she had draped a grey cape of downy fur. The engaged couple held hands and took their place in front of Walter Wagner. He was trembling with fear. He still couldn't get over the fact that he was standing face to face with the master of Germany. His voice unsteady, the functionary began reading the two standard pages on the obligations of marriage in the Third Reich. As he read out these obligations, Walter Wagner realised that they could not be fulfilled. Trained and conditioned to respect in a literal sense the rules decreed by the Nazi regime, he didn't know what to do. He lacked so many official documents, such as the clean criminal record (to which Hitler could not have laid claim, having been condemned to five years in prison after his failed putsch in 1923), the police certificate concerning their good morals, or the couple's assurance of political loyalty to the Reich. It represented an impossible task for the civil servant. However, the Führer couldn't wait. In the end, the man decided to make an exception and stipulated in black and white on the marriage certificate that the couple had cited exceptional circumstances due to the war to free themselves of the usual obligations and time limits. So it was only on the good faith of the engaged couple that the registrar could validate their purely Aryan origins, and the fact that they did not carry hereditary illnesses.

Then came the essential question. Wagner cleared his throat and got down to business: "In the presence of witnesses, I ask you, my Führer Adolf Hitler, if you wish to join Frau Eva Braun in matrimony. If so, I ask you to reply with a 'yes.'"

The ceremony lasted only ten minutes. Just long enough for the couple to reply in the affirmative, sign the official documents, and congratulate one another. Eva was no longer called Braun, but Hitler. The bride was so moved that she made a mistake when signing the marriage certificate. She began signing with a capital B for Braun before catching herself. The B is clumsily crossed out and replaced with an H for Hitler.

The reception that followed lasted only a few minutes. The Führer's room had been chosen to welcome the few high-ranking guests still present in the bunker. Weary generals, depressed Nazi officials, and three women on the edge of a nervous breakdown, Magda Goebbels and Hitler's two personal secretaries. They were all allowed some cups of tea and even some champagne. Only Traudl Junge, the youngest of the secretaries (she was only twenty-five) did not take advantage of this rare moment of relaxation. She barely had time to present her congratulations to the new couple before anxiously disappearing.

"The Führer is impatient to see what I have typed," she writes in her memoirs. "He keeps coming back into my room, looking to see how far I've got; he says nothing but just casts restless glances at what remains of my shorthand, and then goes out again." Traudl Junge was busy tidying up what Hitler had dictated to her just before the wedding ceremony. His will, or more precisely his wills. The first, a personal one, the second longer and political. In his personal will, Hitler began by justifying his sudden marriage to Eva Braun. As if in his eyes such a gesture, quite unusual for a man who had been living as man and wife with a woman for so many years, needed explanation. "I have decided, before the end of my earthly career, to take as my wife that girl who, after many years of faithful friendship, entered, of her own free will, the practically besieged town in order to share her destiny with me." A generous gesture, but one with a price: death! In the next paragraph, he indicates that his wife will follow him to the grave. On that occasion, if he mentions suicide, he never mentions the word itself. "I myself and my wife – in order to escape the disgrace of deposition or capitulation – choose death. It is our wish to be burnt immediately on the spot where I have carried out the greatest part of my daily work in the course of twelve years' service to my people."

Eva Braun, if she was directly concerned by these words, did not involve herself in the writing of the will. Was she even aware of the "wedding present" that her husband was preparing for her?

Traudl Junge read through her notes once more. She was aware of the historic dimension of her task, and couldn't afford to make a mistake. When, thirty minutes earlier, Hitler had asked her to follow him into the "conference" room of the bunker, she had expected to find herself typing up new military orders. As usual, she had sat down at her typewriter, the one that was specially designed with big letters so that Hitler could read them without making an effort. But then, breaking with his usual habits, he said: "Take shorthand notes directly on to your pad." After a brief moment's reflection, he had continued: "This is my political testament ..."

After the war, Traudl Junge never tired of telling the press, writing in her memoirs and communicating to the Allies, the disappointment that this text inspired in her. She had expected so much, something like an epilogue that could have given a meaning to all the suffering unleashed by Nazism. Making intellectually acceptable the blood-drenched madness of a disaster that had been on the cards since the publication of *Mein Kampf* in 1924. Instead, the secretary heard the same Nazi logorrhoea that she knew so well. And still those special formulas of the language of the Third Reich. A Jewish-German intellectual, the philologist Victor Klemperer, analysed that Nazi language and gave it a name: LTI (for *Lingua Tertii Imperii*). Victor Klemperer observed the expansion and universalisation of this new form of expression over the twelve long years of the Third Reich. Staying in Germany, he had to hide and narrowly escaped the death camps. It was only after the fall of the Hitler regime that he was able to publish, in 1947, his work devoted to LTI. In his view, it respected perfectly established rules. Its goal was to adapt to the new man that the regime claimed to have created for centuries to come. LTI had been invented as much to frighten the enemy as to galvanise the people. Its vocabulary stressed action, will, and strength. Like a drum roll, words were repeated, hammered out emphatically and with great aggression. Words that made the worst acts of cruelty sound ordinary. So one did not kill, one "purified." In the concentration camps, one did not eliminate living beings, but "units." As to the genocide of the Jews, it became only a "final solution."

Hitler's political testament is in itself one of the best examples of this language. The Führer begins by presenting himself as a victim, then very quickly rages against his perennial enemy: the Jew.

It is untrue that I or anyone else in Germany wanted war in 1939. It was wanted and provoked solely by international statesmen either of Jewish origin or working for Jewish interests. I have made too many offers for the limitation and control of armaments, which posterity will not be cowardly enough always to disregard, for responsibility for the outbreak of this war to be placed on me. Nor have I ever wished that, after the appalling first World War, there would ever be a second against either England or America. Centuries will go by, but from the ruins of our towns and monuments the hatred of those ultimately responsible will always grow anew against the people whom we have to thank for all this – international Jewry and its henchmen.

Traudl Junge did her best to replicate the Führer's style as faithfully as she could on the basis of her notes. Beneath her master's fevered gaze, she went on typing as quickly as she could on her typewriter. The passage that follows evokes, without explicitly mentioning it, the fate that the regime reserved for millions of Jews.

I have left no one in doubt that if the people of Europe are once more treated as mere blocks of shares in the hands of these international money and finance conspirators, then the sole responsibility for the massacre must be borne by the true culprits – the Jews. Nor have I left anyone in doubt that this time millions of European children of Aryan descent will not starve to death, millions of men die in battle, and hundreds of thousands of women and children be burned or bombed to death in our cities without the true culprits being held to account, albeit more humanely.

In spite of the deadly outcome of the conflict provoked and fanned by his aggressive politics, Hitler had no regrets.

After six years of war which, despite all setbacks, will one day go down in history as the most glorious and heroic manifestation of the struggle for existence of a nation, I cannot abandon the city which is the capital of this Reich. Since our forces are too meagre to withstand the enemy's attack and since our resistance is being debased by creatures who are as blind as they are lacking in character, I wish to share my fate with that which millions of others have also taken upon themselves by remaining in this city. Further, I shall not fall into the hands of the enemy who requires a new spectacle, presented by the Jews, for the diversion of the hysterical masses.

I have therefore decided to stay in Berlin and there to choose death voluntarily when I determine that the position of the Führer and the Chancellery itself can no longer be maintained.

In the second part of his testament, he officially confirms his decisions concerning the exclusion of Himmler and Göring, whom he subjected to public scorn. "Göring and Himmler irreparably dishonoured the whole nation by secretly negotiating with my enemy without my knowledge and against my will, and also by trying illegally to take control of the state, not to mention their perfidy towards me."

Then he appointed his successor at the head of the Third Reich: Grand Admiral Dönitz. He received the title not of Führer, but of President of the Reich. Goebbels was appointed chancellor. In all, a dozen or so ministries were doled out to the last remaining loyalists, not to mention the general staff of the army, the air force, and the navy. So many virtual posts, given that the Nazi state and war machine were on the brink of imploding.

Hitler concluded with one final piece of advice: "Above all, I recommend that the rulers of the nation and their subjects meticulously adhere to the racial laws and ruthlessly resist the poisoner of all nations: international Jewry."

Traudl Junge was about to finish when she was interrupted by a visibly overwhelmed Goebbels. He had just learned of his appointment as chancellor. He refused it categorically, because it meant that he would have to survive his master. That was impossible. At the risk of complicating still further the task of secretary, the head of German propaganda decided to dictate his own testament to her on the spot. "If the Führer is dead my life is pointless," he laments with tears in his eyes. Then he too dictates his testament. The style is typically Nazi again. It concerns his loyalty to Hitler and his decision not to survive the fall of National Socialism in Germany. He includes his whole family in his desire to die. "Bormann, Goebbels and the Führer himself keep coming in to see if I've finished yet. They make me nervous and delay the work," Traudl Junge reports. "Finally they almost tear the last sheet out of my typewriter, go back to the conference room [and] sign the three copies ..."*

*Traudl Junge, *Until the Final Hour*, p. 185.

It was four o'clock in the morning by the time Goebbels, Bormann, and Generals Burgdorf and Krebs signed Hitler's political testament as witnesses. Three copies were handed to three messengers. Each of them was given the grave and perilous task of conveying the precious document outside of Berlin. One to Grand Admiral Dönitz, in the north of the country, another to Marshal Schörner (the commander of the central group of the German army), currently retrenched in the Czech region, and the last to the head-quarters of the Nazi Party in Munich.

Exhausted, the Führer went to bed. He would not rest for long.

A new Russian attack on the bunker woke him suddenly at six o'clock in the morning. Cries rang out around him, some people being sure that the Chancellery was already surrounded. The emergency door of the shelter was believed to be under machine-gun fire. Would it hold for long? Hitler looked at the cyanide capsule that he always kept in his pocket. A doubt nagged at him. Wasn't it Himmler who had given him the capsules? And what if it was a trap? Himmler would only need to have replaced the deadly poison with a powerful sleeping pill, and he would be captured alive by his enemies. To be absolutely sure, he wanted to test one of them on somebody. But on whom?

It was to be his dog, the faithful Blondi. The German sheepdog that he loved so much. To make him swallow the poison, the Chancellery dog-keeper would have to intervene. The animal fought back. It took several men to hold its mouth open and crush the capsule with a pair of pliers. Blondi soon went into convulsions and, after several minutes of intense suffering, died in front of her master's eyes. Hitler watched his animal without a word. He was reassured; it was definitely cyanide.

The occupants of the bunker couldn't bring themselves to wait for certain death without trying to flee. But for that they would need Hitler's authorisation. Without that, they were bound to end up with a Gestapo bullet in their heads. Several young officers got the green light from the Führer. "If you bump into Wenck outside," he said to them, "tell him to hurry up or we're lost." The Luftwaffe colonel Nicolaus von Below also decided to try his luck. He left the bunker during the night of the 29 to 30 April and headed west. He was given two letters: one from Hitler for Marshal Keitel, the other from General Krebs for General Jodl. Just like Hanna Reitsch the previous day, no sooner had he left the Chancellery than von Below burnt the two letters. For fear that they might fall into the hands of the enemy, he claimed. More probably the better to conceal his identity if he was arrested by the Russians. In the end, it was the British who would capture him, much later, on 8 January 1946. In any case, the war was lost, he would argue to the British officers who questioned him. So what did those letters matter? Before destroying them, von Below did take the trouble to read them. And from memory he gave the gist of them to the British Intelligence Bureau in Berlin in March 1946. According to von Below, this was what Hitler wrote to Marshal Keitel:

"The battle for Berlin is drawing to a close. On other fronts too the end is approaching fast. I am going to kill myself rather than surrender. I have appointed Grand Admiral Dönitz as my successor as President of the Reich and Chief Commander of the Wehrmacht. I expect you to remain in your posts and give my successor the same zealous support as you have given to me. [. . .] The efforts and sacrifices of the German people in this war have been so great that I cannot imagine they have been in vain. The final objective remains to win the territories in the east for the German people."

Hitler clearly set out his decision to commit suicide. As the British officer who signed the report on von Below rightly observed, nothing proved that Hitler had actually written those words. But "they coincide with other evidence obtained from other sources."

If, for von Below, the night of 29 April marked the end of weeks of mental torture in the Führerbunker, for Hitler the nightmare continued. In the middle of the night he received some devastating news, a hint of what was to come. He learned that his faithful ally, the one who had so inspired his beginnings, Benito Mussolini, was dead. The Duce had been executed the day before by Italian partisans while trying to escape through northern Italy disguised as a German soldier. It wasn't so much the death of his ally that chilled Hitler's blood as the fear of the similarity of their two fates. The Italian dictator had been killed like a dog with his mistress Clara Petacci after a sham trial. Then their corpses were displayed in Milan, in Piazza Loretto, hanging by their feet. The enraged crowd savagely mutilated the bodies. Only the intervention of Allied soldiers who had come to liberate the country brought a halt to these scenes of collective hysteria. Mussolini would be buried secretly the same evening in a cemetery in Milan.

Hitler was terrified. Undergoing a similar humiliation was out of the question. He told Hans Baur, his personal pilot: "The Russians will do anything to capture me alive. They are capable of using sleeping gas to stop me from killing myself. Their objective is to put me on display like an animal in a zoo, like a trophy of war, and then I will end up like Mussolini."

30 APRIL 1945

"Where are your planes?"
(Hitler to his personal pilot, Hans Baur)

"Wenck? Where is he?" It was one o'clock in the morning and the same question was still being asked in both bunkers. When would Wenck's attack save him? The Führer couldn't hold out for much longer. For several weeks he had spent his nights pacing the corridor of his lair, seeking sleep that he couldn't find. Besides, by night, by day, all of these notions had become abstract by virtue of living underground, far from any natural light. The damp air of the shelters attacked the skin and the respiratory tracts. Was that also what disturbed everyone's minds, making even the toughest people so fragile? Or the certainty that these wrecks of the Third Reich were destined for absolute hell?

Their few contacts with the outside world were shrinking the range of possibilities still further. Soldiers covered with dust, their eyes filled with alarm concerning their own survival, came regularly to deliver their reports. The battle was lost: that was the essence of what they said. The Russians were crushing everything in their path. They were advancing towards the Reichstag building (the Reich assembly), and were no more than three hundred tiny metres away from the New Chancellery. Or, to put it another way, a rifle shot away.

At about two o'clock the answer that everyone was waiting for arrived by cable: Wenck's army was still fighting valiantly, but couldn't get through to Berlin, let alone rescue Hitler.

So it was over.

"How long can we hold out?" The Führer's question no longer concerned Germany as a whole, nor even Berlin, but just the bunker. How many days, how many hours, before the final assault? The officer standing in front of him stood to attention and answered without a moment's hesitation: "Two days at the maximum."

It was now 2:30. All the women who were still in the area around the New Chancellery, principally servants, were assembled in a dining room. There were about ten of them, standing very straight. None of them knew why they had been woken up in the middle of the night. All of a sudden Hitler entered the room. He was followed by Bormann. The scene was set out in a report by the British secret services drawn up on 1 November 1945 from the stories of eyewitnesses. The dictator appeared abstracted, his eyes glazed, as if he were under the influence of medication, of drugs. He greeted them one by one with a handshake, then muttered a few barely intelligible words about the traitor Himmler, the gravity of the situation, and, particularly, of his decision to evacuate the zone. He thus freed them of their oath of loyalty to him. His only advice: flee to the west, because the east is totally controlled by the Soviets. Fall into their hands, he reminded them, and you are certain of being raped and ending up as a soldiers' whore. He finished speaking, then suddenly exited the room with Bormann. The participants were left on their own. For a few seconds they stood there petrified. Their Führer had just abandoned them to their miserable fate.

It was now the turn of the generals and the inner circle to receive the same orders. Meanwhile, Eva Hitler tidied her things away in her little bedroom. She called in Traudl Junge, who picked up her notebook, imagining that she too wanted to dictate her testament. Far from it. Deep in a wardrobe filled with dresses and fur coats, she beckoned the young secretary over. "Frau Junge, I would like to offer you this coat as a farewell gift," she said. "I've always liked to have well-dressed women around me, and now it's your turn to have them and enjoy them."* The silver fox fur cape was the one in which she had been married.

At eight o'clock in the morning, the order to evacuate the government building was finally made official. Hitler had just dictated it to Bormann. Immediately, small groups organised themselves. Each one wanted to try their chance. Some opted for the south-west, others for the north. The Russians could patrol the city, but they didn't know Berlin, let alone its network of underground channels or the twists and turns of the Berlin underground. Escape was still possible. The pilot Hans Baur was bursting with enthusiasm. At last he was going to have a purpose. He ran to see the Führer and tell him he was ready to get him out of Berlin. He knew where to dig up some planes in the capital. Baur had thought of everything. He would then take Hitler to refuge far away. There were still some friendly countries like Japan, Argentina, and Spain ... "Or, if not, with one of those Arab sheikhs who have always been friendly towards you in relation to your attitude towards the Jews."†

To thank his excited pilot, Hitler left him the big painting that hung on the wall of his office. It showed Frederick the Great, the famous King of Prussia, the typical incarnation of the so-called "enlightened" despot. A political and military point of reference for the Führer. Baur was mad with joy. Many people in the bunker thought it was a Rembrandt, and that it was utterly priceless. In fact, according to Heinz Linge, it was a work by Adolph von Menzel, a German painter who died in 1905 and was very popular in his own country. "It cost me 34,000 marks in 1934," the Führer added with the precision of an accountant. A sum equivalent to almost 400,000 euros today. "It's yours." Then, in a low voice, he added: "Where are your planes?"

*Traudl Junge, *Until the Final Hour*, p. 172.
†Hans Baur, *I was Hitler's Pilot*, op. cit., p. 188.

Heinz Linge, the Führer's personal valet, was also making himself busy. At dawn, his master confided to him that the "hour of truth" had sounded. He advised him to escape towards the west, and even to surrender to the British and the Americans. He confirmed his decision concerning giving the portrait of Frederick the Great to Linge, and absolutely maintained that, even in these moments of chaos, his will was to be respected. The painting became an obsession for the Führer. He wanted to protect it from the looting that would follow the fall of the bunker. Linge assured him that he would take care of it in person.

Reassured, Hitler went to take a rest in his room for a few hours. He lay down fully dressed and ordered his SS guards to stand outside his door.

At about one o'clock he came out to have lunch with his wife, his two secretaries, and his nutritionist. For several days he had refused to share his meals with men. Around the little table, everyone tried to maintain a dignified attitude. But the conversation was stilted. No one had the heart to chat as they had done even the previous day.

Once the meal was over, Eva Hitler left the table first. The secretaries also disappeared to smoke a cigarette. They were joined by Günsche, the Führer's austere aide-de-camp. He told them that the master wanted to say his goodbyes to them. The two young women stubbed out their cigarettes and followed the impressive SS officer – he was 1.93 metres tall, six foot four – to join a small group. The last loyalists waited there, in the corridor: Martin Bormann, Joseph and Magda Goebbels, Generals Burgdorf and Krebs, and Linge. It was almost three o'clock when the door of the antechamber opened. Hitler came out slowly and walked towards them. The same ceremony was repeated. His soft, warm hand gripped the hands that were extended towards him. He murmured a few words and left immediately. Eva Hitler appeared more alive than ever. Her hair, which she had just had done, shone brilliantly. She had changed her dress, and was wearing one that her husband was particularly fond of, a black dress with an edging of roses printed around the neck. She kissed the secretaries one last time, asked them to escape as quickly as possible, and joined Hitler. Linge closed the door and took up position outside the Führer's apartments. Everyone was now free to pursue their own fate.

1 MAY 1945

"Hitler is dead. He fought to his last breath for Germany against Bolshevism."

(address by Grand Admiral Dönitz on Radio Hamburg)

Where is Hitler? In the middle of the night, in the streets of Berlin, the words rang out like a burst of machine-gun fire. The Russian soldiers had learned by heart that phrase in German: *"Wo ist Hitler?"* Where is Hitler? For the general staff of the Red Army, the issue was vital. Marshals Zhukov and Konev, who were in charge of the assault on the German capital, had received two missions from Stalin: to conquer the city before the arrival of the British and the Americans and to catch Hitler. Neither Zhukov nor Konev had any intention of disappointing the master of the Kremlin.

Very quickly they understood that Hitler was hiding near the New Chancellery. The crazed defence of the Nazis around the imperial quarter gave them a clue as did the size of their forces; and then there were all the witness statements from civilian and military prisoners: "Hitler declared that he would remain in the city to the end," they said. "He would be locked in a bunker."

It seemed inevitable now that they would catch him. The symbols of German power fell one after the other. The Reichstag had been taken the previous evening, at about ten o'clock. The flag of the Soviet Union now flew over the ruins of its dome. On the ground, the battles continued to rage with cruel intensity. In fifteen days, the battle of Berlin had claimed at least 20,000 civilian and 200,000 military lives in both camps. It was one o'clock in the morning, the last few metres leading to the government buildings were gained at the cost of the blood of hundreds of soldiers. The last SS regiments fanatically defended the smoking ruins of the New Chancellery.

Suddenly, as if by magic, silence fell. Then a single shot and no more screams. The whole area was plunged into an unreal calm. Two men in Wehrmacht uniforms felt their way across the charred stones and the shapeless rubble of what had once been one of the most beautiful streets in Berlin. The infantry general Hans Krebs spoke reasonably good Russian. It was because of this linguistic skill and his status as head of the land army that he risked his life in the middle of the worst combat zone in Berlin. The orders he received in the Führerbunker had been clear: he had to attempt to negotiate with the Soviets. Beside him, an officer, Colonel von Dufving, had been given the task of assisting him and, if necessary, of protecting him. Certainly, a few hours previously, an agreement had been concluded between the two warring forces to let them pass freely, but would the Russians respect it?

The two German soldiers were quickly led to the nearest Soviet command post, the post of the 8th Army led by General Vasily Chuikov. Of humble origins, indefatigable and intransigent with the enemy, he was the son of a Russian peasant, a colossus with rustic manners. Hans Krebs, on the other hand, embodied the German military aristocracy. Shaven-headed, he had put on his finest military costume with his Iron Cross clearly in evidence and a long, impeccable leather coat. As one last flourish he wore a monocle in his left eye. The two men were almost the same age, the Russian forty-five and the German forty-seven. But in all other respects they were opposites. Chuikov had thick black hair, his forehead furrowed with deep wrinkles mixed with startling scars, heavy, severe eyebrows, a flattened nose, his skin thick and soft from heavy drinking, and most of all, incredible teeth, all of them false, made of silvery metal. It only made his grimacing smile all the more menacing. Krebs remained rigid in the face of the animal power exuded by his enemy. In the photographs taken by the Soviets during those negotiations, the anxiety of the German general is palpable. Krebs committed one first mistake. He stood to attention and gave his best military salute. He thought he was in the presence of Marshal Zhukov. Chuikov was amused by his confusion, and turned gleefully towards his officers. Krebs managed to catch a few words that the Russians exchanged in front of him, notably when Chuikov uttered a thundering: "We'll have to finish them all off!" which did not presage anything good.

At last the Russian general telephoned Zhukov and said, "Personally, I wouldn't stand on ceremony. Unconditional surrender, and that's that." During the phone call, the attitude of the Soviet soldiers who were present worried the two Germans. Their hatred was palpable. Krebs was even violently taken aside by a colonel, who wanted to remove the pistol that he wore in his belt. It took several other officers to calm him down. For his part, Zhukov confirmed that no negotiation was conceivable in the absence of the Allies.

Krebs then played his last remaining card. He held out a document that he had taken from von Dufving's saddlebag. It was a letter from Goebbels addressed to the "ruler of the Soviet people." It said that Hitler had killed himself the previous day and had passed on his power to Dönitz, Bormann, and Goebbels.

Hitler dead! The Russians hadn't expected that. Zhukov was given the news almost immediately. The information was too serious, and he decided to call Stalin straight away. It was four o'clock in the morning in Moscow and the Soviet dictator was asleep. "I'm ordering you to wake him up," Zhukov shouted at the officer on duty. "It's urgent, and it can't wait till tomorrow."[*] The announcement of the suicide vexed the head of the Kremlin: "So

---

[*]Elena Rzhevskaya, *Carnets*, op. cit., p. 227.

that's the end of the bastard. Too bad he couldn't be taken alive. Where is Hitler's body"*

Meanwhile, at 3:18, an urgent radio telegram reached the general staff of Grand Admiral Dönitz in Plön. It was signed by Goebbels and Bormann:

Grand Admiral Dönitz (personal and secret)
To be conveyed only by officer.

Führer died yesterday, 1530 hours. In his will dated April 29 he appoints you as President of the Reich, Goebbels as Reich Chancellor, Bormann as Party Minister, Seyss-Inquart as Foreign Minister. The will, by order of the Führer, is being sent to you and to Field Marshal Schoerner and out of Berlin for safe custody. Bormann will try to reach you today to explain the situation. Form and timing of announcement to the Armed Forces and the public is left to your discretion. Acknowledge.

Signed: Goebbels, Bormann.†

A few hours later, at about seven o'clock, Radio Hamburg interrupted its schedule and broadcast an extract from Wagner's *Twilight of the Gods*. Then a communiqué was read several times. It indicated that Hitler was still supported by his troops in Berlin. Two hours later, a sombre voice warned listeners that a solemn announcement was due to be broadcast. Against a background of funeral music, Dönitz's voice rang out. "German men and women, Wehrmacht soldiers: our Führer, Adolf Hitler, has fallen. The German people bow in grief and veneration."

★   ★   ★

*Zhukov (Marshal), *Memoirs*, New York, Delacorte Press, 1971, p. 622.
†Karl Dönitz, *Memoirs, Ten Years and Twenty Days*, Barnsley, Frontline Books, 2012, p. 452.

End of the day in the Führerbunker in Berlin. General Krebs was back. The Russians categorically rejected his offer of a ceasefire. They demanded an unconditional surrender. Most of all they wanted Hitler's body to prove that he was really dead and not in flight.

2 MAY 1945

"Hitler has escaped!"
(Soviet Press Agency TASS)

The 2 May edition of *Pravda*, according to a dispatch from the Soviet Press Agency TASS:

> Late yesterday evening, German radio broadcast the communi-
> qué from the so-called "Führer's headquarters," stating that
> Hitler died on the afternoon of 1 May. [. . .] These German radio
> messages are probably nothing but a fascist trick: by broadcasting
> the news of Hitler's death, the German fascists hope to give him
> the chance to leave the scene and go into hiding.

PART III

THE INVESTIGATION (II)

MOSCOW, DECEMBER 2016

It's impossible to ignore the proximity of Red Square. Christmas garlands and decorations frame a forest of little rectangular chalets singing the praises of Russian popular art. In an uninterrupted torrent, Muscovites in gaudy anoraks slalom among the stalls. Laughing, they hurry down the long pedestrian Nikolskaya Street towards the crimson walls of the Kremlin. The ones most vulnerable to the cold, or the least well covered-up, find an oasis of warmth by passing through one of the grand entrances to Gum, Moscow's historic commercial centre. You can't miss this great stone and glass ocean liner of a building opposite Lenin's mausoleum. The temple to bourgeois hyper-consumption stands in contrast with the grim, dark marble sarcophagus of the master of the Russian Revolution. As if to taunt old Vladimir Ilyich, Gum has even been decked out with a thousand bright lights for the New Year celebrations, and its ostentatious window displays burst with Western luxury goods. A few foreign tourists, happy to test the heat-protecting properties of their fur hats, brave the polar wind. As if amazed by their own resistance to the cold, they take selfie after selfie with their mobile phones on the end of fragile telescopic perches. It'll soon be Christmas.

Our present is waiting for us at the other end of the tourist quarter.

Here I am back on Russian territory. After a phone call from Lana the previous week, I made my mind up. "It's okay, she told me, I've been given the green light and I'm taking the first flight from Paris to Moscow." So here we are, Lana and I, bang in the middle, near the Kremlin.

We still don't know the nature of the present as we pass through the crowds coming in the opposite direction along Nikoskaya Street.

The darkness of the Russian winter days makes the biting cold feel even more intense, even though, at only minus 15 degrees, the temperature is acceptable to a Muscovite. The appearance of cars with blue lights marks the end of the pedestrian section of the street. In front of us is a monumental square of the kind that the Russians are so good at building. At its centre, a snow-covered central island. Then, further off, a building with Italian-inspired orange pastel tones. The rigour of its architecture, stripped of decorative flourishes, gives it an immediately recognisable commanding quality. Lubyanka Square, with the notorious Lubyanka building bounding one side.

Lubyanka equals KGB, KGB equals terror. If the history of the Soviet Union has its shadowy areas, the Lubyanka is definitely its black sun. For decades, Number 2 Bolshaya Lubyanka housed the secret services of the Communist regime, the KGB. Not only its administrative service, which, with a simple stamp, dispatched deportees to the Siberian camps. No, hidden deep within this Lubyanka address are the interrogation rooms and a prison. For generations of Soviets, entering this building amounted to a death sentence, or at least the certainty of disappearing for many years. Some of the most important Nazis, imprisoned after the fall of the Reich, endured their worst torture sessions between these thick walls. Since 11 October 1991, the KGB has ceased to exist, having been partially replaced in 1995 by the FSB which is still based at 2 Bolshaya Lubyanka. That was where we were due to have our meeting. A meeting to try and consult the secret reports into Hitler's death, the ones that haven't yet been declassified. Particularly the ones about the discovery of the alleged body of the Führer. More than seventy years after the demise of the Third Reich, the Hitler file is still partly confidential, and comes within the competence of the secret services.

Quite quickly, thanks to our contacts at GARF, the Russian State Archives, we came to learn that one of the keys to the Hitler mystery dwelt at the heart of the FSB. Like a giant jigsaw puzzle scattered by a temperamental child, the pieces of the "H file" have been distributed among different Russian government services. Was it done deliberately so as not to leave such a secret in the hands of a single administration? Or was it just the result of a hidden war between bureaucrats jealous of their archive dossiers? The USSR, and then today's Russia, have been skilled at creating and maintaining these administrative quarrels, the perfect illustration of a paranoid system. Whatever the truth of the matter, consulting these documents is like a treasure hunt whose rules vary between one contact and another. Stalin would not repudiate such methods. GARF gets the bit of skull that they claim belonged to Hitler, the Russian State Military Archives get the police files of the witnesses of the Führer's last days, and the TsA FSB have the file about the discovery and authentication of the body. A chaotic spread of resources for anyone hoping for any kind of simplicity in the consultation of documents. People such as historians and journalists. The proliferation of pitfalls and authorities to be persuaded means that the slightest inquiry into the disappearance of the German dictator quickly becomes both infernal and exhausting, in terms of time and money.

It is now three months since we first made our application to the FSB. That was last October. Three months of waiting. Silence. Nothing. And then an answer. "No. Don't even think about it. Impossible." Lana knows the Russian mentality well enough not to give up at the first refusal. So she started writing new mails, and then going directly to the offices in question. Persuading people is her major gift. To increase our chances, she approached the media service of the Ministry of Foreign Affairs. Alexander Orlov is the man who deals with journalists covering stories on Russian territory. He was the one who got me my temporary Russian press card, without which I wouldn't be able to conduct this investigation. Alexander speaks French and knows about our research into

Hitler. He's bound to have contacts with the FSB. Lana is sure of it and she gets in touch with him. The result is a long time coming, but then there's a call from Alexander. "Yes. Next week. Wednesday!"

The day before the meeting, when I've just booked in at my Moscow hotel, Lana tells me that it's not going to happen on Wednesday now. It's all been cancelled. In fact not cancelled, but postponed. Postponed to when? Maybe Thursday. On the phone, Lana negotiates and argues. "He's come specially from Paris," she explains to Alexander. "When is the French journalist going home?" he asks. "Ah, Friday! What time flight? 1:30 pm! Then the meeting will be on Friday at 10:00. The person who will see you is called Dmitri. Be on time!"

Apart from the surprise, even the joy, of a positive response, one question eats away at us: why? Why this sudden U-turn by the Russian authorities? Why would the FSB hand over secrets that had been so closely guarded for over seventy years? Why us? Let's be frank. Lana and I very quickly came to doubt our importance for them. Not because we doubted the seriousness of our project, or the solid foundations of our professional reputation, but that couldn't be enough.

There had, of course, been Lana's patient, dogged work on the different bureaucratic wheels of the Russian administration. Not to mention the support, time and again, of her well-placed friends in the spheres of "Putinian" power. That combination seemed perfect when it came to removing obstacles in the way of our researches in the State Archives (GARF). It allowed us to obtain green lights from the relevant services relatively easily. And, above all, the definite permission to consult documents that few researchers, particularly foreign ones, could have got hold of. But the FSB archives are from another world, a closed world. All the more so since Putin took over the country. In the Yeltsin era, in the 1990s, you could get hold of anything if you poured money into it; today that's impossible. Besides, everyone we met in the course of this investigation told us over and over again: the Hitler file is a Kremlin matter. No decision can be taken without agreement from the top levels of the state, or at least without their knowledge.

The most credible hypothesis we were able to come up with did not work in our favour. It could be summed up in a word: manipulation. What if granting us access to the files on Hitler's death was useful to Russian state propaganda? Just like in Stalin's day, immediately after the war, Moscow is suspicious of the West, of Europe, and primarily of the United States. Diplomatic tensions have been mounting between the White House and the Kremlin for a decade, and you don't have to be a genius to sense the cooling of relations between the Western powers and Russia. And yet our investigation into Hitler is taking place within that tense context. It gives Moscow the opportunity to remind the whole world that it was the Red Army that defeated the Nazis and broke Hitler. The proof being the ultimate trophy of the Second World War: the remains of the Führer's corpse, in fact a piece of his skull. Producing this evidence today is a reminder that Russia is a great nation, a power that can once again be counted on.

And who better to convey that message than a team of international journalists: Lana is Russian-American, I'm French.

That's our hypothesis. For want of certainty, it encourages us to remain vigilant.

You might think that the wounds of the Second World War are finally healing as the last actors in that drama succumb to sickness or old age. The last days of the Führerbunker and its inhabitants have been known about for decades. There is no shortage of eyewitness testimonies or reference works. We know who among the inhabitants of Hitler's shelter was arrested by the Soviets, the British, or indeed the Americans. We know who died, too. The visual proof exists for all of them – except Hitler and Eva Braun.

★　　★　　★

To prepare for our meeting with the FSB, Lana and I returned to the indisputable facts of the fall of Berlin.

On 2 May 1945, the first Soviet troops attacked the Führerbunker. In Hitler's apartments, they found some injured people who were too exhausted to flee, and three corpses. These were Generals Krebs and Burgdorf, as well as the head of Hitler's bodyguards, Franz Schädle. All three had chosen to commit suicide. No trace of Hitler. The previous day, as we saw earlier, an official message signed by Goebbels and Bormann and conveyed to the general staff of the Red Army announced the death of the Führer. Immediately informed, Stalin issued the express order to find his enemy's body. All the secret services of the Soviet Union and the elite military units were informed of their new mission.

That was how, a few hours after the taking of the Führerbunker, the bodies of Joseph and Magda Goebbels were found, photographed, and filmed. Those were the facts.

Let's come back to the Goebbels case for a moment. There is no mystery about him. His suicide is confirmed by the existence of numerous documents, and especially photographs and videos. The fanatical master of Nazi propaganda took his own life and dragged his wife and six children with him into his final act of madness. It was 1 May 1945. Having received the order from Goebbels in person, the last SS men in the bunker burnt his corpse and that of Magda, his wife. Then they ran for it in the hope of escaping the Red Army. In their haste, they forgot, or didn't take the time, to deal with the bodies of the children. Contrary to the plan, they would not be burnt.

The Soviets found the bodies of the Goebbels couple as soon as they entered the shelter. This is the account given in a "Top Secret" NK report by the NKVD, the People's Commissariat (equivalent to a ministry) for Internal Affairs. It is dated 27 May 1945. It was sent directly to one of the most powerful and feared men in the USSE, the head of the NKVD, Lavrenti Beria.

On 2 May 1945 in Berlin, a few metres away from the air-raid shelter in the grounds of the Reich Chancellery, which has recently held Hitler's headquarters, the charred corpses of a man and a woman were found; it is also noted that the man is of small stature, his right foot is in a semi-folded position in a charred orthopaedic shoe, and on his body were found the remains of the NSDAP party uniform and a party badge damaged by fire.

By the head of the two corpses lay two Walter No. 1 pistols.

The Goebbels children were not found until later. The officer who signed this report, Lieutenant General Aleksandr Vadis, was hard-bitten, a man inured to the horrors of the war of extermination that the Nazis waged against his country. Vadis wasn't just anyone, in Berlin he led a very secret and very violent unit of SMERSH, the Soviet military counter-espionage service that operated between April 1943 and May 1946. And yet in his report he has difficulty concealing his dismay:

> On the 3rd of May of this year, in a separate room in the bunker of the Reich Chancellery, 6 corpses of children were found laid out on beds – five girls and one boy wearing light nightshirts and bearing signs of poisoning.
> [. . .]
> The fact that the corpses of the man, the woman and the six children are in fact those of the Reich Propaganda Minister Dr. Goebbels, his wife and his children, is confirmed by the testimony of several prisoners. It should be noted that the most characteristic and convincing statement is that of the dentist of the Reich Chancellery "Sturmbannführer SS" Helmut Kunz, who has been directly implicated in the murder of the Goebbels children.
> Interrogated on this matter, Kunz declared that as early as 27 April Goebbels' wife asked him to help her kill her children, adding: "The situation is difficult, and plainly we will have to die." Kunz gave his consent to this act.
> On 1 May 1945 at midday, Kunz was summoned to the infirmary of Goebbels' bunker, in the grounds of the Reich Chancellery, and once again it was Goebbels' wife, then Goebbels himself, who

proposed killing the children, declaring: "The decision has already been taken, because the Führer is dead and we must die. There is no other way out."

After which Goebbels' wife handed Kunz a syringe filled with morphine, and he gave each of the children an injection of 0.5 ml of morphine. —Ten to fifteen minutes later, when the children were half asleep, Goebbels' wife introduced a crushed capsule containing cyanide into the mouth of each of them.

In this way all six of Goebbels' children, from the age of four to fourteen [in fact Helga, the eldest, was only twelve] were killed.

After the murder of the children, Goebbels' wife, accompanied by Kunz, went into Goebbels' study and informed him that it was all over with the children, after which Goebbels thanked Kunz for his help in the murder of the children and dismissed him.

According to Kunz's testimony, after the murder of the children, Goebbels and his wife also went to commit suicide.

The Russians agreed to pass on this confidential information to the Anglo-American Allies. Goebbels was a considerable trophy for the Kremlin. A trophy that was worth displaying to the whole world. Because there had not been enough petrol and time to take the cremation to its conclusion, Joseph and Magda Goebbels were easily identifiable. The Red Army hurried to broadcast photographs and films of their spoils. The bodies of the children were taken from the room where they had lain and placed in the gardens of the Chancellery near the remains of their parents. The two bodies, blackened by the flames, monstrous piles of flesh, lay next to frail children wearing white pyjamas. They looked as if they had just fallen asleep. The morbid display was horribly effective. The Soviets wanted to appeal to the emotions. Their message to the world was clear: look what the Nazi leaders are capable of! Look at this monstrous regime that we have defeated!

Photographs, films, everything was in place for the accreditation of Goebbels' death. Certainly, the German Propaganda Minister embodied a large part of the totalitarian insanity of the Nazi regime, and his corpse symbolised the fall of Nazism. Certainly, for a few hours he had been the Chancellor of the Third Reich after the death of Hitler. So why did the Soviets not broadcast similar pictures and publicly exhibit corresponding documents for the keystone of the Nazi regime: the Führer? Even today there is no official visual proof of the charred body of Hitler or his wife.

Are we to believe that the Red Army didn't take the time to photograph or film the remains of their greatest enemy? If not for the press then at least for Stalin? All the more so since, after the fall of Berlin on 2 May 1945, at the slightest suspicion of the discovery of Hitler's body, films were shot and photographs taken. In some of these one can see Soviet soldiers proudly presenting a dead man with a small moustache, bearing a vague resemblance to the German dictator. The Russian chiefs of staff wanted to authenticate these "pseudo-Hitlers." To do so, they asked the Nazi officers they had taken prisoner to identify them. A Soviet diplomat who had met the Führer when he was alive was sent from Moscow to participate in the identifications. In the end the result was negative in every case. Officially, none of the bodies shown was Hitler's.

Very soon the most outlandish rumours began to circulate. Was the dictator really dead, or had he fled? The stubborn silence of the Soviet authorities only amplified these stories, and unleashed the Hitler mystery.

★   ★   ★

A mystery that we hope to penetrate in the archives of the FSB seven decades after the fall of Berlin. As long as we are granted permission to authenticate the documents we are allowed to examine. In Russia, trust is a desirable but not obligatory precondition.

It is in this deliberately cautious frame of mind that we walk towards the offices of the TsA FSB. In contrast with the other pavements lining Lubyanka Square, the one that runs along the façade of the Lubyanka remains surprisingly empty. Not a pedestrian in sight. Just two uniformed policemen, truncheons in their hands. Our arrival does not go unnoticed. They watch us out of the corner of their eyes. There are no signs indicating the entrance to the building. With our noses in the air and our hesitant walk, we must look like lost tourists. One of the two cops comes towards us with a cross expression on his face. "Photographs are forbidden on this pavement," he begins by warning us. "You mustn't stay here, sensitive area, cameras everywhere," he goes on, pointing with the end of his truncheon at the many cameras bolted onto the window ledges. Our answer amazes him. We're there because we want to go in, not take photographs, just go in. "Are you sure?" the policeman says, as if he's sorry for us. Then he continues, turning up the collar of his thick lined jacket, "That's the entrance there." It's in the middle of the building, framed by a heavy block of granite, dark, grey, and sad, with the emblems of the former Soviet Union just above it. If this entrance was chosen to make an impression on the visitor, that goal has been perfectly achieved.

Dmitri is already waiting for us inside. A soldier in ceremonial dress stands between him and us. He must be close to six foot six. Without a word, he brusquely extends a hand towards us. "Passports!" Dmitri explains with a fixed smile. At that precise moment, Lana doesn't know if I'm going to be able to obtain authorisation to get through the double security door. A stranger in the offices of the FSB, and a journalist to boot – that's a lot to ask of a Russia in the middle of an international diplomatic crisis. Would a Russian journalist be invited into the offices of the DGSE in Paris, or MI5 in London? Not necessarily. In emails and phone-calls, Lana has found some good arguments for persuading the FSB. But everything could stop at the last minute. A few days previously, the Russian ambassador in Turkey was shot live on television by a Turk in the name of the jihad in Syria. At that point Dmitri nearly cancelled everything. Who knows whether the Kremlin might have changed its mind this morning? Our investigation into the disappearance of Hitler would be halted right there, on the landing of the FSB headquarters, only a few feet away from the confidential evidence.

LUBYANKA, MOSCOW, DECEMBER 2016

The rules are clear. You don't touch anything. You don't film anything without authorisation, and you wait. Lana listens and nods, then translates the recommendations detailed by Dmitri in the lift. Our contact is trying to be nice. He's obviously trying. The men who receive us on the third floor not so much. Like Dmitri, they wear a severe uniform: black suit, black tie, white shirt. Unlike our host, their faces remain impassive. Neither aggressive nor suspicious, and certainly not benevolent. Real faces of bad guys from a fifties spy film.

Dmitri leads the way towards a corridor covered with a drab-coloured carpet that gives it an ageless patina and adds to the "hammer and sickle" atmosphere of the place. We are now surrounded by three FSB officers. No one speaks. The mediocre lighting doesn't illuminate the whole of the endless corridor. From where we are we can't even see the end of it. It must pass through the whole of the building, at least thirty or forty metres. The walls are punctuated at regular intervals by light wood-panelled doors. None of them is open. No names, just numbers to distinguish them from one another. On this floor alone, on this façade, there must be about twenty doors on either side. But are there any staff? The silence is total. Approaching one of the doors, I slow down and listen. Nothing. Not a murmur. Only our footsteps echo in spite of the reasonable thickness of the carpet. The Overlook Hotel in *The Shining* would seem almost welcoming and desirable compared with this floor on the Lubyanka.

"Here it is. Come in! Take a seat." Our little group has joined two new members of the black-suit-black-tie-white-shirt gang. They were waiting silently outside one of the panelled doors. This one has the unusual quality of being open. The invitation to sit down and make ourselves comfortable is not rejected. And no questions are asked without a great deal of preliminary thought. The room where we have been asked to sit is an office of about ten square metres. Curtains have been carefully drawn over the window. A round table, a glass-fronted bookcase and poor-quality shelves, some Russian flags, a television, a sofa in mad leather, and even a synthetic mini-Christmas tree blinking nervously: the interiors of Russian administrative offices really do all look identical. Except that here the emblems of the FSB are proudly fixed to a wall. A sword covered with a shield emblazoned with the two-headed eagle of the Russian coat of arms reminds us that we aren't in just any federal administrative office. Dmitri has disappeared. Time passes slowly but surely. A man, on the short and squat side, has joined us in the office. He doesn't speak, and doesn't answer Lana's questions. He looks at us, observing us openly without bothering to pretend otherwise. Outside, in the corridor, the two people we just bumped into are discussing something. Some voices carry more than others. Particularly a woman's voice. She has just arrived, and doesn't seem happy to see us. What are they going to agree to show us? What orders have they received? To get things clear in my mind, I decide to take a look. I've barely headed towards the door when our invigilator is standing in my way. I improvise: "Wee-wee! Toilets?" My innocent air does nothing to soften the behemoth. I repeat my request. "Toilets? WC?" I know he understands. The man hesitates, gestures to me to wait and then leaves the room. A moment later, Dmitri appears and asks me to follow him. Here I am in the corridor again. I pass through the group I heard in heated discussion before. There are at least seven men and one woman. The woman is wearing a severe dark suit. Her blonde hair cut strictly at the back of her neck adds a little colour to this monochrome universe. Taller than most of her colleagues, and with shoulders at least as wide as theirs, she clearly shows me that our presence within these walls is an insult to her principles. Even from behind, I feel that her eyes never leave me. Another door, again without a name. Dmitri opens it. There are the toilets.

"They will bring the files at any moment." When I get back to the office, I am welcomed by a triumphant Lana. While I was away, she was given confirmation that we would be shown the secret documents. So much the better, because I only have an hour and a half ahead of me before I have to go to the airport. All of a sudden, the whole group from the corridor bursts into the little office. The woman comes first. She carries some files in her arms in front of her as if they are holy relics. That and a big shoe box. Behind her, two men are delicately setting down a tailor's dummy covered by a dust cover.

Now everything's happening very quickly. The woman arranges the files and the box on the table, the two men finish setting up the dummy on our left, and the others just watch. Some of them are sitting on chairs, some are standing up. There are so many of them that they can't all get into the room. We contemplate the scene without daring to open our mouths for fear that it's all going to stop.

"The rules are as follows ..." In a firm voice that brooks no opposition, the blonde woman sets out, one by one, the conditions that will govern the consultation of the documents. Lana listens, concentrating hard, hands crossed behind her back like a schoolgirl facing a teacher. She whispers a simultaneous translation for me. "Photographs are allowed, but only of documents. It's completely FORBIDDEN to take a picture of any of the members of the FSB that you see here ..." The word "forbidden" is given such emphasis by the secret service official that I even understand it in Russian. "And we will check each photograph that you take. Only the pieces selected by our services will be accessible to you. You will easily recognise them by the bookmarks slipped into the files." A quick glance allows me to estimate the number of those bookmarks, and hence the number of documents allotted to us. There must be ten or so. It's a good start, I reassure myself. "We've also brought you the physical proof of the capture of Hitler's body by our troops." Lana just has time to translate that last phrase when, like a pair of cabaret conjurors, the two men near the tailor's dummy remove the sheet. They get the surprise effect that they're after. A mustard-yellow jacket appears. It looks old but perfectly preserved. On one of the outside pockets, at chest level on the left, three badges are pinned: a medallion circled with red and white, a swastika at its centre, a military medal, and one last dark badge showing a military cap over two crossed swords. "This is Hitler's tunic," our FSB contact informs us. The three badges are perfectly identifiable: the medallion is none other than the official badge of the Nazi Party, the military medal an Iron Cross first class, and the last decoration the badge of those wounded in the First World War. Exactly the same as the ones regularly worn by Hitler.

"Where was this jacket found?" Our question immediately irritates the young woman. Would we dare to doubt the authenticity of the jacket? Which would amount to calling them liars, no more and no less. Dmitri intervenes. "Soviet troops recovered it on the spot, in the area around the Reich Chancellery." Did it really belong to Hitler? Or is this a piece of theatrical staging, perfectly credible, but unverifiable? In the end it doesn't matter. We're not here to look at bits of fabric, but to obtain irrefutable evidence of the death of Hitler on 30 April 1945, and particularly details of the discovery of his body by the Soviets. Neither Lana nor I are particularly fascinated by these Nazi objects. Quite the contrary. Our lack of enthusiasm at the sight of the clothing and the medals prompts Dmitri to speed up the schedule. He gestures to his colleague to get on with the demonstration. With a heavy sigh she asks us to approach the round table. The files are just in front of us. The little chest that looks exactly like an old shoe box, a bit like the one at GARF with the skull fragment, has been set down a little further away, out of reach of our hands. "You'll see that one later!" My lingering glance at the box has not gone unnoticed. "Right, here are the files. They contain the confidential documents concerning Hitler's corpse." Open, look, photograph, quickly, as quickly as possible. I have only a few minutes before I have to leave. Am I allowed to sit down to consult them? I ask the question. Lana can't translate, she's busy with Dmitri. I try speaking in English. Clearly the woman understands. "Da, da," she replies. I open the first file, careful to respect the instructions about the bookmarks, and careful to avoid making the slightest mistake.

It's a typewritten report. Poor-quality, almost rough paper. Creases show that it has been folded in four. The edges are worn and slightly torn, as happens when you transport a document in too small a pouch. Some of the letters have only been half-printed at the outset: the typewriter ribbon must have been worn out. A lot of details to suggest that the text wasn't typed in an office in normal conditions. Was it in the ruins of a Berlin ravaged by bombing raids?

I immediately look at the date. Even though I don't understand Russian, I can still read it. "Year 1945, month of May, 5th day." The report states that the corpses of a couple have been found. The information is set out concisely, precisely, without interpretation. Including the information about the identity of the bodies.

I, Guards Chief Lieutenant Alexei Alexandrovich PANASSOV and private soldiers Ivan Dmitrievich CHOURAKOV, Yevgeny Stepanovich OLEINIK and Ilya Efremovich SERUKH, in the city of Berlin, near HITLER's Reich Chancellery, close to the spot where the corpses of GOEBBELS and his wife were discovered, beside HITLER's personal air-raid shelter, discovered and seized two burnt corpses, one female, the second male.

The bodies discovered were seriously damaged by fire and impossible to recognise or identify without further investigation.

The corpses were in a shell crater, about 3 metres from the entrance to Hitler's bunker, and covered with earth.

The bodies are stored in the "SMERSH" counter-espionage department of the 79th army corps.

The text concludes with four signatures, those of the four soldiers who made the discovery.

г. БЕРЛИН. действующая армия.

А К Т
===========

1945 года, мая месяца " 5 " дня.

       Мной гв. старшим лейтенантом ПАНАСОВЫМ Алексеем
Алексондровичем и рядовыми ЧУРАКОВЫМ Иваном Дмитриевичем,
ОЛЕЙНИК Евгением Степановичем и СЕРОУХ Ильей Ефремовичем ,
в г. БЕРЛИНЕ в районе рейхсканцелярии ГИТЛЕРА, вблизи места
обнаружения трупов ГЕББЕЛЬСА и его жены, около *личного*
бомбоубежища ГИТЛЕРА были обнаружены и изъяты две обожжен-
ных трупа, один женский, второй мужской.
       Трупы сильно обгорели и без каких-либо допол-
нительных данных опознать невозможно.
       Трупы находились в воронке от земли, в 3-х мет-
рах от входа в Гитлеровское бомбоубежище и засыпаны слоем зем-
ли.
       Трупы хранятся при отделе контрразведки "СМЕРШ"
79 стрелкового корпуса.

КОМАНДИР ВЗВОДА ОКР " СМЕРШ " 79 СК
      ГВ. СТ. ЛЕЙТЕНАНТ -   *Панасов* / ПАНАСОВ /

РЯДОВОЙ ОКР " СМЕРШ " 79 СК -   *подпись* / ЧУРАКОВ /

РЯДОВОЙ ОКР " СМЕРШ " 79 СК -   *Олейник* / ОЛЕЙНИК /

РЯДОВОЙ ОКР " СМЕРШ " 79 СК -   *Сероух* / СЕРОУХ /

*Original report by the Soviet secret services on the discovery, on
5 May 1945, of the corpses of a couple outside Hitler's bunker.
The document is still kept in the archives of the FSB.*

The next document is a map painstakingly drawn by hand and coloured. The quality of the paper seems to be just as poor as the other one, but this one has not been folded or damaged. The word "map" is written in large letters at the top, and just below it: "Place of the discovery of the corpses of Hitler and his wife." It is a drawing of the garden of the New Reich Chancellery done with great detail and respect for proportions. It is scattered with little numbered dots, representing the exact spots where the bodies of Joseph and Magda Goebbels were found, as well as the ones believed to be those of Hitler and his wife. The document is signed by Guards Commander Gabelok, on 13 May 1945.

What has happened between the first document, signed on 5 May, in which nothing indicates that the bodies discovered are those of Hitler and Eva Braun, and the one dated 13 May, in which they seem to have been identified? The two reports are only a week apart. No sooner has Lana finished translating them than I loudly express my doubts and questions in French. How were the Russians able to identify the charred bodies with any certainty? I turn towards the FSB staff members around us. As diplomatically as possible, Lana and I try to find out more. To start with, we thank them. Through them we have the proof that the Soviet authorities thought they had found Hitler on 5 May 1945. But that can't be enough for our inquiry. In the office, the atmosphere becomes a little more tense. Perhaps they weren't expecting such a reaction. "Which camp are you in?" the young woman snaps severely at Lana. "Are you Russian or American?" Lana tries to maintain her smile as best she can. Since she won her green card by lottery in 1997 and then got an American passport, she's used to this kind of remark. Traitor to her motherland, no less! "Aren't these documents enough for you?" the FSB official goes on. "You're like those American journalists who refuse to believe that we found Hitler first. You're after a scoop." Our conversation is taking a bad turn. Voices are raised behind us, things are getting heated. A bald man rises abruptly from his chair and leaves the room. Is that a sign that it's all over already? But we have so many documents to consult, and there's that box taunting us

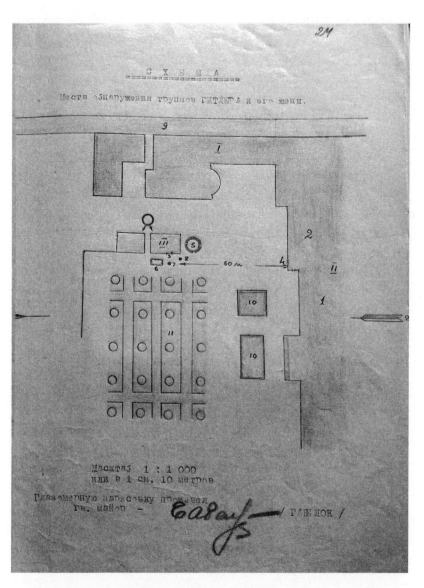

Map of the discovery of the probable bodies of Hitler, Eva Braun and Joseph and Magda Goebbels outside the emergency exit of the Führerbunker in Berlin. The map was drawn on 13 May 1945 by Soviet investigators. Number 6 indicates the spot where the charred bodies of a man and a woman were found. Number 7, the place where the Goebbels corpses were incinerated. Number 8, the likely place of the incineration of Hitler and his wife (TsA FSB).

from the end of the table. I leave Lana to try and soften the woman, who is clearly opposed to our presence, and turn towards Dmitri. I'm sure he must speak English or French.

"Do we have a problem?"

Rather than answer, he gestures to me to be patient. After several long minutes the bald man comes and stands in front of me and holds out a big brown paper envelope. "Open, open!" I do so, as Lana explains herself more and more excitedly to her compatriot. Or semi-compatriot, I should say.

Mug shots, or not really mug shots, more anthropometric photographs, in black and white verging on sepia. They are enlargements. One shows a quite young man with his hair slicked back. His name is written in big Cyrillic letters: Echtman F., followed by a date: 1913.

On the other, a woman, also in the prime of life, wearing a gingham blouse. Her name written in Russian is translated as Hoizerman K., just beside another date: 1909.

Anthropometric photographs taken by Soviet investigators of Fritz Echtmann, Hitler's technician-prosthetist. (TsA FSB).]

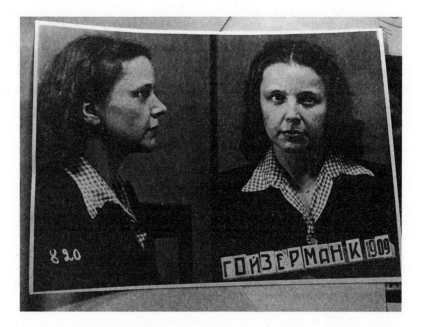

Anthropometric photographs taken by Soviet investigators of Käthe
Heusermann, assistant to Hitler's personal dentist (TsA FSB).

In fact the two individuals are Fritz Echtmann (with two n's) and
Käthe Heusermann, the two Germans who took part in the dental
identification of the bodies found outside the bunker. Fritz
Echtmann, as a technician-prosthetist, worked with Hugo Blaschke,
Hitler's personal dentist; Käthe Heusermann was Blaschke's assistant. Two biographical files accompany the photographs. We learn
that in 1951 they were both sentenced to ten years' forced labour by
the Soviet Union. One for "having been dental prosthetist to Hitler
and his close circle," the other "for having served Hitler, Himmler
and other senior fascists." On the other hand, nothing on the conclusions of their macabre forensic examination, no photograph of the
teeth in question. The bald man who handed me the kraft envelope
notices my huge disappointment, not without a certain satisfaction.
Is this really all they have to give us? Our allotted time is trickling
away. We only have half an hour left. My visa expires this evening,

and they know that my flight to Paris takes off in the afternoon. While we despair of obtaining concrete information, formal proof, our severe and taciturn "friend" takes some latex gloves from a pocket of her skirt. Gloves like the ones used by surgeons. At last, without a word, she picks up the "shoe box," sets it down firmly in the middle of the table and removes the lid. As if drawn by a magnet, Lana and I immediately lean forward to catch a glimpse of its contents. No sooner have we realised what we are dealing with than the young woman is roughly manipulating the objects in the box. I hear myself shouting "stop!" I don't know which of the two of us is more surprised by my daring. None the less, she obeys and puts everything back. I want to take the time to discover and understand what we have in front of our eyes. Too bad if I miss my plane. Discreetly, I signal to Lana to do the act that we've perfected together. The principle is a simple one: Lana talks and talks without interruption. Her task is to keep the minds of our interlocutors busy and let me observe and take photographs, as many as necessary. It's quite simple and, thanks to Lana's uncommon ability to talk for hours at a time, fiendishly effective. Without having to be asked, she launches into a monologue directed at our hosts.

The box is full of thick layers of cotton wool. Three objects are set on top of it, occupying all the room in it. The biggest consists of a large curved metal rod connected to a leather membrane the size of a leg below the knee. Immediately I think of the orthopaedic apparatus that Goebbels wore because of his club foot. Is it his? The whole thing is blackened and badly damaged as if burnt by a violent but short fire.

There is also a small golden object that has also been severely damaged by fire. It is a cigarette case. The inside is equally charred, but an engraved signature can be very clearly made out. It is the image of Hitler's. I recognise that kind of stripe, like a lightning flash, crossed with a small line at the bottom, and that characteristic capital H. Below it, a date: 29.10.1934. Was it a present from the Führer to Magdalena Goebbels? Is this the "cigarette case" mentioned in the NKVD report from 28 May 1945? It said: "The woman's body had on it a gold cigarette-case damaged by fire ..." It would match. If it is authentic, the object was signed on 29 October 1934. On that date, Hitler had recently concentrated all powers in Germany. With the death of Marshal President Hindenburg on 3 August, he became both chancellor and president of the German state. And then he became the Führer.

But back to Moscow. I concentrate on this last object, the one that intrigues me the most. A small square box with a transparent lid. Written on one of the sides, in French and Russian, are the words "25 cigarettes No. 57, Société Bostanjoglo." Apparently it was a box of cigarillos. I can see the inside through the transparent lid. Not a sign of any tobacco, but more cotton wool, on which the remains of a human jawbone have been thrown at random. A jawbone broken into several pieces. Even though I don't say a word, the gloved hands of the FSB official delicately open the box and take out the four parts of the jaw one by one. Lined up in front of me are twenty-four teeth fixed to blackened bony tissue. Most of them false or covered with implants and gold bridges. I can only make out a few natural teeth, perhaps three or four. The others are made of either porcelain or metal. The man, or woman, to whom they belonged, had absolutely terrible teeth. "That's the proof that you were looking for." Arms crossed, and her expression still just as severe as before, my demonstrator for today at last decides to address me in English. I am bold enough to ask her for confirmation: "Are these Hitler's teeth?" The "da" which is all I receive by way of answer is supposed to satisfy me. It doesn't. Or at any rate it isn't enough for me. Since we're here, I'm going to take all my time and photograph these teeth and the remains of jawbones that go with it from every imaginable angle.

While Lana goes on deluging everyone else with her torrent of words, I manage to make myself understood to my watchdog. One by one, I ask her to position the human fragments in front of me. From the front, from the back, from either side, I don't want to leave anything out. And, most importantly, there is this very unusual bridge connecting two teeth by passing in an arch over a third.

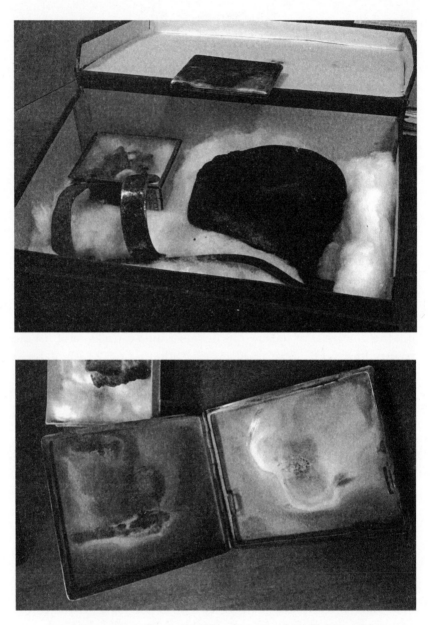

Box containing, according to the FSB archives, Joseph Goebbels' prosthesis as well as Magda Goebbels' gold cigarette case given to her by Hitler. Also visible is the small box supposedly containing Hitler's teeth.

My photographic session comes to an end. Tensions ease. I save Dmitri and his colleagues from Lana's logorrhoea and thank them. They have played the game. At least partly, because we still haven't seen any photographs from the time of the corpses of Hitler or Eva Braun. "There aren't any," Dmitri cuts in. Of course we don't believe a word of it. But it doesn't matter. We are pursuing our inquiry. The puzzle is slowly beginning to come together. It was the forensic examination carried out by Hitler's personal dental prosthetist and his assistant that would have persuaded the Soviets in May 1945. They were the ones who laid hands on the body of the Nazi dictator.

"Before you leave, look at this ..." Dmitri holds out one of the files that we hadn't yet consulted. He opens it up on one of the bookmarks placed there earlier on. "This is what was done to Hitler's body after it was formally authenticated."

I avidly decipher a few words in the document. At the top of the page on the right, "Top Secret," the general title, "File," the date, "4 June 1945," and the signatures as well as the stamp at the bottom of the page. Lana translates the rest for me:

As the result of later research on 5 May 1945, a few metres away from the place where the bodies of Goebbels and his wife were found, two badly burned bodies were found in the crater of a bomb: the body of the Reich Chancellor of Germany Adolf HITLER and the body of his wife Eva BRAUN. These two bodies were transported to the "SMERSH" counter-espionage of the 3rd Assault Army in the district of Buch in Berlin.

All the bodies brought to the "SMERSH" department of the 3rd Assault Army were subjected to a medico-legal examination and presented for identification to individuals who knew them well when they were alive.

After being subjected to medico-legal examination and the entire set of identification procedures, all the bodies were buried near the Berlin district of BUCH.

Because of the redeployment of the "SMERSH" counter-espionage department, the bodies were withdrawn and transported first to the area around the town of Finow [60 km north of Berlin], then on 3 June 1945 to a place near the town of Rathenow [80 km west of Berlin], where they were buried once and for all.

The bodies are in wooden boxes and have been buried at a depth of 1.7 metres and placed in the following order:

From East to West: HITLER, BRAUN Eva, GOEBBELS, Magda GOEBBELS, KREBS, the GOEBBELS children.

The western part of the grave also contains a basket with the bodies of dogs, one of which belonged to HITLER in person, and the other to BRAUN Eva.

The location of the buried bodies is as follows: Germany, province of Brandenburg, near the town of Rathenow, forest to the east of the town of Rathenow, on the motorway from Rathenow to Stechow, just before the village of Neu Friedrichsdorf, 325 metres from the railway bridge, gap in the forest, from the stone post number 111 – to the north-east as far as the stone marker bearing the same number 111 – 635 metres. Then from that marker in the same direction to the next stone marker bearing the number 111 – 55 metres. From this third marker due east – 26 metres.

The grave has been flattened out at ground level, and small pine seedlings have been planted on the surface forming the number 111.

The map with the diagram is attached.

This file exists in three copies.

I was also allowed to photograph a hand-drawn map, carefully coloured in green and red. It shows very precisely where the remains of the Nazi ruler were buried. The town of Rathenow was not chosen at random by the Soviets. This small town which had about ten thousand inhabitants in 1945 and was situated in the Red Army-controlled zone was easily and quickly accessible from Berlin.

/ с востока на запад:/ ГИТЛЕР, БРАУН Эва, ГЕББЕЛЬС, магда
ГЕББЕЛЬС, КРИС, дети ГЕББЕЛЬСА.

В западной части ямы находится также корзина с двумя трупами
собак, принадлежавших одна - лично ГИТЛЕРУ, другая - БРАУН Эве.

Местонахождение закопанных трупов: Германия, Бранденбургская
провинция, район и гор. Ратенов, лес восточнее гор. Ратенова: по
шоссе с Ратенова на Штехов, недоходя дер. Ной Фридрихсдорф, что
325 метров от железнодорожного моста, по лесной просеке, от каменного столба с числом 111 - на северо-восток до каменного 4-х гранного столба с тем-же числом 111 - 635 метров.От этого столба в том-
же направлении до следующего каменного 4-х гранного столба с тем
же числом 111 - 55 метров.От этого 3-го столба строго на восток -
26 метров.

Закопанная яма с трупами сравнена с землей, на поверхности
ямы внсажени из мелких сосновых деревьев число - 111.

Карта со схемой прилагается. Акт составлен в 3-х экз.

ПРЕДСЕДАТЕЛЬ КОМИССИИ - полковник   /Мирошниченко/

                                                     /Горбушин/

                                                     /Быстров/

                                                     /Горохов/

                                                     /Белобрагин/

                                                     /Вакалов/

          Красноармеец   /Хайретдинов/

          Красноармеец   /Терляев/

Original of the map drawn by Soviet counter-espionage on 4 June 1945 showing the burial place of Hitler and his wife, Goebbels and his wife and General Krebs (TsA FSB).

So if we are to believe this document, on 4 June 1945 Hitler's body was found, identified, and buried with great secrecy in the Soviet zone of defeated Germany. However, officially, Stalin informed the whole world, and his Anglo-American Allies first and foremost, that Hitler was definitely still alive and that he had escaped! Why adopt such an attitude?

Before replying, we must immerse ourselves once again in the days that followed the fall of Berlin. Starting with 2 May 1945 …

BERLIN, 2 MAY 1945

The capital of the Third Reich has just fallen. Some hours previously, at about 8:30 in the morning, the military commander of Berlin, General Helmuth Weidling, had ordered his troops to stop fighting. A decision taken immediately after the announcement of Hitler's suicide. Weidling believed that the disappearance of the Führer freed the men from their vow to fight to the death. "On 30 April 1945, the Führer took his own life and thus abandoned those who had sworn loyalty to him. [...] Every additional hour of battle prolongs the suffering of the civilians of Berlin and of our wounded," he wrote in his public declaration. "In accord with the High Command of Soviet troops, I order you to stop fighting immediately."

For the Allied staff, a new race against the clock began. Who would be first to lay hands on the Nazi dictator? Was he really dead, or was it a trick by the Nazis? The Soviets had the advantage of the terrain. The city remained under their control until the Potsdam Conference on 17 July 1945. Berlin would then be divided into four zones, one for each of the Allies: the United States, United Kingdom, France and, of course, the Soviet Union. The district around the Chancellery where the Führerbunker was located would be in the sector under Russian command.

Since they didn't know with any certainty and didn't just want to imagine things, the Soviet, American, British and, to a lesser extent, French investigators would spend the next few months questioning, counter-questioning and checking. And always that same question: what happened in the Führerbunker on 30 April? All those Nazis who had, intimately or otherwise, witnessed Hitler's final hours became essential sources of information. And at least on the Soviet side, prisoners were immediately placed in solitary confinement. The secret services of the USSR almost systematically refused to share what they knew with their allies. No sooner was the war over than suspicion, indeed defiance, gained the upper hand.

The Russian archives of that period offer a gripping picture of those investigations carried out in the emergency setting of occupied Berlin. Stalin wanted to remain the sole conqueror of Nazi Germany, and didn't for a moment envisage sharing his victory or his ultimate trophy: the Führer's body. For the Soviet investigators, the task was twofold: to get there first and find Hitler.

Moscow mobilised the best parts of the secret services and the Red Army. Those men and women knew they would be putting their careers, even their lives, on the line within a few days.

Step one: find witnesses.

★ ★ ★

On the morning of 2 May 1945, while most of the German troops in Berlin capitulated, the area around the New Chancellery had still not been secured. In spite of their fury and their determination to die rather than lay down their arms, the last Nazi fanatics ended up being swept by machine-gun fire and shells. Immediately, the underground shelters were inspected by the troops of the 3rd Shock Army. They discovered terrified men and women almost deafened by whole days of bombing. They were wounded, tired, hungry. Some of them wore civilian clothes, others German army uniforms. The chaos was total. How could anyone recognise the members of Hitler's inner circle in this crowd? A security cordon had been put in place. No one was to be allowed to leave without being questioned. But everything was going too quickly, and the risk of suicide attacks remained real. After a few hours the Soviets had to admit: everyone close to Hitler had escaped.

Apart from Joseph and Magda Goebbels, Krebs, Burgdorf and Schädle, who had committed suicide, everyone had left the bunker the previous night. It was difficult to know with any certainty how many people had still been inside Hitler's shelter. At the maximum, about thirty, including at least four women, three secretaries, and the Führer's personal cook. Their escape began at around 11 o'clock at night. To limit the risk of being captured, they divided themselves up into a dozen small groups. At thirty-minute intervals they left the government district via the tunnels of the underground. Once they were in the open air, amid the hubbub of the bombs and the street fighting, some tried their chances westward, others towards the north. A few exceptions aside, they wouldn't stay free for long. Most of them would fall into the hands of the Red Army within a few hours. The others would be arrested by the British or the Americans. In the general confusion, they joined thousands of German prisoners and tried to melt into the crowd by trying to pass for private soldiers. Heinz Linge, Hitler's valet, had teamed up with Erich Kempka, the Führer's personal chauffeur. The two men quickly parted ways as they progressed along the blazing streets. Linge decided to seek refuge in the tram tunnels. As he approached a passageway leading to the surface, he thought he heard German soldiers. "From above I heard the call: 'German panzers are advancing. Come up, comrades!' I leaned out of the shaft and saw a German soldier. He looked towards me and beckoned. Scarcely had I left our hiding place than I saw all the Soviet tanks around me."* The German soldier was bait for capturing fugitives. Linge hurried to remove the SS badges from his uniform, the silver eagle and the swastika, as well as his rank. The strategy worked, because the Russian soldiers, so overjoyed by the end of fighting, even offered him cigarettes. His true identity would only be revealed several days later thanks to the carelessness of another eminent member of Hitler's close guard: his personal pilot Hans Baur.

Erich Kempka was luckier. On 2 May, while escaping and after leaving Linge, he was quick to swap his SS uniform for civilian clothes.

*Heinz Linge, *With Hitler to the End*, op. cit., p. 210.

A few hours later, when he was checked by the Red Army, he was easily able to pass for a German worker. He managed to leave Berlin and got to Munich a few hours later. In the end he was captured by the American forces that occupied that part of Germany.

Bormann, Hitler's personal secretary and certainly his closest confidant, was nowhere to be found. Rumours soon began to spread. He had fled with Hitler, some people claimed; he was killed while trying to escape, others said. In the end his body was found in December 1972 in Berlin, during some road maintenance. In 1973 he would be identified by a comparative examination of his teeth against his dental file. Then, in 1998, tests were carried out on DNA taken from the supposed bones of Bormann and compared to those of his children. The results were positive.

During May 1945, the Soviets captured more prisoners from the Führerbunker than all the Allies put together had managed to do. But it didn't make their investigation any less complex, especially because of the internal quarrels raging within the different army units and the many Soviet secret services. Everyone jealously guarded their spoils of war and resisted allowing their "precious" prisoners to be interrogated by anyone other than their own services. The man in charge of the first investigation into Hitler's death was Aleksandr Anatolevich Vadis, the head of the SMERSH unit of the 1st Belorussian Front. The 1st Belorussian Front, led by Marshal Zhukov, was one of the main Soviet army units involved in the battle of Berlin. SMERSH was created in 1934 specifically to hunt down deserters, traitors, and other spies within the Red Army. SMERSH is the contraction of two Russian words: *Smiert Shpionam*, which may be translated as "Death to spies." Very quickly, SMERSH became a counter-espionage service directly attached to Stalin's authority. Vadis was one of Stalin's men. In May 1945 this brilliant officer was thirty-nine and held the rank of lieutenant general. Vadis was anything but a beginner. He had joined the security service of the Red Army in 1930, Soviet counter-espionage in 1942 and then SMERSH the following year. A convinced Stalinist, with a formidable sense of political intrigue, he escaped the successive military purges leading up to the war against Germany. Stalin considered him one of the best men in his counter-espionage service. Logically enough, Vadis was granted every power to take his investigation to its conclusion. He was answerable to no one in Berlin. He reported only to Stalin and his closest circle, including the head of security for the USSR, Lavrenti Beria. No one else was informed of his mission. Even Hitler's conqueror, Marshal Zhukov, was kept at arm's length. He would never know anything about Vadis's work. And besides, from the afternoon of 2 May, when the Führerbunker was definitely secured by the soldiers of the Red Army, the men of SMERSH of the 1st Belorussian Front took control of it, expelled the Soviet army, and forbade access even to senior officers.

On 27 May 1945, Vadis sent the report that Moscow had been so eagerly waiting for. In spite of the means at his disposal, Stalin's envoy hadn't performed any miracles. For want of time, he was unable to interrogate the last witnesses to Hitler's last days. On the other hand, the master spy was able to present the result of the autopsy carried out on the alleged corpse of the Nazi dictator.

But before that, he explained the circumstances under which the body was located.

On 5 May, on the basis of witness statements of an inmate, the officer from the security police of the Reich Chancellery, Oberscharführer [adjutant] Mengershausen, two burnt bodies of a man and a woman were discovered and exhumed in the city of Berlin, in the grounds of the Reich Chancellery, near the emergency exit of Hitler's bunker. The bodies were found in a crater created by a shell and covered with a layer of earth. They were so badly burned that without additional data they could not be identified.

As so often with the Soviet secret services, the information contained in their reports had to be checked with extreme care. Here, Vadis was lying.

Elena Rzhevskaya was an interpreter within the SMERSH team

of the 1st Belorussian Front, as was Lev Bezymenski, but within the 1st Belorussian Front itself. They were in Berlin on 2 May 1945. According to them, Hitler's alleged corpse was not found on 5 May 1945 but on the previous day, and not on the instructions of Oberscharführer Mengershausen but by chance, thanks to the Soviet soldier Private Ivan Chourakov. According to Rzhevskaya and Bezymenski, Churakov, in the company of Lieutenant Colonel Klimenko of the 3rd Schock Army, had returned to inspect the place where Joseph and Magda Goebbels had been discovered on 2 May. It was 11 o'clock on the morning of 4 May when, just beside them, from a shell crater, Churakov called to Klimenko: "Comrade Lieutenant Colonel, there are legs here!"* The men started digging and disinterred not one body but two. Klimenko did not imagine for a moment that these might be the remains of Hitler and his wife. So he gave the order to have them re-interred. He did so because the previous day another body had already been identified by some Nazi prisoners as being Hitler's. At 2:00 pm, Klimenko learned that, in the end, the authentication was not conclusive: they couldn't be sure it was Hitler. The next day, on 5 May, Klimenko asked his men to dig up the two bodies found the previous day and inform his hierarchy.

This version of the discovery of the supposed bodies of Hitler and Eva Braun is a partial match with the secret document in the FSB archives that we have been able to examine – the document co-signed on 5 May 1945 by the same Private Chourakov about the discovery of two charred bodies. On the other hand, there is no mention anywhere of Lieutenant Colonel Klimenko. Elena Rzhevskaya also wondered about the officer's extraordinary discretion. He simply replied: "I never delivered a report about the bodies to anybody."†

As to the burnt bodies revealed on 4 May 1945, Elena Rzhevskaya

---

*Lev Bezymenski, *The Death of Adolf Hitler: Unknown Documents from Soviet Archives*, New York, Harcourt, Brace & World, 1969, p. 45.

†Elena Rzhevskaya, *Carnets*, op. cit., p. 273.

claimed to have seen them: "The human remains, disfigured by fire, black and horrible, were wrapped in grey, soil-stained blankets."*

Had Vadis, only, been informed about the conditions under which the two corpses had been found? As the uncontested head of counter-espionage in Berlin, it was his duty to know everything. But even if he did know that version, his decision to hide it remains compre-hensible. He didn't want to inform the Kremlin about the weird discovery. Still, he was taking a considerable risk in altering the truth. All the more so since everything had been recorded in a report sent to Moscow. Vadis was unaware of that detail because, as usual, the Soviet authorities kept all their information close to their chests, even within the secret services.

The other thing Vadis neglected to mention was that the two bodies had been stolen from the 5th Shock Army, which had been entrusted by Moscow with control of the Chancellery district. Stolen by members of its SMERSH unit. They had taken the initi-ative of not letting the 5th Shock Army get their hands on such precious booty. Discreetly, during the night of 5–6 May, the human remains were wrapped in blankets and placed in ammuni-tion boxes. Elena Rzhevskaya was involved in this kidnapping: "the bodies were passed over the garden gate and loaded onto a truck."† That was the perfect illustration of the absurd internal conflicts within the Soviet units. For the SMERSH commandos, if those bodies did indeed belong to Hitler and his wife, no one but them in Berlin must know. On 6 May, the two boxes were stored in the new headquarters of SMERSH, in the Berlin district of Buch.

Vadis obviously didn't say a word about this "theft" in his report. He wanted to keep the secret about the existence of these bodies.

But let's return to his report about the interrogation of Mengershausen, which he conducted on 13 May 1945:

*Ibid., p. 276.
†Ibid. p. 277.

Mengershausen announced that he had recognised the bodies of the man and the woman as those of the Chancellor of the German Reich, Hitler, and his wife, Eva Braun. He added that he had personally seen their bodies being burned on 30 April in the following circumstances: on 30 April, at 10 am, Mengershausen was in the security service of the Reich Chancellery, patrolling the corridor with the kitchen and the dining room of the Reich Chancellery. At the same time, he had the task of keeping watch over the garden of Hitler's bunker, which was 80 metres from the building where Mengershausen was working.

During his patrol he met Hitler's orderly, Baur, who informed him of the suicides of Hitler and his wife Eva Braun.

An hour after the meeting with BAUR, leaving the terrace 80 metres from Hitler's shelter, Mengershausen saw Sturmbannführer GÜNSCHE, personal aide-de-camp, and Sturmbannführer LINGE, Hitler's valet, leaving the shelter by the emergency exit carrying in their arms Hitler's body, which they placed a metre and a half from the exit. Then they went back in, and a few minutes later brought the body of his wife Eva Braun and set it down near Hitler's body. Beside the bodies there were two canisters of petrol; GÜNSCHE and LINGE began pouring it over the bodies and then set light to them.

When the bodies were reduced to ashes, two men from Hitler's personal guard (whose names are unknown to him) who had come out of the shelter approached the burned bodies, put them in a hole dug by the impact of a shell and covered them with a layer of soil.

Vadis based his entire demonstration on the witness of a single German soldier, Harri Mengershausen. But the scene that he described so precisely was played out 80 metres away. A respectable distance that made all identification risky. Vadis was plainly aware of this, as the next part of his report reveals:

Asked how he recognised the bodies that had come out of the bunker as those of Hitler and his wife Braun, the prisoner Mengershausen stated: "I recognised Hitler from his face, his size and his uniform."

The SS adjutant even managed to give some details concerning the clothing: Hitler was wearing black trousers, a tie, a white shirt; Eva Braun a black dress. "I've seen her several times in that dress," Mengershausen added. "I also knew her face very well. It was oval, the nose straight and thin, the hair light-coloured. So since I knew Frau Braun well, I can affirm that it was her body that was removed from the shelter."

Once again, Vadis probably didn't imagine that he could convince his superiors on the basis of a witness statement of a low-ranking SS man. While he was well aware of this, as in a good detective novel he also knew how to spin out the suspense. Here is his trump card, the one that he would claim as his ultimate proof:

The fact that the corpses discovered are really those of Hitler and his wife is confirmed by the statements of Heusermann, the technical assistant to the dentist Blaschke who tended to Hitler, his wife Braun, Goebbels and his family, as well as other rulers of the Reich.

Käthe Heusermann, Vadis's treasure, his key witness. She was the young woman whose biography and anthropometric photographs have been handed down to us by the services of the DSB. The identification of the most wanted man on the planet rests entirely on the shoulders of a medical assistant in her early thirties.

Wasn't this another instance of slightly shaky testimony? Vadis had no choice. His services had looked everywhere in Berlin, and there was no sign of the dentist Blaschke. According to Heusermann he had taken refuge in Berchtesgaden, far from the Soviet-controlled zone. That was true. Blaschke would be captured by the Americans. In the absence of the dentist, Vadis had to make do with his assistant. That was why he tried to stress Käthe Heusermann's expertise.

During the interrogation she revealed that she had on several occasions helped Dr Blaschke in the treatment of Hitler and Braun's teeth. Furthermore, she had described in detail the state of the teeth in Hitler's upper and lower jaw [. . .].

It was only after checks on the young woman's real knowledge of Hitler's medical dossier that the jaws were presented to her.

Having identified these bridges and teeth as belonging to Hitler, Heusermann declared: "I state that the bridges and teeth presented to me belong to Hitler according to the following indications: on the upper jaw presented here I see a clear scratch left by the drill when the gold bridge after the 4th tooth had been sawn. I know this trace very well, because the operation had been performed in autumn 1944 by Dr Blaschke with my participation to remove Hitler's sixth tooth. Here we also see all the characteristics of Hitler's bridges and teeth about which I had given depositions during my interrogation."

Vadis's demonstration stops there. He does go on to cite one other witness, Fritz Echtmann, the other German prisoner mentioned by the FSB during our visit. A dental prosthetist, he had also worked with Hitler's dentist. Vadis used him to identify Eva Braun's teeth.

And where were the remains of the two bodies? Vadis lingers at length on the jaws but remains curiously brief concerning the autopsy on the bodies.

After examination of Hitler's charred body and that of his wife Braun, the forensic team concluded that because of the great damage done to the body and the head by the fire, no visible signs of serious injuries were discovered. In the oral cavities of Hitler and Braun they found the remains of crushed capsules of cyanide.

Laboratory analysis of these showed that they were identical to those detected in the bodies of Goebbels and members of his family.

Nothing more. And yet the forensic examination surely deserves more than a few lines at the end of the report.

The details of that autopsy remain confidential even today. Neither at GARF nor at TsA FSB were we able to consult the complete conclusions.

At most we managed to glean factual information disseminated in other confidential reports. That is how we know the identities of the team that carried out the medico-legal study led by the coroner of the 1st Belorussian Front, Lieutenant Colonel Faust Chkaravski. We also know that the examination took place in the north-east of Berlin, in the district of Buch, on 8 May 1945, the day of the signing of the German surrender.

As to the results of the autopsy, this is what we found in an NKVD report dated 19 January 1946.

The presumed body of Hitler
(file dated 8 May 1945)
No visible signs of severe fatal damage or illness were discovered on the severely fire-damaged body.

The presence in the oral cavity of the remains of the crushed · glass capsule, the obvious smell of bitter almonds coming from the corpse and the results of the forensic analysis of the internal organs with the detection of cyanide led the commission to conclude that in the present case death was caused by cyanide poisoning.

The presumed body of Eva Braun
(file dated 8 May 1945)
On the roughly charred body traces of fragmentation wounds to the rib cage were found, with haemothorax, damage to the lung and the pericardium and six small metal shards.

Also, in the oral cavity, the remains of a crushed glass capsule were found.

Taking into consideration the presence of the capsule, the smell of bitter almonds which was apparent during the autopsy on the corpse as well as the result of the medical-chemical study of the organs of the body, which detected cyanide in them, the commission concluded that in spite of the presence of the severe injury to the rib cage, the direct cause of death was cyanide poisoning.

The commission also notes that because of the marked changes to the body caused by fire, the only proof regarding the identification of the corpses can be given by the analysis of teeth, of crowns and dentures which are preserved in the oral cavity.

For greater detail about the autopsies, we must turn to Lev Bezymenski, the bilingual Russian-German interpreter who served in the Red Army. In 1968, it was as a journalist that this Soviet citizen wrote a successful book about the death of Hitler and had it published in West Germany. Europe was embroiled in the Cold War and the USSR was under the leadership of Leonid Brezhnev. The publication of such a book was possible only if the Soviet authorities gave their agreement, and above all if they considered it to be in their interest. This point is not unimportant. Was Bezymenski telling the truth, or was he passing on propaganda from the Communist regime? Be that as it may, he explains in great detail how Soviet forces found Hitler's body and how they succeeded in identifying it.

He even allowed himself the luxury of illustrating his words with hitherto unpublished documents such as photographs of Russian soldiers outside Hitler's bunker. The caption states that they are busy "disinterring the bodies of Hitler and Eva Braun." There are also two photographs of members of the autopsy commission standing neatly in a row, with the bodies of General Krebs and Joseph Goebbels in front of them. No photograph of the autopsy of Hitler or Eva Braun however – the man in charge of the autopsy,

Faust Chkaravski, claims that he was forbidden to photograph it.*
Bezymenski did, however, publish two poor-quality photographs in
which one can see two wooden boxes filled with a shapeless dark
mass. If we believe the captions, these photographs show the
remains of Hitler and Eva Braun.

Apart from these historic iconographic pieces, Bezymenski
claims to have obtained all the autopsy reports on the bodies discovered in the Führerbunker. Those of Goebbels, of General Krebs, of
the two German shepherd dogs and, of course, the bodies claimed
to be those of Hitler and Eva Braun.

The tone employed in this book is deliberately political. For
example, Bezymenski writes that "the medical evidence, inciden-
tally, refutes the frequent declarations in western historical studies
on the fact that General Hans Krebs, the last head of the general
staff of the German land army, died like a soldier by killing himself
with his weapon. [. . .] The medical conclusions say: 'Death by
cyanide poisoning.'"†

It is all in this passage: the almost ideological opposition to the
West; here the Soviet truth is based on scientific facts and can see
through Western manipulations. Then there is the denigration of
the Nazi enemy. So Krebs killed himself with poison, the act of a
coward in the eyes of the Soviets. For Moscow, a real soldier would
only commit suicide with a bullet.

Something that holds even more for a war lord.

It is no surprise that the autopsy on the body attributed to Hitler
gives the following results according to Bezymenski:

> The man is almost 165 centimetres tall (according to the state-
> ments of his personal physician, Dr. Morell, Hitler was 176 centi-
> metres tall and weighed 70 kilos), and his age between fifty and
> sixty (estimation based on his general development, the size of
> the organs, the state of the lower incisors and the right

*Elena Rzhevskaya, Carnets, op. cit., p. 339.
†Lev Bezymenski, The Death of Adolf Hitler, op. cit., p. 57.

premolar). Some pieces of glass from a medical capsule were found in the mouth. The forensic examiners stress "the typical smell of bitter almonds coming from the bodies, and the forensic examinations of the internal organs which established the presence of cyanide ..."

The commission reached the conclusion that "death was caused by cyanide-based poison."[*]

The Soviet medical team also recorded the absence of part of the skull: the part from the back left, which was supposed to correspond to the piece stored today in the GARF archives.

According to Bezymenski, the doctors claimed to smell a strong odour of bitter almonds from these charred bodies, which had been buried, on the understanding that they were those of Hitler and his wife, five days earlier. Is it possible for cyanide to emanate such an odour with such persistence? And why does Bezymenski not retranscribe the results of the toxicological analyses of the organs of the two bodies? He writes only: "The chemical tests of the internal organs have established the presence of cyanide."

It was of no consequence to the former Red Army interpreter. The goal was to present as certain the cause of the death of the man under examination: poison. At no point is the impact of a bullet mentioned. If this body was that of Hitler, it would have meant that the dictator had committed suicide with a cyanide capsule.

QED: Hitler was a coward like the head of his chief of staff, General Krebs, and of course Goebbels.

This desire on the part of the Kremlin to present the Nazi leaders as "subhuman" is apparent from the announcement of Hitler's suicide to Stalin. On no account was his enemy to pass for a hero. So, if the German dictator stayed in Berlin to the end, in spite of the bombs, it was not because he was courageous, but because of his destructive madness.

The Lieutenant General of SMERSH, Aleksandr Vadis, says

[*]Ibid., p. 67.

exactly the same thing in his report dated 27 May 1945 and addressed to Beria, Stalin's right-hand man.

Beria took account of it and then passed it directly to Stalin.

As to the proof that the body was indeed Hitler's – the teeth. They were sent secretly to the Kremlin.

The H file was about to be closed. Stalin could tell the whole world that he had found Hitler, that he was dead, that he had died like a coward in his rat hole.

Except that one man had revealed to the NKVD secret services that Vadis and SMERSH were wrong. This man was none other than Otto Günsche, Hitler's aide and bodyguard. He too was captured by the Soviets after his attempt to escape the bunker, and very quickly identified. His first interrogation called everything into question. He was categorical on the matter: the Führer had fired a bullet into his head!

MOSCOW, MARCH 2017

Normally, only the family is authorised to consult this file. Vladimir Ivanovich Korotaev tells us this again. Even though it has been declassified and lost its "classified on grounds of national security" status, the military "Otto Günsche" file remains confidential. "Except if a member of his family formally used a request," he insists, abruptly closing the brown cardboard dossier, which bears the stamp MVD SSSR (Ministry of the Interior, USSR). On the cover it says in big printed letters: "Personal File: Günsche Otto Hermann." The same Otto Günsche who was Adolf Hitler's personal aide-de-camp until his death. One of the few witnesses to the final act of the drama in the Führerbunker. Vladimir Korotaev is the deputy director of the "Rossiiskii gosudarstvennyi voennyi arkhiv," the Russian State Military Archives. A state organisation holding almost 7.3 million documents concerning Soviet armed forces, then the Russian armed forces, as well as the military intelligence services. It also contains all the official documents of the Third Reich seized by Soviet forces at the end of the Second World War, including the personal files of the Nazi leaders, Goebbels' private journal, and Himmler's work diary. From our very first meeting, Vladimir has been more than courteous, almost kind. In his fifties, with "salt and pepper" hair and a short beard, he speaks quietly and says little. On the other hand, he does have a rare ability to listen. When I speak to him, his pale blue eyes don't leave me for an instant. His face betrays no emotion, no reaction, like a wax mask.

Lana had contacted him some weeks previously, after our visit to the offices of the FSB. Before leaving the Lubyanka again we had requested some advice from Dmitri, our "case officer" in the Russian secret services. How should we approach the military archives? Did he have a name he could suggest to us? Perhaps a telephone number? "Work it out for yourselves" was all he would give us. "We have nothing to do with the military, this is the FSB. You've got the wrong institution." Who says the Russians aren't touchy? "Why do you want to waste your time in the military archives?" An old journalist's reflex led me not to divulge all my information. Particularly to an eminent member of the FSB. Mightn't he intervene to block our access to the military files? It was on the advice of the State Archives of the Russian Federation, GARF, that we were trying to get into the Red Army archives. "If you want more information on Günsche, that's where you've got to go," we were told by Dina Nokhotovich, the ancient archivist and keeper of Hitler's skull. "You will want to consult the files of the Frenchmen taken prisoner by the Red Army in 1945." Improvisation is a fragile art. Dmitri didn't react to the answer I gave him. He said goodbye to us once more and walked us to the exit, to the pavement, to be precise. Well outside the building.

Military archives. The epithet "military" had added a hint of extra anguish for Lana and me. Was there a Russian institution as reluctant to talk to foreign journalists as the FSB? Yes, the army. How were we, Lana with her dual Russian and American citizenship, me as a Frenchman, going to get into those archives? Contrary to our expectations, it wasn't as complicated as all that. The mother of a friend of Lana's had once worked as a historian in the Russian State Military Archives. Admittedly she's retired now, but she still has excellent contacts with the current directors. She was the one who passed Vladimir Korotaev's name to Lana. From their first telephone conversation, Vladimir was won over. He imposed no conditions, he required no special authorisation from an official authority. He didn't have to give an account of our request either to the Kremlin or to his superiors. "Just tell me what you're looking for about the Third Reich," he replied simply. "Hitler? Hitler again?" The deputy director's voice changed immediately. Lana insisted. She altered her voice, making it both sweet and pleading. In the end he replied crisply: "One or two days. Give me time to find the right files." Forty-eight hours later, Vladimir returned Lana's call; he had found everything. The meeting could be arranged. The following week. At the end of the day, at 5:00 pm. In Moscow, the public services close their offices early. By 5:00 pm most Russian civil servants are long gone. A meeting so late in the day could not be a coincidence. Vladimir wanted to be sure that no one would see us in the archive offices. He would be alone.

It was already fifteen minutes past five and our taxi was hopelessly stuck on Patriarshy Bridge in the centre of the city. The driver had abandoned the very idea of getting anywhere and plugged a DVD player into his cigarette-lighter socket. He offered us a disheartening vision of local pop song videos full of young women who were delighted to writhe around in hot pants. Traffic jams make Moscow an impossible place to live, Lana reflects at length. The age of the empty Moscow boulevards has succumbed to the siren songs of liberalism. Old Soviet Ladas and Volgas have made way for cheap Asian cars and a flood of saloons and obese European four by fours.

How long would it take us to get to Vladimir's office? "An hour …" the driver replies, tapping his GPS. "Perhaps a little less, a little more …" The melted snow so typical of the late Russian winters softly coats the windows, emphasising the depressing aspect of our situation. All of a sudden Lana gets out of the car and calls to me to wait for her. Given the state of the traffic, that shouldn't be too difficult. Less than ten minutes later, when we have struggled barely fifty metres on, she reappears, her hair white with snowflakes, clutching a plastic bag. "This will help us apologise," she says triumphantly, brandishing a bottle of Armenian cognac. 'Everyone loves this in Russia," she assures me.

"Really, really sorry, a thousand apologies," I repeat in Russian the words that Lana is trying to teach me. I want to say them as correctly as possible to Vladimir when we finally get there. It's past 6:00. The Russian military archives building, very socialist-Communist in style, is all concrete and opaque windows in a grim area on the edge of the city. It's empty, or pretending to be empty. From outside, not a single light is shining in any of the ten or so floors. Only the ground floor is still illuminated.

The heavy front door closes behind us with an intimidating crash. Mouse-grey marble panels cover the entrance from floor to ceiling, creating the impression of an abandoned church nave. Perhaps not the best way of encouraging the circulation of heat. Our noisy entrance at least has the merit of making a head appear from the imposing wooden counter barring the way to the stairs. The head belongs to a woman in army uniform. She gets to her feet slowly as if the simple fact of moving requires a painful effort. Even her taciturn presence warms our hearts, proving as it does that the building hasn't been abandoned since the fall of the Soviet Union. The very "vintage" furniture gives the opposite impression. Like that orange-brown Bakelite telephone or the Plexiglas clock with its hands in the form of swords. Objects from the Communist era that still accomplish their duties perfectly. The clock is on time and the telephone works, as our hostess demonstrates in front of our very eyes. "Two. Yes, there are two of them, Deputy Director. No, I can't let them go up. You'll have to come and get them. Yes. Yes. They're waiting." The conversation was a short one. The woman soldier delicately sets down the old telephone receiver and gestures to us to wait.

"We're sorry, Vladimir, we're so sorry. Really embarrassed." Did he even understand that rumbling noise I made that was supposed to sound like Russian? The deputy director of the Russian State Military Archives keeps us waiting for about ten minutes. Then he turns up looking annoyed. In answer to our apologies he gives us a frowning half-smile, turns on his heels and sets off back towards the stairs from whence he came. Lana pushes me in the back to follow him. "It's all fine," she whispers to me, "he hasn't put his coat on. That means he isn't going to leave straight away."

The Günsche file, impossible! Goebbels' private journal, why not, but Günsche, absolutely not. Vladimir insists, it is out of the question to consult the personal file of the SS man Otto Günsche.

And yet there it is, in front of us. Vladimir has taken it from the shelves where it is stored and prepared it especially for this meeting.

He has opened it up and shown us some ID photographs from the times, then nothing. Or almost. As if it were a happy coincidence, a fortuitous act of providence, the deputy director stands up and asks us if we would excuse him. "I'm going to get some other files from one of our stores. I'll be away for about ten minutes. Wait for me here …" We watch him leave without a word. Then Lana smiles at me and says, "Go on!"

I turn the pages, my breath short, my hands clumsy. Otto Günsche is right in front of us. His life as an SS man, as Hitler's personal bodyguard and as a prisoner of the Soviets. So many historical and previously unseen documents. Our investigation is taking a new turn. Günsche is the only member of Hitler's inner circle who never agreed to write his biography. He was a quiet man who refused to give anything away in interviews. Apart from some answers that he gave to the American journalist James O'Donnell, until his death in 2003 at the age of eighty-six, Günsche avoided the media. His only statements were given to the Soviet secret services. But given reluctantly, and under constraint.

The first page of his personal file is merely his identification papers prepared by the directors of the Ministry of Interior Affairs on 4 June 1950, or five years after being captured in Berlin. This was a standard form for all prisoners in the Soviet Union. Apart from the handwritten words in bold red ink: "Special supervision." Ref. 4146 Günsche Otto is not a prisoner like the others. Apart from the basic information such as his date of birth (1917), place of birth (Jena, Germany), height (193 centimetres), place of imprisonment (POW camp no. 476), the handwritten addition indicates that the prisoner requires additional guards. It is also specified that Günsche is in an appropriate state of health and that, in his prison, "he has no infectious illnesses." The other pages are dog-eared and of different sizes, some barely any larger than the pages of a pocket diary. Most of them are written by hand, as if in great haste. Each time the signatory indicates his rank and function. A whole hierarchy of complex designations is revealed: there's a "chief deputy for operational labour," a "behaviour director," a "special head of department" … Often, the notes only concern reports of aggressive behaviour on the part of the prisoner Günsche towards the Soviet Union. The reports continue for only a few lines, requesting appropriate sanctions. An enormous "approved" added diagonally by hand completes the set each time.

In most cases, Günsche is reported by people who share his daily life, German prisoners, former Nazis. The Soviet prison organisation encourages and satisfies the zeal of informers like a man by the name of Nokri. He addresses his letters to "Boss," the head of his unit of prisoners, the 14th Brigade in camp no. 475. Special regime labour camp no. 476 was in the Oblast of Sverdlovsk, deep in the Urals, notorious for the harshness of its climate. The camp was one of the biggest in the Soviet Union.

Both the vocabulary and the writing of the informer lack confidence. Nokri is German and writes very bad Russian. "I received today from the camp guard the order to stack wood in the courtyard of the zone. [. . .] Günsche Otto spoke in the room where the 74 men of the 14th Brigade live. He said: 'I'm not going. The Russians know very well that I refuse.' He said that as if he were our hero, a man above the Soviet authorities. [. . .] Please, Boss, punish this person severely."

The sentence is passed a few weeks later, after a rapid investigation. According to the document that we are holding in our hands, it is established that:

The condemned man Günsche, formerly Hitler's aide-de-camp, expresses révanchiste anti-Soviet opinions and glorifies the old Hitler regime. He deliberately works badly on the works.

It has been decided that the condemned man Günsche should be locked up in a cell as a particularly dangerous element, in total isolation, for a duration of 6 months.

Signed: Investigator in chief of branch No. 5
Captain P. Olenov

Günsche's file consists of about a hundred pages like this. One of them attracts Lana's attention. It is carefully typed, with the word "secret" at the top right-hand side. A stamp in indigo ink with the coat of arms of the Soviet Union completes the official, even solemn appearance of the document. "It's the verdict of his trial," Lana explains. It comes from the military tribunal of the region of Ivanovo, 300 kilometres north-east of Moscow. It is dated 15 May 1950.

The legal investigation and the materials of the trial have identified the following elements:

The accused man GÜNSCHE, a convinced and partisan Nazi devoted in his politics, all the way through his service in the old German army, was an active partisan and participant in the enforcement of Hitler's criminal projects as part of the preparations for war against the Soviet Union.

Before Hitler took power, in 1931 GÜNSCHE joined the fascist youth organisation "Hitler-Jugend," and then in 1934, at the age of 17, he voluntarily joined the SS corps "Leibstandarte Adolf Hitler," as a member of which he was involved in reinforcing the fascist regime in Germany.

In 1936 GÜNSCHE was particularly distinguished in his service, and was transferred to Hitler's personal bodyguard.

During the period of Germany's war against the USSR, GÜNSCHE served in the German army within the division "Lebstandarte SS Adolf Hitler," first as a platoon commander, and then as a company commander with the armoured division.

Finding himself in the temporarily occupied territory of the USSR within his division, he has committed atrocities against Soviet civilians and prisoners of war. The slogan of the SS division was: "We need Russian space without the Russians," calling for the total destruction of the Russian population.

In carrying out this criminal command, the division shot 285 civilians in the region of Zhitomir, hanged 8 people, tortured 73 people to death and starved 25,196 Soviet prisoners of war to death.

From January 1943 until 30 April 1945, GÜNSCHE, as a convinced fascist, served as Hitler's personal aide-de-camp, combining this function with that of Commander of the Reich Chancellery in March and April 1945.

As Hitler's personal aide-de-camp, GÜNSCHE took part in all the meetings held by Hitler about aspects of the war waged against the USSR and peaceful and democratic people.

As Hitler's personal aide-de-camp, GÜNSCHE carried out his different criminal orders and instructions.

[. . .]

On the basis of this evidence, the Military Tribunal found GÜNSCHE guilty of breaching Art. 1 of the Decree of 19/IV-1943 in accordance with Art. 319 and 320 of the Penal Code,

HAS SENTENCED:

GÜNSCHE Otto Hermann, based on Art. 1 of the Decree of the Presidium of the Supreme Soviet of the USSR of 19/4-1943 and in accordance with Art. 2 of the Decree of 26/V-1947 "On the abolition of the death penalty," to imprisonment in a Re-education through Labour of a duration of TWENTY-FIVE (25) years.

GÜNSCHE's period of imprisonment begins on 6/IV-1950.

Otto Günsche was thirty-two years old at the time, and had been a prisoner of the Soviets for almost five years. The identifying photograph that accompanies the sentence shows a prematurely aged man, gaunt but still with a hard, almost threatening expression, like a gauntlet thrown at the Russian authorities. Was the SS officer showing that he wasn't anyone's fool? That his trial was only a masquerade and that his sentence left no doubt of it?

Isn't a sentence of twenty-five years in a camp worse than execution? How could anyone survive a sentence like that in the gulag? In what physical and mental condition would they be when they came out? Günsche would be fifty-seven when he had served his sentence. This former intimate of Hitler's could not accept the prospect of an existence as a jailbird. "The verdict may be appealed before the appeal jurisdictions of the Military Tribunal of the troops of the MVD of the district of Moscow," he was informed in writing. He had seventy-two hours to do that. A few pages later we find the result of his appeal. On 21 October 1950, or five months after his trial, Günsche was summoned before the judges again.

239.

С П Р А В К А

На жителя села Церпеншлейзе, района Бернау - ВЕЛЕР Густава

ВЕЛЕР Густав, 1886 г.рождения, уроженец с.Доротенталь, крайс Гренвальде /Померания/, немец, член СА, женат, происходит из крестьян, проживает с.Церпеншлейзе, района Бернау, работает кровельщиком.

ВЕЛЕР Густав, имеющий сходство с Гитлером, проживал до 1944 г. в г.Берлин по улице Ционскирхштрассе, 23, а с 1944 г. по настоящее время проживает в с.Церпеншлейзе.

ВЕЛЕР Густав в 1924 г. был осужден на 3 года тюремного заключения, за подделку денежных знаков, которое он отбыл. В январе месяце 1932 года ВЕЛЕР вступил в члены СА, откуда через 2 месяца был исключен потому, что он не выполнил приказания подстричь волосы. ВЕЛЕР Густав, с приходом Гитлера к власти, в 1933-1934 г.г. неоднократно вызывался органами гестапо, где ему предлагали в связи с тем, что он похож на Гитлера, подстричь волосы и сбрить усы, но он этого не делал. В 1934 г. ВЕЛЕР был вызван лично Гимлером, который также предлагал ему снять волосы и сбрить усы, за что обещал ему 1000 марок. При этом Гимлер, по словам ВЕЛЕР, угрожая ему, заявил:

"Если Вы еще будете носить волосы так, как наш фюрер, то Вы исчезнете навсегда."

В результате частых вызовов в гестапо ВЕЛЕР Густав пытался отравиться светильным газом.

ВЕЛЕР в национал-социалистической партии не состоял и компрометирующих материалов на него не добыто.

НАЧАЛЬНИК ОПЕРСЕКТОРА ПРОВИНЦИИ
БРАНДЕНБУРГ - ГЕНЕРАЛ-ЛЕЙТЕНАНТ

/П.ФОКИН/

"22" января 1946 г.

Soviet investigation into a doppelgänger of Hitler (GARF archives).

Here is the report:

In his application for judicial review, Günsche claims that he has
committed no crimes, and requests that the sentence be annulled.
Having found no reason to annul or modify the sentence
IT HAS BEEN RULED:
The sentence passed on the condemned man Günsche Otto
Hermann should remain in force, and his application for judicial
review should not be sustained.

Death, deportation, difficult prison conditions – the SS Sturmbannführer (commander) was prepared for all of those when he
decided to escape from Hitler's bunker. But he surely hadn't
expected the incredible treatment that Stalin would reserve for
those who had been close to the Führer.

★   ★   ★

1 May 1945, in the Führerbunker. General Krebs had failed. The
attempt to mediate with the Soviet chief of staff begun the previous
evening had not been a success. The hope of an armistice had gone
up in smoke. The Russians were demanding an unconditional
surrender. The end was close and inevitable for the last residents of
the imperial bunker. All day everyone had been preparing for an
almost impossible operation flight. It was nearly 10:00 pm when the
first group set off on a desperate course. Günsche was one of them.
The two secretaries and Hitler's nutritionist went with him, along
with Bormann's secretary. They were escorted by about a hundred
soldiers. All night, together, they tried in vain to force their way
through Soviet lines. On the morning of 2 May they found refuge in
the cellar of a bar on Schönhauer Allee, in the centre of the city.
None of these fugitives knew that the commander of German
troops in Berlin, General Weidling, had given the order to surrender. In the afternoon, Russian soldiers surrounded the bar. "The
war is over. Your commander has signed the ceasefire," they shouted.
Günsche and other German officers hesitated. But they had to face

the facts: fighting had effectively ceased, and they no longer had any choice. Before handing themselves over as prisoners, the German officers helped Hitler's two secretaries, Gerda Christian and Traudl Junge, his cook, Constanze Manziarly, and Else Krüger, Bormann's secretary, to leave the shelter discreetly. For the young women it was worth trying anything rather than falling into the hands of the Soviets. Hitler had warned them that they would be automatically raped. Gerda Christian would manage to get to Bavaria, where she would be arrested by the American army in March 1946. Traudl Junge, after a long journey through Germany, would come back to hide in Berlin, where she would be captured by the Red Army in early June 1945. Constanze Manziarly would never be seen again. Gerda Christian would claim that she saw her being arrested by Russian soldiers on 2 May 1945. On that day there is no trace of her in the Russian archives. Else Krüger would end up in British hands.

It was 10 pm on 2 May 1945 when Günsche surrendered without a fight. The interrogations began. Very quickly his status as an SS Sturmbannführer attached to Hitler's personal staff brought him special treatment. Günsche found himself in the hands of the People's Commissariat for Internal Affairs, the NKVD. This state organisation concentrated the powers of the police of the country and managed the gulags and internal secret services. Günsche made his revelations directly to General Kobulov, the deputy head of the central administration for prisoners of war and internees (the GUBPVI), and to Lieutenant Colonel Parparov, his operational head of department. When questioned on 18 and 19 May 1945, he told them that Hitler had shot a bullet into his head. Oh-so-disturbing information for the Soviet secret services, because it called into question the hypothesis of a suicide by poison. A hypothesis offi-cially preserved and maintained by the Lieutenant General of SMERSH, Aleksandr Vadis.

"Sturmbannführer Linge was outside the entrance to the bunker, near the door to Hitler's office. At about 4:00 on 30 April 1945 he heard a shot." Günsche's answers are recorded as he delivered them, without embellishment or interpretation. Kobulov and Parparov noted each statement with great precision. What they heard both surprised and enchanted them. They had something to bring down their colleagues and, at the same time, their rivals at SMERSH. Kobulov and Parparov hated that counter-espionage service that thought it was all powerful. They were both men of Lavrenti Beria, the dreaded head of the NKVD. Beria hated SMERSH and its leader, General Viktor Abakumov, with a vengeance. The head of the NKVD was suspicious of this secret service that escaped his control. Because while, officially, SMERSH depended on the NKVD, in fact Abakumov often reported directly to Stalin without passing through Beria. The competition between the Soviet secret services couldn't last for long. Stalin's regime only kept the best. And Beria had decided to stay the best.

In May 1945, Lavrenti Pavlovich Beria was forty-six. This pure product of the Soviet Revolution, originally from Georgia, like Stalin, was at the peak of his career. With his pretentious airs of a petty bureaucrat and his ludicrous pince-nez, he didn't look like much. And yet … He was Stalin's deputy in the heart of government, one of the members of the National Defence Committee, and he ran the external intelligence service of the secret police. Hated and despised, Beria was feared more than anything. Violent, ruthless, sadistic, vicious, psychopathic, alcoholic, the black legend of the "top cop" of Stalinist power was not entirely invented, but it needs to be treated carefully. It is true that he had a certain talent for running torture sessions, and indeed for torturing the more recalcitrant prisoners in person. Signing the deportation orders of the "enemy peoples," or more than a million Soviet citizens from minorities (Chechens, Ingush, Germans from the Volga, Tartars from the Crimea …) didn't bother him in the slightest. Stalin suspected them all of collaborating with the Nazis. They would be sent to Siberia and Central Asia to live in inhumane conditions. Only four years after their deportation, their mortality rate rose to 20 per cent. Almost 200,000 failed to survive the treatment dished out to them by the NKVD. Beria took responsibility for the massacre of over 25,000 Polish officers in the forest in Katyn in 1940 without blinking. Nikita Khrushchev would say of him that to reach that level of power in the USSR "he had passed through the different echelons by climbing over a huge number of corpses."* But if Beria could be objectively considered a monster, he was still a politician with a phenomenal survival instinct. He understood very quickly that the fact of being Georgian like Stalin and of being almost insanely loyal to him did not make him untouchable. He could be eliminated from the system at any moment. Didn't Stalin like repeating that there were only two options in the secret service: "promotion or the firing squad"? That phrase came tumbling into his head when he registered the rise to power of his former subordinate, General Abakumov.

Everything about Viktor Semenovich Abakumov was a tremendous source of irritation to him. Being younger – he was nine years his junior – and a Muscovite by birth while Beria was a hick, the son of wretched Georgian peasants, the head of SMERSH had the look of a conqueror, with an open and profound expression. With an almost jet-black shock of hair and square shoulders, he wore his uniform like one of those heroes celebrated in Soviet propaganda. Very much the opposite of Beria who was short-legged – Abakumov was a head taller – almost bald, short-sighted, and running to a paunch, the man that Stalin liked to present as his "Himmler" – in reference to Heinrich Himmler, the man responsible for Hitler's worst atrocities – was physically no match for his direct competitor. Recruited into the special forces of the Red Army at the age of thirteen, Abakumov rose progressively through the echelons of the military before joining the intelligence services. There he became a specialist in surveillance on enemies within. Bugging technologies held no secret for him. Beria was quick to notice this new star. In 1938 he advanced Abakumov's career within the NKVD by appointing him as one of his deputies. He then hoped to turn him into a sort of vassal. But Beria had reckoned without Stalin, who tore

*Secret report presented on 25 February 1956 to the 20th Congress of the Communist Party of the USSR.

Abakumov out of his clutches and in 1943 put him in charge of SMERSH. Now, for the boss of the NKVD, Abakumov became a dangerous competitor and hence a mortal enemy. With tens of thousands of men and women at his service, Beria saw himself as the best-informed man in the country. And soon, thanks to the final victory against Nazi Germany, of a good part of Europe. So it was perfectly normal if nothing that happened in Berlin escaped him, even if he stayed in Moscow, two thousand kilometres away. He learned almost instantly of the discovery of Hitler's supposed corpse. A discovery for which a SMERSH team got all the glory. For Beria, the threat of Abakumov was becoming increasingly apparent. His job was at stake. Luckily, with the arrest of this man Günsche, he still had a good card to play. Thanks to this giant, square-jawed SS man, this killer of Jews and Communists, Beria would be able to prove to Stalin that he was still indispensable.

"How did Hitler commit suicide?" the agents Kobulov and Parparov ask Günsche.

"According to Linge, Hitler fired a bullet into his temple."*

The interpreter at the interrogation was given the task of using exact words to transcribe the prisoner's thoughts as accurately as possible. In case of error, he was reminded that he risked imprisonment in a special camp in Siberia.

Without any apparent emotion, Günsche told them that the suicide of the German dictator occurred just before 4:00 pm on 30 April.

Question: When did you first enter the room where the suicide occurred? And what did you see?

Answer: I went into the room at 4:45. I saw that the mat on the floor had moved slightly and that there was a bloodstain. On the table there were several small boxes containing capsules of

*GARF archives : GARF 9401/2/551, f.58

poison. On the sofa, near the wall, beside the door, there was a pair of shoes. Beside the sofa there were two pistols on the floor. One a 7.65 mm calibre and the other 6.35 mm. These pistols were given to Hitler by a man of Axmann's [Artur Axmann, head of the Hitler Youth] whose identity I do not know.

There was a very strong smell of almonds in the antechamber where Hitler's body lay.

Who is telling the truth? Günsche, with his theory of death by bullet? SMERSH, who were certain that he had killed himself with cyanide? Unless it was both? Unless it was all a huge trick, and Hitler was still alive and kicking?

Beria has no idea. Abakumov, the boss of SMERSH, had sent him the report in which he concluded that Hitler had poisoned himself. To him, Beria, not to Stalin. For once, Abakumov respected the hierarchical route. But wasn't this a way of associating Beria with this investigation, and making sure that they were bound to one another in the event of any possible reproaches from the "Little Father of the peoples"? And another purge of the secret services?

Stalin was not a man to grant his trust easily. Neither was he a man to forgive easily. His victory over Nazi Germany reinforced his power and his popularity within the Soviet Union. On the international scene, he also appeared as one of the strong men of the new world order that was now appearing. Even though, for many people, what he provoked was fear rather than admiration. He didn't care. He had a talent for exploiting fear. During the war, he proved that no one could escape his most severe decisions. Not even his own family. His elder son, Yakov, was already thirty-four in 1941 when he was called up to join the Red Army and fight the Nazis. He was captured on 16 June 1941. His sister, Svetlana, related this tragic episode years later. "My brother was not a great fighter. He was too nice for that. He went to war because our father wanted him to. When he was taken prisoner by the Germans, the Nazi regime humiliated him. He was toured around Germany and presented like a zoo animal. Just imagine, Stalin's son! It was perfect for Nazi propaganda. At the end of January 1943, the German Field Marshal Paulus was captured by our troops in Stalingrad. The Germans thought my father was going to swap him for Yakov. They didn't know him very well." In the end, Stalin's elder son would die a few weeks later, on 14 April 1943, in a POW camp in Germany.

The message from the master of the Kremlin was clear: no special treatment for anyone. Besides, it had already been planned that if Yakov had survived, or even if he had escaped, he would be sent to a special camp in Siberia. "That was how they treated Soviet soldiers who had been through the German prisoner of war camps," Svetlana Stalin says. "They were suspicious of them."

Abakumov and Beria both remembered Yakov's fate. They knew their master's intransigence and cruelty. And above all they knew his rampant paranoia. The slightest error on their part could prove fatal. And all the evidence suggested that the report into Hitler's death contained errors or at least large gaps. At the end of May 1945, Beria was sure of it. The head of the NKVD reread the thirteen pages of the interrogation of SS man Günsche carried out by his men on 18 and 19 May 1945. Did they need to tell Stalin and sow doubts in his mind? Nothing could be more dangerous. Beria chose prudence. The most extreme prudence. He kept his men's work to himself and simply passed the file to Stalin without comment, whether positive or negative.

On 27 May 1945, Stalin held the report from SMERSH in his hands. For the Kremlin, Hitler's death was official.

Günsche, for his part, was just starting to understand that he wasn't about to leave the secret service jails. He was transferred from Berlin to Moscow, headed for the Lubyanka special prison under the control of the NKVD.

★   ★   ★

That same Lubyanka where we were granted permission to look at those teeth that were supposed to have been Hitler's. Back then we were on the third floor. The interrogations of the SS prisoners were held on the first or second floor. We can't help wondering if their groans reached the room where we had our meeting. As we progress with our investigation, that chilling sensation of awakening ghosts barely leaves us now. So much blood, tears, cruelty, inhumanity surrounds our quest like a dark halo. The truth around the Hitler file, even today, hides itself in a nauseating fog under the pretext of secrets of state and struggles of geopolitical influence. Seventy years have passed already, and the question is still a sensitive one. Will the spectre of Hitler one day stop haunting the West?

These reflections filled me as I ran through the Günsche file in the office of the deputy director of the Russian State Military Archives. Lana half-opens the door and glances quickly into the corridor. Not a sound. The building is still fast asleep. We can go on checking the official documents. I pick up a different one. Another German officer. I struggle to decipher his name: Rattenhuber, Johannes.

Soviet military justice file on SS General Johann Rattenhuber (Russian Military State Archives).

No, not Johannes. Johann, I see the photographs of a mature-looking man, his hair almost completely white, still wearing his German uniform. The photograph must have been taken only a few hours after his capture, in early May 1945. Holding his head very straight, and with a steady, cold gaze, this officer is clearly used to issuing orders and being obeyed. A few pages later I find myself looking at other pictures. Is it really the same man? The photograph dates from 1950. Now he's just an old man, a pale copy of the proud German officer he once was. His face is emaciated, his skin tanned by excessive exposure to the cold, a shaggy beard sprouts from hollow cheeks, his hair is coarsely shaven. Who was he? I ask Lana to leave her observation post and come and translate the documents. The man's pedigree stretches over several pages.

Military dossier of Johann Rattenhuber, Hitler's head of security (Russian State Military Archives).]

RATTENHUBER Johann, born in 1897, originally from the village of Oberhaching (Bavaria), German nationality ...

... After Hitler's assumption of power in Germany, in 1933 Rattenhuber was appointed aide-de-camp to the head of the Gestapo, the fascist Himmler and then, in the same year of 1933, was appointed to the post of head of Hitler's personal guard, reorganised in 1934 into the so-called "Reich Security Service" [Reichssicherheitsdienst] ...

... During the period of the war waged by Hitler's Germany against the Soviet Union, Rattenhuber and his subordinates guaranteed the security of Hitler's trains going to the Soviet–German border in 1941–1943, when Hitler, in collaboration with the corps of generals, was elaborating plans to enslave and exterminate the Soviets.

Questioned in the course of the hearing, the defendant Rattenhuber was found guilty on these charges and stated that he was only acting on the orders of his superiors.

This argument of "only obeying orders" was also used by other Nazis in their trials. Notably Adolf Eichmann, the senior SS man in charge of executing the "Final Solution," the extermination of the European Jews. An excuse that was systematically rejected, as here by the Soviet judges:

The defendant's argument that in his practical activities he was guided by orders is false given that Rattenhuber himself occupied elevated posts in the "Reich Security Service" with the fascist government in Germany and in the criminal organisation of the SS.

In his criminal activities he demonstrated diligence and personal initiative, for which he was rewarded by the fascist leaders.

Consequently Rattenhuber was sentenced. But to how many years? Lana runs her finger along the lines of the document until she reaches the sentence. Twenty-five years! Like Günsche. In "re-education through labour camps." It is added that everything that Rattenhuber possessed at the time of his arrest was confiscated from him.

I turn towards Lana. She has suddenly stopped translating. She looks away. What has she read that shocks her like this? She repeats out loud a passage from the trial that she had originally missed:

> ... Apart from the personal confessions of the accused, his guilt was confirmed in the course of the hearing by witness statements from: Eckold, Mohnke, Mengershausen ...

Mengershausen, the SS adjutant who, according to SMERSH, told the Russian soldiers where to find Hitler's corpse.

"Ah, Rattenhuber! He's an important piece in the Hitler file." Vladimir makes us jump. He has come back into the room without a sound. He looks at us both, rather proud of his entrance. We look like children caught red-handed, with our fingers covered with jam. He doesn't seem surprised, and is even amused by our embarrassment. "Rattenhuber was a general who was very close to Hitler, his head of security. You can't take photographs of these documents. Look, why not, but nothing more," he growls. Lana gives him her sweetest look and murmurs some words whose meaning I don't catch. They hit the mark, judging by the smile that lights up Vladimir's face. The deputy director finally throws on the table the files that he had gone to look for.

There are some which are even more important than Rattenhuber. Three key men, Vladimir is sure of it. "Linge, his valet ..." he begins, sliding a cardboard file towards us. He opens another one and puts on his presbyopic glasses: "This one here is Baur, his personal pilot. Here ..." All the files of the military justice system are now piled up in front of us. "With Günsche, Hitler's aide-de-camp, and there you've got the lot!"

Was it these men, or at least their statements, that gave Stalin doubts? Was it because of them that the Hitler mystery survived for so many years?

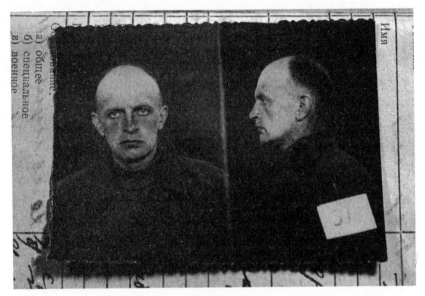

Linge, the valet (Russian State Military Archives).

Baur, the pilot (Russian State Military Archives).

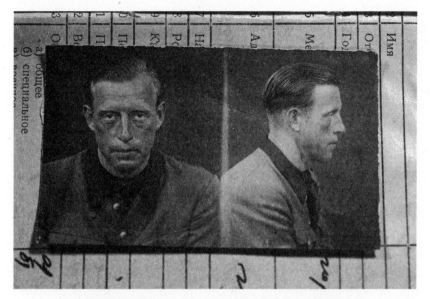

Günsche, aide-de-camp (Russian State Military Archives).

They were all in Hitler's personal service, and all present until the fall of the Führerbunker. They all fell into the hands of the Soviets.

Their interrogations, their imprisonment in special camps, everything is recorded. Among the documents from GARF, the ones passed on by the FSB, and now the ones rediscovered in military archives, we have the pieces to reconstruct the puzzle. At this stage, one thing seems certain: Stalin was informed about the tiniest details concerning the Führer's last moments. But he would go on claiming to the Allies that his troops had not found Hitler.

MOSCOW, MAY 1945

Hitler isn't dead!

On 26 May 1945, Stalin received representatives of the American President Harry Truman in Moscow. They had come to prepare for the future conference due to be held between the Allies in Potsdam in July, about thirty kilometres south-west of Berlin. Truman had just succeeded Roosevelt, who had died of a cerebral haemorrhage at the age of only sixty-three on 12 April 1945. If his mandate had begun under the most favourable auspices – the German surrender on 8 May fell on the day of his birthday – Harry Truman had not yet been put to the test among the Allies, particularly by the most unpredictable of them, Josef Stalin. It was no coincidence that the man he sent to Moscow was Harry Hopkins, Roosevelt's diplomatic adviser and a man very familiar with the Soviet regime. Stalin knew him well, having dealt with him during the darkest hours of the war. The US ambassador to the USSR, William Averell Harriman, went with him. On 26 May, Stalin still hadn't received the SMERSH report on the autopsy of the bodies found outside the bunker. The report would not appear on his desk until the next day. Nonetheless, he was aware of the identification process, and of the high probability that it was indeed Hitler. However, Stalin forgot to inform his American visitors. He even told them a story that would weigh heavily on relations between the two great powers. When Harry Hopkins mentioned his hopes of finding the Führer's body, Stalin replied that "in his opinion Hitler was not dead but hiding somewhere. He said the Soviet doctors thought they had identified the body of Goebbels and Hitler's chauffeur [Erich Kempka], but that he, personally, even doubted if Goebbels was dead [. . .]. He said he thought that Bormann, Goebbels, Hitler, and probably Krebs had escaped and were in hiding."* Stalin outlined scenarios about the flight of the Nazi leaders. Many countries could take them in or help them, he argued. Like Japan and Switzerland. Ah, Switzerland, that bank-turned-state that was overflowing with Nazi gold. Can't we imagine the worst about bankers? As to Japan, don't their myriad islands offer impregnable hiding places? The American diplomats were amazed. How could Hitler have reached the coast of Japan? Stalin had an answer for everything. In a submarine! Harry Hopkins ventured to express his doubts. He told his host that, certainly, he had already heard of a plan involving large German submarines, but to his knowledge none had ever been discovered. What, though, did reality, the possible, the probable have to do with anything? Stalin had said so, and that had to be enough to convince President Truman's emissaries. And convinced they were. Since the dictator was certainly alive they insisted that he be found. Stalin agreed: "I have issued orders to secret services to seek those submarines. As things stand they have found nothing, but I think it possible that Hitler and his acolytes may have left for Japan in one of those submarines."

On 6 June, a new meeting was held between Hopkins, Harriman, and Stalin. Stalin told them that he had still not found Hitler, but was convinced that he had escaped. Hitler was alive, he added. Yet, by this date, he had had the SMERSH report for at least a week. The report which concluded, thanks to the autopsy, that his enemy had committed suicide by poisoning. Stalin had validated this evidence by not asking for a second opinion. He had also been informed that his men had re-interred the bodies of Hitler, Eva Braun, and Joseph and Magda Goebbels near Rathenow on 3 June 1945.

Unfortunately for the Kremlin, a first breach in the secret of the Hitler file was about to appear.

*Foreign Relations of the United States: Diplomatic Papers, The Conference of Berlin (The Potsdam Conference), 1945, Vol. I, no. 24, "Memorandum by the Assistant of the Secretary of State (Bohlen)," pp. 29–30.

On the same day, 6 June, but in Berlin, a Russian press conference was improvised in the offices of the Soviet military administration. American, British, and French reporters attended. They heard an officer from the staff of the Soviet Marshal Zhukov tell them that Hitler had been found and identified with almost a hundred per cent certainty. The next day, the headline of the *New York Times* read: "The identification of Hitler's body almost certain, say Russians."

Stalin reacted immediately, and tried to regain the upper hand. He sent one of his most loyal cohorts, Andrey Vyshinsky, to Zhukov to organise a new press conference. An official one this time. It was held three days later, on 9 June. The proud and martial Zhukov took the floor in his baritone voice. All the Western and Russian journalists based in Berlin were present. "We have not discovered a body that could have been identified as Hitler's." Murmurs spread through the audience. Non-Russian reporters waited for translations to be sure that they had understood the words of the victor of the battle of Berlin. Zhukov got his breath back and continued beneath the steady gaze of Stalin's special envoy. "Hitler and Braun had good chances of escaping Berlin. They could easily have taken off at the last moment because they still had access to a runway." The murmurs grew louder. Hands were raised to ask questions. "All of this remains mysterious," Zhukov acknowledged. "All that I can say is that we have not identified Hitler's body, and that I don't know anything about what has happened to him ... . Now it is up to you British and Americans to find him." Stalin's advisers could not have come up with a better way to destabilise the Allies. Hitler has fled, and it's up to you to capture him, or tell us if he's alive or dead. Because as things stand there is no body, Hitler is not dead. Zhukov had already left the room. A Soviet officer answered the press in his place. He put forward hypotheses, he explained and informed, or rather he spread disinformation. Rumours about his death? Fantastical. Where was he hiding? Why not in Spain, with that fascist Franco?

In this vast deception, the glorious Marshal Zhukov played the role of useful idiot. Everything suggested that he was unaware of the SMERSH report. Even he had been kept out of the biggest secret of the end of the Second World War.

The international press put out the new Russian version.

"Zhukov declares that Hitler may be alive in Europe. He had married his mistress shortly before. Together they may have escaped the German capital by plane."

Spain got wind of the Russian declarations and felt obliged to deny any implication in the supposed escape of the German dictator. On 10 June, the Spanish Minister of Foreign Affairs asserted officially that "Hitler, married or not, living or dead, is not on Spanish soil, nor is he authorised to come, and if he entered Spain he would not receive asylum."

But doubts persisted. The Allied secret services asked the Soviets for access to the Führerbunker and for information to be shared.

Dwight Eisenhower, the American general and commander-in-chief of Allied forces in Europe, personally asked Zhukov whether Hitler was alive or not. On 18 June 1945, when General Eisenhower gave a press conference to the Pentagon in Arlington, Virginia, a journalist was quick to ask him the question that was on everyone's lips: "Do you think Hitler is dead? Are you convinced Hitler is dead?"

Well, to tell you the truth, I wasn't. I was at first. I thought the evidence was quite clear. But when I actually got to talk to my Russian friends, I found they weren't convinced, and I found that it had been erroneously reported from Berlin. I don't know. The only thing I am sure of is what I said in my Paris conference – if he is not dead he must be leading a terrible life for a man that was the arrogant dictator of 250,000,000 people, to be hunted like a criminal and afraid of the next touch on his shoulder. He must be suffering the agonies of the damned if he is alive.*

*Eisenhower Presidential Library, Museum, and Boyhood Home, Abilene, Kansas, United States [Dwight D. Eisenhower's Pre-Presidential Papers, Principal Files, Box 156, Press Statements and Releases 1944–46 (1), NAID, #12007716], p. 4.

Strengthened by the doubts that he had managed to sow, Stalin persisted in his theory of a Hitler who was alive and in flight during the Potsdam Conference held between 17 July and 2 August 1945. He was thus lying to all of his Western allies in turn. This time, he explained that the German dictator, if he was not in Spain, was certainly hiding in Argentina. What was certain, he added, was that he was not in the German zone under Soviet control. These declarations finally shook the certainties of the Anglo-Saxon secret services and prompted them to speed up their own inquiries. If Stalin had wanted to weaken his allies with pointless investigations, he couldn't have made a better job of it.

Argentina, Japan, Spain, and even Chile – so many false trails deliberately laid by the Soviets to throw off the British and American intelligence agencies. The Potsdam Conference concluded with the Hitler mystery. Stalin was radiant. Of the three great men who had fought and defeated Germany, he was the last one still in the saddle. Roosevelt was dead and Churchill, after losing the elections, had stepped down from his post as prime minister right in the middle of the conference, on 26 July.

As to Hitler, Stalin, who was sure that his men had found and identified him, knew exactly where his secret services had buried him. A long way from South America and Japan. More precisely, in the little town of Rathenow, only an hour's drive from Potsdam. Any trace of his interment had been meticulously erased and his location was now a state secret shared only by a handful of people. To remember where the grave was located, Russian agents drew a map with clues worthy of Stevenson's pirates. We had held these confidential documents in our hands in the FSB archives: "The grave has been flattened out at ground level, and small pine seedlings have been planted on the surface forming the number 111. The bodies [. . .] have been buried at a depth of 1.7 metres and placed in the following order: from East to West: HITLER, BRAUN Eva, GOEBBELS, Magda GOEBBELS, KREBS, the GOEBBELS children."

Stalin would never reveal that state secret.

The manipulation of the master of the Kremlin would lead the Allies to work investigating the German zones under their control.

Three months. It took the British only three months. By 1 November 1945, their investigation into what happened to Hitler was at an end. This information was given to a young thirty-one-year-old British historian, Hugh Trevor-Roper. This brilliant Oxford-trained history professor had joined the army as soon as the United Kingdom had gone to war with Nazi Germany, in the "Secret Intelligence Service," to be precise. While he had thought that his time in the army would come to an end along with the war, in the summer of 1945 he was asked to write a report into the disappearance of Hitler. The task was huge, but Trevor-Roper received every imaginable help from London to complete his investigation. For example, he was able to question all the Nazi prisoners held in the British zone, but also those in the American and French zones. As to the Russian zone, it was better to assume that no help would be forthcoming. At best he would be allowed to visit the Führerbunker, which was still in Soviet hands. Trevor-Roper finished his report in late October 1945. A big press conference was planned for 1 November, in the course of which the broad lines of his work would be set out under the title "The last days of Hitler and Eva Braun."

It concluded with Hitler's suicide by bullet and not by poison. A more complete file was sent to the secret services of the three other powers present in Berlin: the Americans, the Soviets, and the French.

Berlin   1 November 1945

From: Brigadier E.J. Foord
To: General B. Conrad, American
Major General Sidney, Soviet
Colonel Puel, French

The attached document concerns the death of Hitler and Eva Braun. It can be discussed at the next meeting of the Intelligence Service Committee.

From the perspective of the constant allusions recently made in the British press about Hitler, it seems judicious to publish a short version for the press.

That will be done today at 5:00 pm.

The attached version is not intended for the press because it contains more details than those already distributed to the press.

By indicating that they planned to make Hitler's suicide public, the British were putting pressure on the Russians. The goal was to stop the disinformation campaign begun by Moscow. However, the British intelligence services acknowledged in a preamble that they had been able to rely on only a small number of witnesses.

The most important are those who were close to Hitler during the last days of his life, who lived with him in the bunker and who took part in the execution of his decisions, including those concerning the elimination of his body. These people were: Dr. Goebbels, Martin Bormann and Dr. Ludwig Stumpfegger [surgeon to Hitler and his team].

But all of these men were either thought to be dead or reported missing. Other important Nazis had survived, however. Some of them were in the hands of the Western forces, and were questioned. There were those who had fled the bunker very early, like Albert Speer, Hitler's favourite architect and his Armaments Minister, or Ritter von Greim, the last Aviation Minister. And those who were believed to be present at the supposed death of Hitler. In summer 1945, there were only a handful of these who had been taken prisoner by the Anglo-Americans, notably Bormann's secretary, Else Krüger, and more importantly, Hitler's personal chauffeur, Erich Kempka. It was Kempka who informed them about the death of the Nazi dictator.

The British could not conceal the relative weakness of their sources. Subtly, they suggested in their document that they knew where the main living witnesses were. On the Russian side.

More details could be obtained from others who were in the bunker on 30 April, including Oberführer Hans Baur, Hitler's personal pilot, who is now a prisoner in a Russian hospital.

The same was true of Hitler's servants.

Of these, the most important are Stubaf [Sturmbannführer] Günsche, his personal aide-de-camp, and Stubaf Linge, his personal valet. All of them took part in the cremation of the bodies of Hitler and Eva Braun. Günsche was reported missing and Linge may be a Russian prisoner of war (one witness believes he saw him in a procession of prisoners in Muellerstrasse in Berlin on 2 May).

On that date Günsche had already been put in solitary confinement in Moscow and was being regularly interrogated, as was Linge.

The head of the RSD [Reichsicherheitsdienst, Reich Security Service], SS Major General Johann Hans Rattenhuber, was in the bunker himself, and would be a first-ranking witness if he were still alive. He has certainly given orders concerning the burial of the human remains of the body (if we accept the Russian war report of 7 May, Rattenhuber was captured by the Russians).

Rattenhuber was alive and shared the same prison – the Lubyanka – as Günsche and Linge in Moscow.

In spite of the lack of witness statements, the British secret services reached the conclusion that Hitler had committed suicide.

On 30 April at 2:30, Hitler and Eva Braun last appeared alive. They walked around the bunker and said goodbye to their direct entourage, the secretaries and the assistants, then withdrew to their apartments where they both committed suicide. Hitler by firing a bullet into his mouth and Eva Braun (although she had been given a revolver) by swallowing one of the capsules of poison distributed to everyone in the bunker.

The work of the British put the senior Soviet officers in a very uncomfortable position. The theory of suicide by poisoning, which they had acknowledged to the Kremlin, was under attack. The British report was added to the statements that Günsche and Rattenhuber had given the NKVD in June, then the statement given by Linge a few weeks later. The option of Hitler having committed suicide by firearm recurred more and more often in the interrogations. And if the men of SMERSH, the ones who had quickly carried out the inquiry into Hitler in May–June 1945, had been mistaken about the form of the suicide and that Hitler had killed himself with a bullet to the temple or in the mouth? That would mean that the body on which the autopsy had been carried out was the wrong one!

The Russian general Ivan Serov was the representative of the NKVD and the supreme deputy commander of the Soviet military administration in the Russian zone of Germany. Serov was in fact one of the most senior Soviet officers in Germany. Beria had chosen him personally for his extraordinary capacity for work, and most of all for his flawless loyalty. In mid-November, Beria received an urgent telegram from Serov. He informed him of the delicate situation facing Vadis and SMERSH.

Top secret
Telegram
From BERLIN
Moscow, NKVD USSR – to comrade BERIA L.P.
The head of British intelligence Brigadier FOORD and the head of American intelligence Brigadier CONRAD have sent the head of the operational group of the city of Berlin, Major General comrade SIDNEV, some documents concerning the deaths of HITLER and Eva BRAUN.

In doing so, Brigadier FOORD and Brigadier CONRAD are asking General SIDNEV to pass them the data of the Russian intelligence service concerning the death of HITLER.

They also indicate that they plan to discuss the question of the death of Hitler at the joint meeting of the general directorship of the intelligence services which is usually held in the presence of General Sidnev.

In this context I would ask you to give your response to the behaviour of General SIDNEV at the next meeting of the joint directorship of the intelligence services on this subject.

I SEROV

20 November 1945

Beria remained suspicious. He wasn't used to sharing documents classified as "secret" with strangers, including military allies. But the opportunity to eliminate one of his competitors, in this instance Abakumov, the head of SMERSH, was too good to miss. By passing the Hitler file to the British and the Americans, he knew that SMERSH's errors would be brought to light.

Hesitating, Beria sought the advice of Vyacheslav Mikhailovich Molotov, the first Vice President of the Council of Ministers and Minister of Foreign Affairs.

TOP SECRET PEOPLE'S COMMISSARIAT FOR INTERNAL AFFAIRS

Copy no. 1

20 November 1945

No. 1298/b

Moscow

To Comrade V.M. MOLOTOV

I am sending you the telegram from comrade SEROV about the request from the Anglo-Americans to give them information about the death of Hitler.

Please discuss this question.

This last phrase is circled and underlined in pencil. This is followed by Beria's signature in red pen.

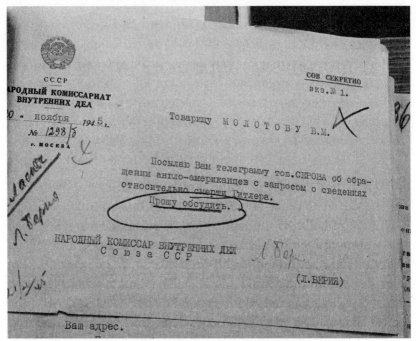

*Secret mail from Beria to Molotov on the Allied request to have access
to the Hitler file, dated 20 November 1945 (GARF archives).*

Molotov saw no objection to the Allied request. His positive
answer gave Beria an ideal alibi. Stalin would not be able to
accuse the head of the NKVD of having placed his rival in an
untenable position. He hurried to warn his agent in Berlin,
General Serov.

To Com. SEROV

We have no objection to the British and the Americans
being given information that you possess about the results of
the investigation into the circumstances of Hitler's
disappearance.

Please also note that the Allies may ask to interrogate some
people who are in our custody: GÜNSCHE, RATTENHUBER,
BAUR and others.

Think carefully and decide under which form this information
may be provided to the Allies.

Signed: L. Beria

Serov would not provide any information because SMERSH refused to collaborate. The conflict between the two Soviet secret services exploded. It was too much for Beria. He wanted to launch a new enquiry into Hitler's last hours, but this time it would be an inquiry conducted directly by his men. Before that, wouldn't he have to give an account to Stalin? Abakumov remained one of the protégés of the master of the Kremlin, and a head-on attack was not an option. A letter explaining the situation should sort things out, Beria said to himself. He asked his assistant, Merkulov, to get to work and find the right words for this most important message.

In fact it was not one letter but two that his assistant had to write. Or more precisely, two versions of the same letter. In one, Beria suggested giving the Allies a translation of the secret report from SMERSH, while in the other he only let the Western investigators inspect the garden of the bunker, at the spot where the bodies had been burnt.

On 19 December 1945, Merkulov delivered both versions to Beria.

Top secret

To Comrade BERIA L.P.

In accomplishing your mission, I present at your convenience two enclosed variants of the note in the names of Comrade STALIN and Comrade MOLOTOV concerning the request of the British and the American to exchange materials about the question concerning the fate of Hitler and Goebbels.

In addition please find enclosed:

Sent by Comrade STALIN and Comrade MOLOTOV concerning the fate of Hitler and Goebbels.

In addition please find enclosed:

Sent by Comrade SEROV the documents provided by the British with the typed translation of this material in Russian.

The identification files and the forensic examination files of the presumed corpses of Hitler, Goebbels and their wives, as well as the records of the interrogations of the entourage close to Hitler and Goebbels, copy no. 3.

(V. Merkulov)

19 December 1945

Beria held all the cards. What version should he choose? And who should he send it to – Stalin or Molotov, the Minister of Foreign Affairs?

He thought for hours. Reworked the wording, crossing out, annotating them time and again. With Stalin, mistakes were impossible, every detail was important and could influence anyone's career, even Beria's, if not his life. So the corpses of Hitler and Eva Braun became the "alleged corpses." Here is the final version:

Top Secret

To Comrade STALIN I.V.

On 16 June 1945, the NKVD of the USSR, under no. 702/b, presented you with the copies received from Berlin by Com. SEROV of the minutes of the interrogations of people from Hitler and Goebbels' entourage in Berlin, as well as copies of the description of his forensic examination of the alleged corpses of Hitler and Goebbels and their wives.

In November of the same year a representative of the British intelligence service in Berlin, and then a representative of the American intelligence service, sent the head of the NKVD in Berlin, Major General SIDNEV, the materials of the inquiry that these services had conducted into this subject which broadly correspond with ours (copies of the English and American documents translated into Russian are attached).

With reference to the fact that some of the people who witnessed Hitler's last days have been arrested by the Soviet authorities, and may complement or confirm the materials in possession of the British, the British have asked for the materials in our possession to be made available to them.

The representative of the American intelligence service in

Berlin has also asked permission to inspect the place, with our representatives, near the Reich Chancellery where, according to the information of the Americans, the corpses of Hitler and his wife (at the time, the alleged corpses of Hitler and his wife), after being subjected to forensic examination, were transferred to another place and buried not far from the Chancellery.

We request that you examine this question.
L. BERIA

At the last minute, Beria changed his mind. He decided only to send the letter to Molotov. Comrade Stalin would never receive the message. And the Allies would never gain access to the SMERSH report. They would only be able to visit the garden of the Führerbunker.

But that wasn't the most important thing. Now that Molotov had been informed of the doubts of the Allies about the non-discovery of Hitler's body by the Soviets, and of the causes of Hitler's death, Beria created the ideal conditions to launch his counter-investigation. This was fully justified. It would be secret and extremely detailed, and would definitively answer the mystery of Hitler's disappearance.

The Code name for the operation: "Myth."

RUSSIAN STATE MILITARY ARCHIVES
MOSCOW, MARCH 2017

The alarm hasn't sounded. So the air is still breathable. Vladimir Korotaev checks that the ventilation is working properly and allowing oxygen to circulate. The protection system of the rooms where the archives are stored might seem outdated, but it proves to be fiendishly effective. To avoid the risk of fire, the oxygen is simply expelled from the room every evening when the offices close.

This security process will start in only thirty minutes' time. Then the alarm will be heard and we will have just a few seconds to evacuate the room. Vladimir has told us several times in the maze of corridors and lifts that has brought us here. As soon as the signal sounds, we must leave immediately. After that it will be too late; the doors will be automatically blocked and the oxygen evacuated. Death will almost certainly follow! "Is there no way of stopping the process, an emergency alarm?" we ask in surprise, running after Vladimir. "No!" His tone does not invite any further questions. And besides, it isn't in our interest to question the security measures in the archives. Or to give Vladimir a valid reason to stop the guided tour that he is giving us.

In theory, we shouldn't be in this part of the Russian State Military Archives. A few minutes before, Lana managed to persuade the deputy director to let us look at the holy of holies, the rooms where all the archives of the Red Army since its creation are stored, but also documents about the Nazi enemy seized during the war. How did Lana persuade him to let us in? Thanks to her usual technique, which is summed up in a word: "psychology." To be frank, she also uses her smile and a perfect knowledge of the Russian mentality. What button did she press this time? "Is that all you have? I'm a little disappointed ..." Self-respect. Lana knew that this was a sensitive area for many men, and staked everything on touching it. Vladimir wasn't expecting that. We were still in his office consulting the last files of the prisoners of war – Linge, Günsche, and the others. But it had taken him some time to locate them on the dusty shelves of the archives. An unfamiliar effort for this senior official, more accustomed to issuing orders than to executing them. As pleasantly as possible, slowly, with precision and persistence, Lana went on ploughing her furrow ever deeper until she touched the nerve and tickled it delicately, just the right amount. "Are there really no other important pieces that might help with our investigation?" She pressed a little more, again and again. Vladimir began by taking his glasses off. He rubbed his eyes as if to dispel some pain. He was hardly tempted by the idea of going back to the archive store and leaving us alone with the files. Sensing his hesitation, Lana pounced: "We can come with you to the archives if you like ..." The suggestion struck him as so out of place that he didn't reply. Then, against all expectations, after looking at his watch, he said simply: "Let's go. We still have a little time."

Two small red electric panes stand over a greenish armoured door. The first one is lit, and bears the words "Automatic Shutdown." The other, which is unlit, reads: "Gas. Do not enter." Behind the door is one of the ten store-rooms of the Russian State Military Archives. There is one on each floor. Inside, the air is dry, and the temperature, lower than in the offices, mustn't rise beyond 18 to 19 degrees. Imposing ceiling lights give off a whitish light that makes the place feel like a hospital. Only every other lamp works, giving the room an atmosphere of permanent twilight. Here we are in the heart of the Russian State Military Archives. Metal shelves about two metres high stretch over an area of at least two hundred square metres. They are all filled with large rectangular cardboard boxes. Inside are paper documents, most of them stamped "secret." With at least fifty shelves, this room alone contains the trifling amount of five thousand boxes. A veritable wet dream for a historian. What mysteries lie in those boxes, right here in front of our eyes? Stalin's secret accords with Chiang Kai-shek against Mao, the Cuban Missile Crisis, Frenchmen arrested in SS units ... So many mysterious files carefully classified and within reach. I open a box at random, typed pages, others on carbon paper covered with obscure diagrams. It would take months and months to analyse, dissect, check. "And nothing is digitised," Vladimir explains in a low voice. So many historical tragedies, so much pain, so many state secrets emanate from these shelves that even without agreeing in advance, all three of us surprise ourselves by talking in a whisper. "You will now have a better understanding of why it's complicated for us to find the documents with any precision." The classification system of the military archives works in the old style: small cards sum up the themes, years, and events for each box but without more details than that. The task becomes more complicated when the documents are in foreign languages. Like the ones that come from the Nazis. "There's nothing that we don't know," Vladimir says in an attempt to moderate our astonishment. "Our historical collection has nothing to teach us. Everything has been declassified, or almost ..." Ah, that "almost" that crops up all too often in our inquiry. The photographs of the autopsy of 8 May 1945 on the alleged corpses of Hitler and Eva Braun? Impossible. Officially, they don't exist. Stalin's orders to hide the truth from the Allies? Likewise. The results of the forensic examination of the bodies? The list goes on. Vladimir hears it and sighs. We're tiring him out. It's time to leave the room. We've had our half-hour. The gas, the oxygen, the ventilation, he lists the security instructions again. We've got to get out of here. Quickly.

The five steel bolts slide with a loud click into the vertical reinforcements of the door. Vladimir turns the handle to check that the double door is well bolted. Then, once the keys are back in the depths of his pocket, he shows us to the lift. The visit is over. It's no surprise that he has carefully left the files concerning the "Myth" operation in the store-room, far from our eyes. The files on Linge,

Günsche, Baur, and Rattenhuber remain hidden away, even today. Luckily we were able to consult them in his office. Briefly, admittedly, but for long enough to make use of the essential parts: the years of solitary confinement, forced labour, and torture. Obscure SS men who had become the prisoners most sought after by the conquerors of the Third Reich. Would violence make them speak at last? Would they confess, complain, crack?

★　　★　　★

No one can stand up to the Butyrka for long. The Butyrka is a prison, the most famous in Moscow. It is on the edge of the city centre and even today it remains a provisional detention centre. In 1945 the Butyrka would make the Lubyanka seem almost like a pleasant holiday retreat. If the cells were cold on winter nights, they were even more unbearable in the summer months when Moscow is crippled by high temperatures. The Butyrka is not entirely devoid of creature comforts, but its conditions are slightly dated. To the eighteenth century, to be precise, the date of its construction. Originally it was an army fortress. Catherine the Great of Russia wanted to feel that she was protected very close to her throne by her loyal Cossacks. Cossacks, however, are very much at home with a lack of comfort. Particularly since they weren't locked up in rooms only a few metres square and, even more importantly, weren't tortured throughout the night by sadistic thugs. Unlike the men who escaped from the Führerbunker.

For reasons of greater efficiency, all the prisoners more or less implicated in the death of Hitler were brought together at the Butyrka in early 1946. To make sure this happened, the NKVD officers had to spend weeks scouring the Nazi POW camps under Soviet control – except the ones under the surveillance of SMERSH, who still refused to collaborate. They were looking for witnesses to Hitler's last hours. Very gradually a precise list of about thirty Nazis was drawn up, and their transfer authorised. The prisoners were then classified according to their degree of importance:

Level 1: people who had had direct contact with Hitler by
virtue of their function
Level 2: the personal guard and the SD (Security Service) guard
Level 3: the service staff of the Reich Chancellery

Level 1 included all those who were the focus of attention of the Soviet secret services. These were given special treatment, especially:

Heinz Linge: Hitler's valet, thirty-two, SS Sturmbannführer
[Commander]
Hans Baur, Hitler's private pilot, forty-seven,
SS Obergruppenführer [Army Corps General]
Otto Günsche, Hitler's aide-de-camp, twenty-eight,
SS Sturmbannführer [Commander]

Some had tried to hide their true identity after their arrest in early May 1945. People such as Linge, the Führer's valet and confident. Arrested in 2 May 1945, he had managed to disappear into the crowd of Nazi prisoners. "I was captured, but that was all. [. . .] No one was interested in me," Heinz Linge notes in his memoirs. He was sent with several thousand other German soldiers to a camp near the city of Poznan, east of Berlin. Interrogated, he told the Soviets that he was just a simple officer from one of the administrative services. His strategy worked marvellously until the intervention of another of Hitler's confidants, the pilot Hans Baur. Having also been arrested by the Red Army and imprisoned in the same camp, he reminded anyone willing to listen of his qualities as a general, and that as such he was to be treated with respect. "As well as being a general, I was Hitler's personal pilot," he would repeat all day. In the face of Soviet disbelief, Baur had an idea. He spotted Linge in the mass of Germans from the POW camp. Good old Linge would be able to testify in his favour, he said to himself. He alerted his jailers, assuring them that Linge would be able to testify that he was indeed Hitler's personal pilot. He knew because he was Hitler's valet. "My disguise was blown. I had to write down the answers to all their questions which I had answered falsely before, but this time honestly."* At least Baur obtained satisfaction. He was taken seriously, and rightly considered as a prisoner of prime importance. He immediately left the wretched camp in Poznan, bound for Moscow and the Lubyanka prison. With Linge. Where torture sessions worthy of their rank awaited.

Level 1 prisoners were separated from one another. But they were not alone in their cells. Each of them shared a cell with another inmate. A German, but one that they didn't know. These comrades in misfortune would soon become their confidants, the only ones willing to support them, to listen to their complaints, their weeping, their rages. To listen to them – oh yes, and listen they did. They were spies, informers, in the pay of the NKVD. Their task was to gather every least scrap of information and to keep an eye on the physical and mental state of their cell-mates. To avoid arousing suspicion, they took advantage of the daily interrogations of the SS prisoners to deliver their reports to their superiors.

> The double agent in Linge's cell code-named "Bremen," states that Linge is in an advanced state of depression. He says, "Finish me off, just kill me! I have already been tortured enough in the Lubyanka, and it's still going on here ..."

The infiltrated agent excelled in the art of managing the mental and physical resistance of the SS man under his charge.

> Agent "Bremen" confirms that Linge is in a depressive state. [. . .] But the agent thinks that the measures taken will have a positive influence on Linge, and will prompt him to collaborate. The agent is sure that Linge knows and is hiding important secret information. The agent has received the order to keep Linge under surveillance and ensure that he does not commit suicide.

Each weak point was used to obtain total collaboration during the interrogations.

*Heinz Linge, *With Hitler to the End*, op. cit., p. 211.

The prisoner Linge is worried that his family might be removed from the German zone under American control by the Soviets to be imprisoned by them in the Russian zone.

Heinz Linge certainly remained the most important of the level 1 witnesses. And one of the most fragile psychologically. Linge was not a born fighter, far from it. The impeccable dark uniform of the SS officer had never been splashed with blood or mud on a battlefield. At most it had received a few drops of French champagne or Hungarian Tokay during an official cocktail party where the drink flowed freely. That lovely uniform of his, which would be brutally torn from him by his jailers. An NKVD report goes into detail:

> After being subjected to a minute search and obliged to swap his military uniform for the filthy, worn rags of a prisoner, Linge arrived in the interrogation room in a state of complete depression.

SS officer Linge had never been subjected to violence before. Throughout the war, he had known only the wordy diatribes of the bosses of the regime and Hitler's mood swings. The atrocities that were taking place in Europe every day on his master's orders remained immaterial concepts as far as he was concerned. The stench of the dead in the concentration camps and on the battlefields; the smell that was a mixture of guts, excrement, and blood – that smell of death did not fill the hushed apartments of German power. How could he imagine it? How could he have any idea of such inconceivable, inhumane matters when he had never once had to confront them? Linge didn't know. He didn't want to know.

He had served as Hitler's valet for ten years. Now that the Nazi regime had collapsed, he was paying the price. And it was a heavy price. His promiscuity, his intimacy with the Führer, brought very special treatment from the Soviets. At the start of 1946 they were convinced that he was the key. Linge became an enormously important figure. But nothing had predestined him for this role.

Heinz Linge was nineteen and a bricklayer when he joined the Nazi Party in September 1932. A few months later he joined the Waffen-SS, the military branch of the SS organisation. In 1935 he was selected along with two other soldiers to enter "the Führer's personal service."

From that point on he never left Hitler. He looked after his wardrobe, his personal effects on his travels, he checked that the servants were looking after his house properly. During the war against Poland, in September 1939, rather than being sent to the front, he became Hitler's one and only butler. The two others who failed to make the grade were sent back to their fighting units. By way of recompense, he was even given the rank of SS Hauptsturmführer [equivalent of captain], and the title of "head of the Führer's personal service staff." At the end of the war, in the shelter of the Führer's bunker and still without having done any combat duty, he was awarded the rank of SS Sturmbannführer (commander).

The agent of cell "V-III" reports that Baur is frightened of physical torture.

Baur didn't live up to the image of the Nazi warrior with nerves of steel cherished by the regime's propaganda either. Like Linge, this postman's son had earned his stripes in the drawing rooms of the Reich Chancellery. Certainly, he went through the test of fire at a very young age. In 1915 he was just eighteen when he took part in the First World War, initially as an assistant mechanic in the air force and then as a pilot. With six officially recognised victories in aerial combat, he gained the much-desired status of aviation "Ace" (to be considered an "Ace," you had to prove at least five victories). After the defeat of Germany in 1918, Baur stayed in the army for a few years. He was demobilised in 1922 with the rank of lieutenant and went on piloting, but as a civilian. In 1926 he joined the new national airline, Lufthansa, becoming a captain. His talents as a pilot and his commitment to the Nazi movement (he became a member in 1926) assured him a brilliant future. As a pilot on the Berlin–Munich line, he met and bonded with certain passengers in dark uniforms. One of these was a man by the name of Himmler, the head of the SS. He was the one who whispered Baur's name to Hitler in 1932. Germany was still a democracy, and was going through an intense general election campaign, both presidential and legislative. The NSDAP, the Nazi Party, had the most to gain. A victory seemed possible, and the power that went with it. Hitler was looking for a good pilot who could transport him from meeting to meeting to help him win elections. Baur accepted. This idea of the Nazi leader was revolutionary. Using the airways to move faster and give speeches in several cities on a single day. None of his adversaries had done that before him. Hans Baur agreed to become the *Ständiger Flugkapitän und Chefpilot des Führers* ("Führer's captain and chief pilot"). He helped him on two occasions, once between 3 and 24 April, then between 15 and 30 June. It was a success. The NSDAP was the first German political party in terms of both votes and number of deputies. After new legislative elections in November of the same year and months of negotiations, Hitler was appointed Chancellor on 30 January 1933. He would never forget Baur's precious help. He immediately made him his personal pilot and refused to be transported by any other. He also awarded him the grade of SS colonel. In 1944, at the age of only forty-seven, Baur would be appointed SS-Obergruppenführer (army corps general) and police generalleutnant (division general). In spite of these two ranks, he would never command either a military unit or a police platoon.

In 1946, this drawing-room "double general," a close confidant of Hitler, suffered badly from his detention in Russian jails. His attempted escape from the Führerbunker on the night of 1–2 May was disastrous. Seriously wounded, he had his right leg amputated in detention. It was a German doctor, another prisoner, who performed the operation. The conditions were far from ideal. "There was no scalpel available,"* Baur remembers in his memoirs, "so the surgeon amputated me with a pocket knife." It was almost certainly a saw.

*Hans Baur, *I was Hitler's Pilot*, op. cit., p. 205.

Psychologically fragile and genuinely terrified by the torture sessions, Baur had no hesitation in denouncing his former SS colleagues to save his skin.

As soon as he arrived in Moscow, he was initially sent to the Lubyanka. After Linge, he denounced the telephone operator at the Führerbunker, SS Oberscharführer (adjutant) Rochus Misch. Sixty years later, Misch would relate in his autobiography:

> In December there began endless inquisitions by Stalinist inter-rogation officers. Baur was beaten and mistreated. Then he made the portentous statement: 'For that you should ask my attendant. He knows more about it than I do."*

This piece of advice would not be without consequences for NCO Misch. He found himself propelled onto the list of impor-tant witnesses. His fate had already been sealed a few weeks previously, when he had suggested helping Baur. The pilot had just had his leg amputated in the camp in Poznan. Misch, who knew him from having bumped into him on several occasions in the Führerbunker, had offered him his services. He changed his bandages every day and saw to it that he was fed. In return, the adjutant hoped to profit from the special treatment normally reserved for generals in the POW camps. This reasoning might have applied in the one controlled by the Western Allies, but not in the Soviet zone. Very quickly the Russians informed Baur that he would be transferred to a sanatorium in Moscow. There, they assured him, he would be treated as his rank of general deserved. He accepted, but only on the condition that his assistant, Misch, could go with him. Baur had a perfect recollection of the scene: "I had succeeded in getting a former telephonist in the Reich Chancellery, a corporal [he was an adjutant[named Misch, allowed as my batman, and now, with some difficulty, I got

---

*Rochus Misch, *Hitler's Last Witness*, op. cit., p. 176.

permission for him to accompany me to Moscow, though I'm not sure that it turned out to his advantage.'*

A gentle euphemism. Rather than in a sanatorium, Baur found himself in the Butyrka, and so did Misch. They met Linge, Günsche and Rattenhuber, who were already settled in their cells. Fleas and cockroaches by the hundred, the icy cold of Moscow nights, barely edible food, the conditions of their imprisonment petrified proud General Baur and his trusty Misch. The bullying began very quickly. Particularly the one that involved cleaning a floor filthy with urine and excrement with only a plain handkerchief. After this came the physical violence during interminable interrogations. Baur couldn't understand what he was doing here. It had to be a mistake. Admittedly he held the rank of general, but he had never been in command or ordered a massacre. And he didn't know Hitler very well either. That was what he endeavoured to explain to his jailers. To prove his good faith and his willingness to collaborate, he quickly denounced Günsche. He was the one who knew everything.

> The agent recorded the following declaration from Baur, which is worthy of attention: "I don't know why the Russians are sure I was the man who knew everything about the Führer. It would have been in their interest to look into his aide-de-camp [Otto Günsche] who was with him in his apartment all the time."

The Russians didn't wait for Baur's advice to take an interest in Günsche. But the SS colossus posed a problem to the NKVD investigators. Unlike Linge and Baur, he proved to be tough. Even "Siegfried," the spy who shared his cell, couldn't soften him. Suspicious and naturally taciturn, Günsche revealed nothing useful.

> According to information from our source [the informer], Günsche abstained from any conversations about Hitler's death [. . .].

*Hans Baur, *I was Hitler's Pilot*, op. cit., p. 200.

The secret services would try to find ways around this. They regularly changed the infiltrated agents, altering their profiles to win his trust. Nothing worked. Günsche wouldn't crack, and didn't change his statements. The SS man might only have been twenty-eight, but he already had a decade's service in the death's-head uniform. He was very familiar with the methods used to break prisoners' resistance.

Otto Günsche was the son of a police officer. He joined the Hitler Youth at the age of fourteen and joined the SS Leibstandarte in 1934, at the age of seventeen. This SS shock troop contained the elite warriors of the regime. It recruited chiefly on the basis of physical criteria. Officers had to be at least 1.80 metres tall (none of the high-ups in the regime fulfilled that criteria: Hitler was 1.76 metres, Himmler 1.74 metres, and Goebbels 1.65 metres), prove "racial purity" without Jewish blood over several generations, and of course swear fidelity unto death to the principles of Nazism. The following year, to celebrate his eighteenth birthday, Günsche joined the NSDAP. This strapping young man, 1.93 metres tall, blond, broad-shouldered and athletic, soon attracted the attention of his superiors. Very logically, he was chosen to join the SS group responsible for Hitler's personal security. That was in 1936, when Günsche was nineteen. On 1 March 1943 he became Hitler's personal aide-de-camp. In that capacity, he followed the Führer through his everyday life. He attended all the military and diplomatic meetings, recorded everything that was said, and executed his orders to the best of his ability. Like Linge, Otto Günsche became one of Hitler's shadows, and the privileged witness of the last months of his power. When interrogated by the Soviets, he claimed to know exactly how the Führer had taken his life. Like Linge, like Baur: On 30 April 1945, Hitler joined his wife, Eva Braun, in his antechamber in the Führerbunker. They committed suicide. A few moments later, the two bodies were burnt in the gardens of the Chancellery and buried.

But the accounts of the three witnesses did not agree on certain details. Linge heard a shot being fired. Günsche didn't. Baur claimed to have said his farewells to the Führer at about 6–7 pm, when the two others swore that he had killed himself at about 4 pm. Who was right? Who was lying?

Beria couldn't afford to make a mistake. Stalin had just relieved him of command of the NKVD. On 29 December 1945, the first Soviet Union spy was replaced by his deputy, Sergei Kruglov. Did this mean that Lavrenti Beria was being sidelined at the end of his bloody career? Was he still a leading figure in the secret services? Certainly, Stalin seemed to be weakening the power of his "Himmler" in the very sensitive sector of state security. But Beria, who had just been given the honorific title of Marshal of the Soviet Union, was an unavoidable presence in the complex equilibrium of Muscovite power. A major piece in the mechanics of repression and surveillance of the country. He was still allowed to keep an eye on all of the secret services as a member of the Politburo and vice-president of the Council of Ministers. Nothing escaped his attention. Certainly not the "Myth" file.

In mid-February 1946 the interrogations began. Methods changed compared to those of SMERSH in May–June 1945. They became more brutal, even extremely brutal.

None of that violence appears in the accounts of the NKVD investigators. Or hardly anything. It's there between the lines, looking at the times of day chosen for the interrogations. Most of them took place in the middle of the night, between eleven o'clock and five in the morning. Some sessions lasted no longer than two hours, some could extend over six hours at a stretch, or even more.

Breaking the body and the spirit, making the adversary vulnerable, shattering his last resistance, the officers of the Soviet special services had nothing to learn from the Nazis. For years they had been torturing "counter-revolutionaries" and other "enemies" of the people; they had perfected the delicate art of interrogation. Asking the same question over and over again, day after day, or rather night after night, can take the prisoner to the brink of madness, as Hitler's former valet was about to find out.

Investigator Schweitzer. Interrogation of prisoner Linge. From 3:30 to 5:30 in the morning, 19 February 1946.

To the statement by the investigator indicating that his previous statements had been checked and judged incorrect, Linge declared that everything he had said three times during the investigation and written in his witness statements corresponded to reality. There is nothing to add or alter.

This is his account of Hitler's death: "Hitler withdraws to his antechamber at about 3:45 pm on 30 April 1945. He joins Eva Braun. Linge remained behind the door all the time. A few minutes later he hears the sound of gunfire. He runs to alert Bormann, the Führer's secretary. Together they opened the door and observed that Hitler and Braun have died. He by bullet, she by poisoning. Then they take the bodies to the garden and burn them."

Linge's hope of an easy ride from the Soviets faded very quickly. The Russian investigation was only just getting under way again. That first meeting with Agent Schweitzer lasted only two hours. Just a taster of the nights to come. Whether Hitler's butler liked it or not, the questions about the dictator's last days were due to follow.

Session with prisoner Linge in Butyrka prison from 11 pm, 19 February, to 5 am, 20 February 1946.

Linge testified once again about Hitler's last day in the bunker of the Reich Chancellery on 30 April 1945.

Six long hours stating the same story over and over again. Linge held out, presenting a version identical to that of the first days of his detention the previous summer. The interrogation had been conducted in Germany. An interpreter officiated throughout the session. The questions resume. This time, he is asked whether at the last minute Goebbels might not have persuaded Hitler to escape. Linge listens and admits that it might have been possible. But a tank would have been required to pierce the curtain of Russian soldiers surrounding the bunker, the former butler explains.

Session by investigator Schweitzer on Linge, from 11:30 pm, 20 February, until 4:45 am on 21 February 1946.

The prisoner Linge was questioned about the people present in the bunker of the Reich Chancellery on the evening of 29–30 April 1945.

According to him there were still fifty-eight of them. He was sure of it and solemnly declared as much.

Back in his cell, Linge boasted to his cell-mate about the lies he had told during the interrogations. The spy "Bremen" didn't miss a word and reported the conversation to his superiors: "Linge does not deliver sincere witness statements because he knows that the Russian authorities will not be able to confuse him in his lies. For the simple reason that there are only two people who know the circumstances of the 'death' of Hitler: him and Bormann. And Bormann is out of range of the Russians." At this time Martin Bormann was still being actively sought. In fact he had not survived his attempt to escape from the bunker on 2 May 1945.

Three almost sleepless nights. Linge couldn't get to sleep in his cell. He came back exhausted from his endless sessions of questioning. And by day the warders kept him from sleeping. It was a rhythm that wasn't about to stop.

Investigator Schweitzer interrogating prisoner Linge from 11:30 pm on 21 February until 4:20 am on 22 February 1946.

During the interrogation, in response to the question concerning the number of people present in the bunker, Linge wished to correct his statement of 20 February 1946.

The first cracks in the valet's depositions. The blows rain down, threats burst his eardrums. For the first time, he returns to his statements, the ones he made the previous day.

From fifty-eight people in the bunker he switches to only twelve that he really saw on the evening of 29–30 April 1945.

The interrogations continue:

On 23 February, 12:30 pm until 4:00 pm.

On 24 February he is allowed a little rest.

On 25 February the night-time sessions resume. From 11:30 pm until 4:00 in the morning.

On 26 February Linge cracks. A week of that treatment has been enough to transform him. When they come and look for him in his cell at 11:00 pm he reacts like a madman and starts screaming. The NKVD agent records the scene in his report.

> Linge exclaims: "I beg you to kill me, anything but torture. If you don't stop I'm going to kill myself." He was informed that everything would go better if he decided to tell the truth at last. Linge became hysterical and shouted: "I tell the truth at every interrogation! I can't make up a different one!" Then he began to cry. When he calmed down, the investigator resumed the procedure and began the interrogation ...

The Soviet reports never linger on the methods used by the investigators. To find out more, we must turn to the prisoners. Linge recorded some traumatising details of his passage through the Soviet dungeons, particularly concerning physical violence:

> Since I would not confirm what the commissar wanted to hear I had to strip naked and bend over a trestle after being warned that I would be thrashed if I did not finally "cough up." Naked and humiliated I persisted with my account. "Adolf Hitler shot himself on 30 April 1943. I burned his body!" The commissar ordered a powerfully built lieutenant holding a whip with several thongs: "Give it to him!" As I cried out like a stuck pig, he observed cynically: "You ought to know about this technique better than us. We learned it from your SS and Gestapo."*

Hans Baur, already considerably weakened by his amputation, was subjected to the same treatment. The night-time interrogations continued with the same recurring question: is Hitler dead?

*Heinz Linge, *With Hitler to the End*, op. cit., p. 212.

At first the German pilot attempted to maintain a dignified composure. He even complained of the comfort of his new prison, and asked to be taken back to the Lubyanka. A request that was obviously refused. Instead, they shouted at him: "You're lying! You're lying! You're lying!" Exhausted and frightened, Baur admitted that in fact he was lying. He didn't know which lie he had told, but he admitted everything. He had only one wish: for everything to stop.

> I went along to my interrogation as usual, and the examiner glared at me and shouted triumphantly: "Baur, you're going to tell us what you know now – or else. In a day or so your wife will be here, and if you don't talk then we'll rip her knickers off in front of you. And if that's not enough we'll turn her over and thrash her. And if even that doesn't loosen you up we'll make her into a whore."*

The threat had its effect. The pilot dropped his mask.

Hitler's suicide? He wasn't there.

The discovery of the lifeless corpses of Hitler and Eva Braun in the antechamber of the bunker? He wasn't there. The cremation of the two bodies in the garden? He wasn't there.

Why these repeated absences at the most dramatic moment in the life of the man he had served so devotedly?

> I was too busy getting my things together for my attempt to flee the area. And it was too dangerous to go into the park of the Reich Chancellery in broad daylight to see the burnt bodies. The whole district was under artillery fire.

Baur no longer tried to put a brave face on his actions. He presented them as they were, warts and all.

As to the details about Hitler's death, he learned them only later on. "It was on 22 or 23 October 1945 in Poznan prisoner of war camp." Two guards from Hitler's personal security staff gave him the information, he said. Baur was quick to tell his questioners the

*Hans Baur, *I was Hitler's Pilot*, op. cit., p. 211.

names of those two soldiers: "They were Bergmueller and Höfbeck."

The Soviets still doubted the veracity of Baur's declarations. They knew that Hitler had personally given orders to burn his body after his suicide, and to make sure that no one would ever be able to find them. But Baur hadn't done anything.

Could they trust him?

When did you last see Hitler?

On 30 April 1945 at about 6:00 or 7:00 pm. He told me of his intention to kill himself. Then I left his apartments to get my things together and flee.

When did you come back to Hitler's bunker?

Two hours later. [. . .] I asked the ones who were waiting there: "Is it over already?" I was told that he had committed suicide with an 8 mm military pistol.

Baur's statements did not agree at all with those of Linge or Günsche.

Günsche repeated the same information at each of his interrogations. Hitler killed himself on 30 April 1945 at about 4:00 pm. It was Linge who found him. On the other hand, when he was only a few metres away from Hitler's antechamber, Günsche didn't hear gunfire. At that precise moment, however, there was no noise in the bunker, just the vibrations of the ventilation system. How could the young SS man not have heard the report?

In the Russian camp, the results of the interrogations were dissected, analysed, and compared.

Two major differences struck them immediately: the time of the suicide.

Between 3:00 and 4:00 pm for Linge and Günsche.

Between 7:00 and 9:00 pm for Baur.

The cause of death:

By firearm for Linge and Baur.

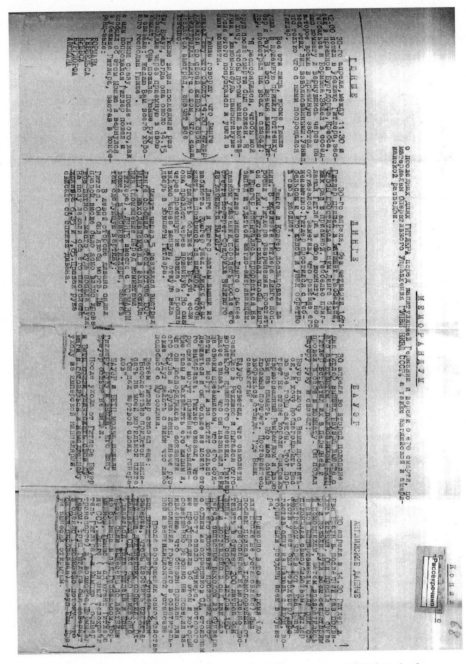

Summaries by the Soviet investigators of the different accounts of Hitler's death.
From left to right, Günsche, Linge, Baur and the Anglo-American investigation.
The Soviets have underlined the most important passages (GARF archives).

Uncertain for Günsche.

After a month of interrogations, they had to admit that the "Myth" file was not getting anywhere. Doubts persisted, indeed they flourished.

At this stage, for the Soviet secret services, Hitler's death remained mysterious.

As to the body they had found, was it his? If so, why did the forensic examiners not notice the impact of a bullet to the head? Unless Linge and Baur were lying?

PART IV

CONCLUSIONS?

MOSCOW, MARCH 2017

We have only two days. That's all the Russian authorities have granted us. Two days to carry out a forensic examination. We had to fight to get even this. "Haven't you ever thought of carrying out scientific tests on Hitler's human remains? Or rather the remains that are potentially those of Hitler?" Alexander Orlov, our contact at the Ministry of Foreign Affairs, didn't expect these questions. It was last December. He got in touch with us again just to know how we had got on with the FSB archives. He'd hoped he was done with us. The teeth, the skull and confidential files, wasn't that enough? "We want to know once and for all, without the slightest doubt …" He's heard these arguments so often, from so many journalists, historians, even scientists. Tests, new technology, with no damage done to the skull or the teeth. Alexander speaks good French. But when he finds himself in a stressful situation, he prefers to reply in his mother tongue, Russian. Lana resumes the conversation. Alexander resists. He claims he doesn't know.

We have only one goal, dear Alexander, which is to put an end to the legends, the rumours of a possible escape by Hitler. Didn't Russia want to know whether it had Hitler's human remains? Unless you're afraid you were wrong for so long? There's only one way to bring this chapter to an end once and for all: let the forensic examiner, Philippe Charlier, come and examine the skull and the teeth.

Silence. Then his voice darkened all of a sudden: "I've got it. I'll give you an answer soon …"

Our reply came in early March. It was: "Two days! One day per archive. Come at the end of the month."

That worked out perfectly. We had also just got the green light for the military archives. We'd be able to kill two birds with one stone.

Dr. Philippe Charlier would be joining us for those important two days. The French forensic examiner and archaeo-anthropologist was the obvious choice for us. In just a few years, this scientist had built up a solid reputation for penetrating historical mysteries. The most famous "murderers" in history speak beneath his skilful fingers. Poison, blade, pistol, nothing escapes him. His accomplishments impress his peers, but also the wider public all over the world. The kings whose remains have passed through his hands include France's Henry IV, Saint Louis, Richard the Lionheart, and legendary figures like Joan of Arc, and the tribune of the French Revolution, the terrible Robespierre. Philippe Charlier liked to publish the studies of his "patients" in the world's finest scientific journals. A youthful man in his forties, enthusiastic, an adventurer (he loved to travel to the remotest spots on the planet to practise his skill), he combined popularisation with a scrupulous respect for classical scientific principles. Hardly surprising that the media saw him as an "Indiana Jones of the graveyards," and passed on in detail each of his new historical autopsies. No way would he be willing to miss the Hitler file.

Two days, then. One day for the skull in the GARF Archives and one more for the teeth in the company of the shady spies of the FSB. GARF and the TsA FSB dragged their feet as they usually did, and talked terms. They all reacted in the same way: "Our country is drowning in forensic specialists. We don't need a foreigner." And they were perfectly right. A Russian would carry out the tests just as seriously, we had no doubt of that. And yet, out of concern for neutrality, as far as we were concerned what was needed was the opinion of a foreign scientist. To our greater surprise, the argument was accepted quite quickly. To avoid any suspicion or pressure from the Russians, we were given permission for the

French doctor of our choice to intervene. We just had to find the dates that would satisfy everyone. Those would be 29 and 30 March.

Moscow, 28 March. I have twenty-four hours to check that everything will be ready for Dr. Charlier's arrival. The Russian capital is calmer than usual. The walls of the Kremlin no longer hum with the babbling of groups of tourists. Lenin's tomb is empty of the devotees of the Communist mummy. In the square are dozens of police officers, truncheons visible, regulation grey fur hats decorated with the insignia of the forces of law and order. They have the closed faces of people who have been given strict instructions. Two hours earlier, a demonstration of opponents of the regime met in the city centre. An insult to Putin. The state powers didn't hold back, and arrested seven hundred demonstrators. The pictures were shown on the news channels all around the world. Russia was going through a major economic and political crisis unprecedented over the past ten years. The country is getting tougher and turning in on itself. Not the optimum conditions in which to investigate the Hitler file. At best, the authorities have neither the time nor the energy to answer our questions; at worst, they see us as a new source of problems. I was barely surprised when I saw Lana in the café where we used to work. Her features were drawn and her gaze uneasy. She didn't have to open her mouth. I understood. They'd just cancelled! Not all of them. Just the TsA FSB. Without giving a reason or justifying themselves. That left us with GARF, the state archives with their bit of skull. They hadn't changed their minds. Not yet.

The people in charge of GARF have stopped replying. We've been waiting in the entrance hall for an hour. It's 3:00 pm on 29 March, and Philippe Charlier's plane has just landed at the international airport of Sheremetyevo, an hour away from the centre of Moscow. Yesterday, Alexander Orlov had personally intervened on behalf of Lana. FSB cancelled, "date doesn't work," but not GARF. "Come on, they're waiting for you." Had they really said that? I ask Lana the question one more time. She sighs: "He said exactly those words." So, the people in charge of the state archives know that we're here, and that a French expert has come specially from Paris to examine the bit of skull, the one they keep in a miserable little computer-disk box! So why is no one replying to us? Even our passes aren't ready. We confirmed a meeting about the skull with Dr. Charlier. The teeth would be later, another time. "When?" he had worried, rightly. Soon. We were using the same methods as the Russian authorities: vagueness and hope. Philippe Charlier reassured us immediately. "Don't worry, I'll find a window when the time comes, don't you worry about that. I'm really interested in the project; you can count on me. But we're okay about the skull?" In principle, yes. But we're seething with rage in an empty waiting room. Do they even know that we're here? Are they playing with our nerves for fun? Or is it just an illustration of the atavistic incompetence of the post-Soviet bureaucracy?

A woman in her sixties is sitting behind the only counter in the room. She's the one who issues the passes. An oh-so important job that gives her the perverse opportunity to be as rude as she wishes, without the visitors to GARF daring to fight back. Right now she is eating a kebab and reading a glossy magazine without paying us the slightest attention. "They're going to phone and tell her to prepare our documents," Lana guesses, trying to remain optimistic. "It's only a matter of minutes." Nikolai Vladimirsev, the archivist with the waxy complexion, finally decides to come and save us. He has brought out the passes. The lady finished her sandwich long ago, and has started reading another magazine. She doesn't even look up when we leave. Stay calm and polite, it's all only a test. It doesn't matter, because the skull awaits our forensic examination. Philippe Charlier should be joining us in about half an hour. We just have time to check that everything has been put in place. "The skull isn't ready?" I can't believe what Nikolai has just told us. And yet he confirms as much with his usual nonchalance. Nothing has been prepared. His opal eyes have never looked as bright as they do right now. "We will wait for Dr. Charlier before we put everything in place," he goes on as we cross the courtyard of GARF towards the head office. "Nothing will begin before he gets here. And for your information, everything must be finished before the offices close at 5:30."

Here we are again in this room where we were shown the skull last year. Only the decorations on the walls have changed. Instead of the revolutionary posters from 1917, a series of black-and-white photographs of the imperial family, the family of Nicholas II, the last tsar of Mother Russia. Should we see this as a desire on the part of the Russian regime to bring back the country's imperialist past? I don't dare to elaborate on this ideological choice in the company of Nikolai, and even less of Dina Nokhotovich, who has just joined us. The head of the department of the secret collection clearly didn't expect to see us again. As usual, her manners are dictated by her mood. It's late afternoon, and Dina seems irritable and doesn't respond to our greetings. I recognise the big shoe box that holds the bones attributed to Hitler. It protrudes slightly from the little supermarket trolley that Nikolai never takes his eyes off. The trolley has been placed carefully at the end of the table. The same big wooden table. "Is there any chance of opening the box?" Lana translates my request. Neither of the two archivists replies. As if they can't hear her, or no longer understand Russian. At last Nikolai reacts. Without a word, he sits down beside his little trolley, folds his arms defiantly and looks us up and down. The atmosphere of our meeting is becoming awkward. The silence is heavy. Lana breaks it. "Isn't Larisa, your director, going to join us?" Anxious now, we even find ourselves wishing she was there. Clearly Dina and Nikolai aren't keen on our forensic project. We need to know if this is merely a case of insubordination, two clerks uneasy with the idea of some strangers manhandling their "treasure." Or, more generally, if the directors of GARF have found their own way of obstructing our work.

Philippe Charlier has just called us. He's at reception, opposite the woman with the newspaper. She clearly doesn't want to let him in. Nikolai agrees to move. Very slowly, he adjusts his hat on his sparse, straw-coloured hair, slips on his coat and comes with me. Imperturbably he greets the French expert with a frosty *"ztrast-vuyte"* (hello). I tell Dr. Charlier about the complexity of the situation. I do so discreetly, because French is a language that many Russians understand, having learned it at school. In the Soviet era, French often replaced English as a compulsory foreign language. And Nikolai is easily old enough to have been a schoolboy under the hammer and sickle. "I understand, I'll adapt," the doctor murmurs. "I'm used to it." Some positive vibes at last. Philippe Charlier has plenty of those. He adds, entering the room where Lana and Dina are waiting for us: "I'm going to have access to the skull. And that in itself is extraordinary."

We think we know why our contacts are being so frosty. A big thank you to Professor Nicholas (known as Nick) Bellantoni of Connecticut University. That American professor of archaeology examined the skull in 2009 and declared that it belonged to a young woman! As we were given to understand at our first meeting with GARF staff last year, his little adventure traumatised Dina and Nikolai. Since that scandal, no scientist has been allowed anywhere near the human fragments. Philippe Charlier is the first. And he is kept under close attention. Nikolai stands a few centimetres away from him, ready to intervene if necessary.

First stage: observation. The French forensic expert picks up the diskette box holding the bit of skull. He brings it to his face and examines it from every possible angle. Nikolai opens his mouth and holds his hands out in front of him as if in a reflex. He is outraged. Normally he is the only one allowed to touch this little box. Dina pulls a face to express her own disapproval. Philippe Charlier is oblivious. All of his attention is focused on the bones. His confident attitude disconcerts the Russian archivists, who don't dare to oppose him. For now ...

"The first important thing you need to know is that it's impossible to determine the sex of this skull just with a visual analysis." The scientist speaks without hesitation. He goes on: "Does it belong to a man or a woman? No one can say with any certainty.

It seems to me risky at best to make a diagnosis on such tiny fragments of bone. We have only the back left-hand part of the skull
at our disposal. That part never gives a clue about its sex. I'm categorical on the matter." In just a few minutes, Philippe Charlier has
demolished part of his American colleague's theory. Bellantoni
claimed that the structure of the bones, too fine, too fragile, did
not correspond to those of an adult male. "Wrong!" The
Frenchman has no doubt. "On a skeleton, the diagnosis of sex is
performed only on the pelvis. It's unthinkable with a skull, a
mandible, or a femur. And you would need to have the whole
skull. Which is not really the case here." And the age? Bellantoni
reached the conclusion that the skull was that of someone aged
between twenty and forty. But Hitler was fifty-six. How did the
American get there? "He must have based his theory on the degree
of closure of the sutures at the level of the skull." Quite correct.
In many interviews, the archaeologist from Connecticut makes no
secret of his reasoning. It is based on the sutures that hold the
plates of the skull together. This is what Nick Bellantoni says in a
video shot by his university in Connecticut "Normally, as you age,
they close down [. . .], and these are wide open. An individual, I
would have expected, twenty to forty years old."* Philippe Charlier
is able to study the sutures in question very closely. "I wouldn't
risk giving an age to a bone like this based only on the gap in the
sutures. They vary so much between one individual and another.
It's possible that my sutures are completely closed like those of an
old person, while my grandmother's were open when she died. I
insist, you can't give the age of this skull on the basis of the sutures.
Particularly when you only have a third of the whole of the skull.
It doesn't hold up."

"Niet!" Dina isn't happy. "Niet!" Nikolai agrees. Lana argues:
we've got permission. "Niettt!" Dr. Charlier was about to put his
sterile gloves on. He wanted them to open the diskette box for
him so that he could take out the piece of skull. Lana had

*https://www.youtube.com/watch?v=ZqrrjzfnsVY

translated the question with a certain restlessness. The reply from the two archivists was as cold as a Siberian winter. We're not opening it. Certainly not for a foreign scientist or some journalists. Dina says it again, on the brink of rudeness. Negotiation is no longer an option. The temperature in the room is starting to rise. Philippe Charlier intervenes calmly: "It doesn't matter. We'll do it without. Can I go on observing the skull anyway?" Nikolai didn't expect such a calm reaction. The scientist turns towards him. He is a good head taller. "Just look, I won't touch." Dina finally says, "Da."

"Then I will continue my observations. I will take my time, and too bad if they hoped to go home early this evening." Lana takes advantage of the moment to escape into the corridor and call Alexander Orlov for help. After ten rings he finally picks up. The situation, the refusal, the obstacles erected by the archivists, Lana lets her distress spill out. Alexander is getting weary. He replies that there's no longer anything he can do for us. "Sort yourselves out!"

It's nearly six o'clock. Nikolai consults his watch. He taps his foot impatiently. The French expert feels the tension mounting around him. Unflappable, he taps all the information he has managed to glean into his computer. It will help him to write his report. Ultra-high-definition photographs of the skull and all the objects on the table will complete his work and allow him to verify his forensic examination. "Vascular orifice (right-hand unilateral parietal foramen), star-shaped loss of substance on the left parietal ..." When he is working, the expert on the dead has no interest in the living people around him. Not even the crafty Russian archivists. "Look at this, for example, it's very interesting ..." He points at an orifice perfectly visible on the top of the skull. "This is clearly a bullet wound. The projectile passed through the head from side to side and emerged at the level of the parietal bone. This is an exit wound, not an entry wound. Its shape is typical, splayed towards the outside. It is about 6 millimetres wide. That isn't to say that the calibre of the ammunition was 6 mm. I can't establish a diagnosis of the calibre on the basis of an exit wound. The bullet could easily have fragmented or been deformed." On the other hand, what seems certain in his eyes is the moment when the bullet went off. "It was fired at a cool, damp bone," he confirms. If it is Hitler's skull, the bullet was fired either while he was alive, or shortly after his death.

The investigation is proceeding at a crazy pace. Now the forensic expert's attention is drawn by blackish traces on the skull. "These are residues of the burial medium, definitely soil. You can also see traces of carbonisation. They prove that it has undergone prolonged thermal exposure. This person was burnt at a very high temperature." According to the survivors of the bunker, almost two hundred litres of petrol were used. "That's perfectly consistent," Charlier says. "Burning a body is very difficult. To make a human corpse disappear completely, it would take at least 100 kilos of wood or several hundred litres of petrol. A body is full of moisture. Hence, in many cases, the heterogeneity of the carbonisation."

Nikolai listens as if he understands every word uttered in French. He almost relaxes. A hint of admiration appears in his eyes. Behind him, the whole of the Hitler file has stayed in the caddy. I can't help consulting those dusty old documents again. I can easily decipher the signatures of the Soviet rulers of the time. Names that have become familiar to me from having studied them so much: Beria, "Stalin's no. 1 cop," Molotov the diplomat, Abakumov the ambitious spy ... I'm looking for one passage in particular. The one concerning an interrogation of Heinz Linge, Hitler's valet. The report dates from 27 February 1946. It's typed and signed by the Nazi prisoner at the bottom of each page. I show it to Philippe Charlier.

Question: Tell us about the events that took place on 30 April 1945 in the bunker of the former Reich Chancellery.
Answer: At about 4:00 pm, when I was in the room outside Hitler's antechamber, I heard a shot from a revolver and smelt gunpowder. I called Bormann, who was in the next room.

Together we went into the room and saw the following scene: facing us, Hitler was lying on the sofa on the left, one hand dangling. On his right temple there was a large wound caused by a shot from a revolver. [. . .] On the floor, near the sofa, we saw two revolvers belonging to Hitler: one a Walther calibre 7.65 and the other a 6.35. On the right, on the sofa, Eva Braun was sitting with her legs bent. She had no trace of bullet wounds on her face or her body. Both Hitler and his wife were dead.

Question: Do you remember clearly enough that Hitler had a bullet wound in his right temple?

Answer: Yes, I remember clearly. He had a bullet wound in his right temple.

Question: What size was this wound to the temple?

Answer: The orifice of the entry wound was the size of a three-mark piece [Linge would say in other reports: "a wound the size of a pfennig piece," author's note].

Question: What size was the exit wound?

Answer: I did not see an exit wound. But I remember that Hitler's skull was not deformed, and that it remained complete.

The description of the wound broadly corresponds to the visual examination carried out by Charlier. If at this stage it remains impossible to determine the identity of the skull, the evidence agrees. Even better, the valet's witness statement sheds new light on the matter for the forensic examiner. Notably the fact that the skull remained intact in spite of the shot. "If he really fired into his right temple, the exit of the bullet through the left parietal seems logical. And we have a way of knowing whether Linge lied or not. We can in fact check the hypothesis of a shot fired in the mouth." What? "Thanks to the teeth! If we find traces of powder on the teeth or the gums, it's a good argument in favour of an intrabuccal shot having been fired." Those famous teeth which are in the archives of the FSB, and to which access has, for the time being, been delayed.

Dina has had enough, she wants to leave. It's 6:30 pm; we've overshot closing time at GARF by half an hour! "Can we come back tomorrow? And continue with the analysis of the skull as well as the pieces of sofa?" Lana shouldn't have spoken. Her question irritates the old archivist. "No! You have no authorisation for tomorrow. Finish for today. I will leave you for another few minutes."

Philippe Charlier doesn't understand a word of Russian, and hasn't grasped the exchange between the two women. The archivist's rude tone of voice tells him nonetheless that the situation is deteriorating. But he keeps his calm and turns his attention to the other pieces of the puzzle set out in front of him. Apart from the bit of skull, he is able to observe the wooden structures of the sofa, including the head-rests. As well as the photographic report from the time of the counter-inquiry into Hitler's suicide in April–May 1946. This series of black-and-white photographs that we saw last year shows the site of the suicide, with traces of blood on the sofa and the wall. "We can't talk about blood traces," Charlier says prudently. "At this stage we can only talk about traces of blackish drips." More than half a century has passed, and they still appear on the light-coloured wood, probably pine, of Hitler's sofa. The passing of time and GARF's very poor conservation conditions have not erased them. If these are authentic pieces and not a trick perpetrated by the Russian secret services. Anything is possible in this inquiry, including the worst. "I think it would be difficult to make such a forgery," Philippe Charlier reckons. "All of these traces can also be found identically in the photographs from 1946. It would demonstrate astonishing counterfeiting skill if it was a copy." Lana tells Charlier: "You can touch them if you like, you can handle them; look here, where there are traces of …" The forensic expert utters a cry as he sees the journalist bringing her hand towards the object. "No! Don't touch! You'll contaminate this piece of evidence with your DNA." Lana apologises with an embarrassed laugh. "That's exactly what you mustn't do," Charlier says apologetically. "And it's bound to have happened several times. That's why I'm not expecting much from these bits of sofa. They have been badly preserved in non-sterilised fabric. Plainly this wood has been touched by numerous hands, directly, without protective gloves. And that's without the spittle that many observers have deposited on them. The only DNA that one would find here will be from a few minutes ago. Hitler's will have disappeared long ago." Then, after a moment's thought, he goes on: "We can hope for nothing from that side. Unless …"

While he leans over them, keeping a respectable distance (without running the risk of adding his own DNA by tiny drops of sweat or saliva) from one of the pieces of sofa, the forensic expert has another idea. He turns his attention towards the photographs from the Soviet inquiry. Then back to the pieces of evidence. That back-and-forth movement speeds up. He picks up one of the chairs around the table and begins a strange demonstration. "This is very interesting. Exciting. Look …" His enthusiasm even communicates itself to the two archivists, who are drawn to him in spite of themselves.

"Let's imagine that the victim is on this chair. He has just fired a bullet into his skull. His head is on the head rest, the blood flows and bounces off the floor, causing splashes. He talks quickly, waving his hands around. Wounds to the head always bleed abundantly. The blood must have flowed in large quantities, even for only a few minutes, the few minutes between the shot and Bormann and Linge's arrival in the antechamber. The blood spread across the floor, thick, heavy, dark, whether on the concrete or on a carpet. Carpet or concrete, it doesn't really matter. There will have been so much blood that a puddle has formed, and the drops that are still falling splash the sofa, but not just anywhere: under the sofa. And here are those splashes!" On one of the pieces of the sofa tiny dark stains mingle with the natural veins of the wood. Sometimes, depending on the lighting, they almost disappear. The scene of the crime, of the suicide to be precise, is coming into focus. Does Charlier's hypothesis agree with the witness statements? Linge, the valet, and Günsche, the personal aide-de-camp, came into the room. They told the Soviet investigators who had taken them prisoner what they saw.

Interrogation on 26–27 February 1946 of prisoner of war Linge Heinz, former Sturmbannführer SS.
Linge: "There was a lot of blood on the carpet and on the wall near the sofa."

Interrogation of prisoner of war Sturmbannführer SS and Hitler's servant, Günsche Otto, 18–19 May 1945.
Question: When did you first enter the room where the suicide occurred and what did you see?
Answer: I entered the room at 16:45. I saw that the carpet on the floor had moved slightly and that there was a bloodstain.

After the liberation of the Soviet camps in 1955, Linge's interminable interrogation sessions in the Russian prisons would resume: "'How much blood sprayed on the carpet?' 'How far from Hitler's foot did the pool of blood extend?' 'Where was his pistol exactly?' 'Which pistol did he use?' and 'How and where was he sitting exactly?' These were some of the stereotyped, endlessly repeated questions I was obliged to answer."[*]

Philippe Charlier is able to give those answers. Or at least some of them. He abandons the pieces of wood, which are unusable for DNA tests, and comes back towards the bit of skull. He picks up the box. He plays with the light to get a better look at the dark traces that cover part of it. "As I thought," he says under his breath, as if talking to himself. "These are not organic remains from an individual. No skin or muscle. It's all been burned. I clearly see traces of carbonisation. They prove that it has undergone prolonged thermal exposure." The expert is more interested in other stains. "I think we are looking at traces of soil here. Perhaps even traces of corrosion or rust. Do we know where the skull was discovered?"

Thanks to the files found in the archives, we know quite precisely.

*　　*　　*

[*]Heinz Linge, *With Hitler to the End*, op. cit., p. 213.

Go seven decades into the past – to 30 May 1946. Thirteen months after Hitler's suicide, the area around the Chancellery in Berlin was subjected to a new inspection, organised within the top-secret context of the "Myth" file, launched on 12 January 1946 by Beria's successor in Internal Affairs, Sergei Kruglov. Teams of investigators brought in especially from Moscow got to work in the Führer's headquarters. They had received very precise orders from their superiors:

Top Secret

"APPROVED"

Vice Minister of Internal Affairs

of the Union of Soviet Socialist Republics

Colonel General: I. Serov

16 May 1946

Plan of operational investigative activities into the circumstances of Hitler's disappearance.

In order to clarify the circumstances of Hitler's disappearance, the following measures must be undertaken:

I

1. Draw a map (to scale) of the location of the new and old Reich Chancelleries as well as Hitler's shelters (bunkers); photograph the sites.

2. Proceed to the internal inspection of Hitler's shelters as follows:

a) draw a map of the arrangement of the rooms in the bunker.

b) photograph the rooms occupied by Hitler and Eva Braun.

c) proceed to the inspection of all furniture preserved in these rooms, as well as the walls, floors and ceilings, for a possible detection of any traces that might shed light on the circumstances of Hitler's disappearance.

d) inquire into the question of the current location of the furniture previously removed from the bunker and examine them.

e) in order to identify the preserved furniture and establish their arrangement in the rooms occupied by Hitler and Eva Braun, Linge, Hitler's former valet, should be brought to the site after having been previously questioned on the subject.

f) Study the place where the corpses of a man and a woman were found by the exit to the shelters in the garden of the Reich Chancellery for a possible detection of objects that might be of importance to the inquiry.

3. Inquire into the location of the personal objects that previously belonged to Hitler and Eva Braun but which were removed from the bunker. Examine these.

II

4. Perform a new medico-legal autopsy of the bodies of a man and a woman discovered in the garden of the Reich Chancellery during the first days of May 1945 to establish the age of the deceased, the signs and cause of their death.

5. To this end it is necessary to exhume the bodies and transport them to the locations specially equipped for the purpose in the hospital in Buch.

On the basis of the results of the activities listed above and the materials previously collected, investigations will have to be undertaken according to a new plan.

The principal goal of the teams of the Ministry of Internal Affairs was to find the missing part of the body found in May 1945. In their autopsy report dated 8 May 1945, the forensic examiners had recorded the absence of the back left-hand part of the head. Very quickly, in May 1946, two pieces of skull were disinterred in the garden, three metres from the entrance to the Führerbunker. Precisely where the alleged bodies of Hitler and Eva Braun had been found on 4 May 1945. One of the pieces had been pierced by a bullet. Might that fragment of bone not be the missing piece of the puzzle? In that case, the theory of suicide by poison was seriously weakened. What if it was true that Hitler had committed suicide not with cyanide but with a bullet? The discovery of these two bits of skull might put an end to speculations about his death. For that to happen, it was enough to check that the bones belonged to the corpse attributed to Hitler. Nothing could be simpler, since the Ministry of Internal Affairs was fully supportive of the inquiry. Except that the corpse in question was still kept under the jealous surveillance of the Ministry of Defence.

For several months, the head of Soviet counter-espionage, Viktor Abakumov, had enjoyed almost total impunity in the chain of command of the USSR. Stalin had made him his new right-hand man. Abakumov took advantage of the fact to act as he saw fit. So on his own initiative, on 21 February 1946, the SMERSH officers based in Germany moved the corpses not only of Hitler, but also of Eva Braun, of the Goebbels family (parents and children) as well as that of General Krebs. Until now these bodies had been buried in a wood near the little town of Rathenow. No justification was given at the time to the Soviet authorities.

Top Secret
ACT
21 February 1946 3rd Shock Army of the Soviet Occupying Troops in Germany
The Commission [of SMERSH] has drawn up the present act stipulating that on the above date, in accordance with the instructions of the head of the counter-espionage service "SMERSH" of the Group of Soviet Occupying Troops in Germany, Lieutenant General Comrade Zelenin, near the town of Rathenow, we have exhumed a grave of bodies belonging to:
– German Reich Chancellor Adolf Hitler.
– His wife Eva Braun.
– The Reich Propaganda Minister, Dr. Josef Goebbels.
– His wife Magda Goebbels and their children – son Helmut and daughters Hildegard, Heidrun, Holdine, Hedwig [only five out

of six children are listed; Helga, the eldest daughter, is missing]
- The head of the general staff of the German Army, General Krebs.

All of these bodies, consumed by putrefaction, are in wooden boxes and have been transported in this state to the city of Magdeburg, to the headquarters of the counter-espionage department "SMERSH" where they were reburied. They were buried at a depth of 2 metres in the courtyard of number 36 Westendstrasse, near the stone wall to the south of the courtyard, 25 metres from the garage wall of the house to the east.

The grave has been filled with earth and flattened at ground level, giving the spot the appearance similar to the surrounding landscape.

Why move such important corpses? Abakumov did this to keep control of his "trophy." The headquarters of SMERSH in Magdeburg, 150 kilometres south-west of Berlin, offered perfect protection against the "snoopers" of the Ministry of Internal Affairs. It was quite natural for the bodies to be moved there. It was most important that they should not be taken to the Berlin hospital in Bunch for a new autopsy.

The Kremlin supported Abakumov, because a few weeks later he was appointed Minister of State Security with the rank of general. Then he was appointed a member of the committee of the Politburo of the Soviet Communist Party, in charge of legal affairs. At the age of only thirty-eight, he was not only untouchable but also terribly dangerous for anyone daring to challenge him. A position that he planned to exploit.

The request by the "Myth" file team to perform a second autopsy on the bodies moved to Magdeburg was rejected out of hand by counter-espionage. But the directives of the Ministry of Internal Affairs did not lack clarity. Lieutenant Colonel Klausen, in charge of the inquiry in Berlin, brought with him a mission order that he thought was sufficient.

May 1946

Top Secret

To the Deputy Head of the Operational Department of Gupyi, MVD (Ministry of the Interior), USSR, Lieutenant Colonel Klausen.

These orders have priority. You must leave for the city of Berlin under the command of Lieutenant General Serov in order to carry out the special mission of the Ministry of Internal Affairs of the Union of Soviet Socialist Republics.

We ask all military organisations of the MVD and the occupying Soviet administration to support Lieutenant Klausen in every possible way from his arrival at his destination until his return to Moscow.

Deputy Minister of Internal Affairs of the Union of SSR

Lieutenant General Chernishov

This mission letter did not make enough of an impression on the SMERSH agents. They were answerable to the Ministry of Defence and had nothing to do with the other ministries. Because of their refusal, no one would ever be able to compare the two fragments of skull with the rest of the male corpse, either in 1946 or in any other year. Never. In spring 1970 all the bodies buried in Magdeburg and under the control of counter-espionage were definitively destroyed. This decision was taken at the highest level of the state by one Yuri Andropov, future leader of the Soviet Union (from 1982 until 1984). In 1970, Andropov already occupied a key post in the nexus of the country's secret services. He was the all-powerful "President of the Committee of State Security in the Council of Ministers of the USSR." In short, the man was in charge of all the Soviet spies. No "special" operation could be decided without his agreement. Like the one code-named "Archive," for example.

Purpose of the operation: to exhume and physically destroy the remains buried in Magdeburg on 21 February 1946 in the military town on Westendstrasse near house no. 36 (now Klausenerstrasse), which are those of war criminals.

Why decide twenty-five years after the fall of the Third Reich to destroy these skeletons? Did the Kremlin fear that the state secret might one day be revealed and that Hitler's body, if it was indeed his, might fall into the hands of the Western Allies? Or, more simply, did the Soviet rulers want to move on from an old story and get rid of defeated enemies once and for all? Moscow would not have to justify its act, because it was secret.

A colonel from the Special Department of the KGB ran this highly sensitive and confidential mission. In the early 1970s, Europe was in a state of major geopolitical tension. The German zone under Soviet administration had declared its independence from the rest of Germany in 1949. It took the name GDR, the German Democratic Republic, and obeyed the orders of Moscow. This was the era of the bipolar world (on one side the capitalist camp dominated by the United States, on the other the Communist camp led by the USSR), and the fear of a Third World War. Officially, Moscow continued to deny that it was in possession of Hitler's body. Operation "Archive" intervened in this complex geopolitical context. Everything had to be totally secret. As usual, the Kremlin was suspicious of everyone, first of all its own men. Precise instructions had been issued in this spirit.

For the operation to be put into effect, it will be necessary to proceed as follows:

1. Two to three days before the start of works on the burial place, the men of the protection platoon of the SD [Special Department – author's note] of the KGB have to set up a tent large enough for the activities covered by this plan of action to be carried out beneath it.

2. The protection of the means of access to the tent after its establishment must be carried out by the soldiers and, when the work is being carried out, by the operational personnel specially dedicated to operation "Archive."

3. Organise a hidden post from which to supervise the house near the site of the operation and inhabited by the local population in order to detect any potential visual observation. In the case of the discovery of any such operation, take measures to counteract it on the basis of the current situation.

4. Perform the excavation at night, place the remains found in specially prepared boxes, evacuate them in the vehicles of the engineering regiments and armoured vehicles of the GSVG [Group of Soviet Forces in Germany] in the region of the "rotten" lake (Fall See) (district of Magdeburg GDR) or incinerate them and throw the ashes into the lake.

5. Document the execution of the activities indicated on the plan by the writing of acts:

    a) act of exhumation of the interred remains (in the act indicate the state of the cases and their content, the procedure of placing the latter into prepared boxes);

    b) act of incineration of the contents of the interment.

    The acts must be signed by all operation agents listed above [. . .].

6. After the removal of the remains, the place where the interment took place must be returned to its original state. The tent must be removed 2–3 days after the major work is complete.

7. The "cover legend" given that the operation is being carried out in a military town where access is forbidden to the local population, the need for an explanation of the causes and nature of the work, may apply only to officers, members of their families and civilian functionaries of the army general staff living in the territory of the town.

The justification of the "legend." The works (installation of the tent, excavation) are carried out with the intention of verifying the depositions of a criminal held in the USSR, according to which precious archive documents may be found in this location. [. . .]

Mission orders for the KGB secret operation "Archive" concerning the complete destruction of the bodies of Hitler and Eva Braun, 26 March 1970. This document is stored in the archives of the FSB in Moscow.

It is rare to be able to consult such a Soviet secret services document. Even though it is over seventy years old, it remains confidential. It is no coincidence that it is preserved today in the archives of the FSB (ex-KGB). It shows us the internal working of a special operation with the use of "legends," scenarios intended to offer a credible cover to spies. What is surprising in the present case is that this "legend" was intended to fool soldiers of the USSR.

Operation "Archive" was officially taken to its conclusion. The alleged bodies of Hitler and his inner circle, Eva Braun, the Goebbels family, and General Krebs, have been definitively destroyed. At least that is the version provided by the Soviet secret services and validated even today by the Russian authorities. Here is that report in its entirety:

Top secret

Unique copy

Series "K"

Magdeburg (GDR)
u.m. [military unit] No. 92626

5 April 1970

ACT

(On the physical destruction of the remains of war criminals)

According to the plan of operation "Archive," the special group consisting of the head of the Special Unit of the KGB in the Council of Ministers of the USSR u.m. No. 92626, Colonel Kovalenko N.G. and military men of the same unit, Commander Chirikov V.L and Senior Lieutenant Gumenuk V.G., on 5 April 1970 has incinerated the remains of war criminals after removing

Unique copy of the report on the success of operation "Archive" carried out by the KGB, dated 5 April 1970 and stored in the FSB archives in Moscow.

them from their place of burial in the military town at Westendstrasse near house No. 36 (now Klausenstrasse).

The destruction of the remains was effected by means of their combustion on a pyre on waste ground near the town of Schönebeck, eleven kilometres from Magdeburg.

The remains were burnt, crushed to ashes with coal, collected and thrown into the River Biderin, which is confirmed by the present act.

Head of Special KGB Unit u.m. No. 92626

★   ★   ★

As in the days of SMERSH and the NKVD, quarrels between different Russian administrations continue even today. The flag has changed, but not the mentalities. As proof of this, will our authorisations to study the skull carry much weight with the two GARF archivists? Philippe Charlier consults the photographs of the Chancellery garden, taken in May 1946 when the fragments of skull were brought to light. A pile of metal debris covers ground violently ripped open by the artillery fire of the battle of Berlin. A small cross drawn in pencil on the photograph indicates the exact place where the two bits of skull were found. Just outside the entrance to the bunker. It was only later that the Russian scientists put the two fragments together to make one. The one archived in the offices of GARF.

"So these bones were buried under rubble in the middle of large numbers of metal objects …. This is important information. Remind me how long this bit of skull has been under the ground?" Each piece of information has its own importance. "Buried for over a year in this ferrous pool? That would be a match. At any rate, the scenario is not out of the question," Charlier reflects. "In plain terms, the bits of skull that we have in front of us show every sign of having been buried for a long time in corrosive ground."

Those are the positive points. Now for the negative ones.

"Isn't handling the skull under your surveillance exactly what we came here to do?" Philippe Charlier tries to persuade the archivists in his turn. Dina is unwilling to yield. She asks Nikolai. He replies by picking up the box holding the piece of skull. "Another time," he says without looking at us. When? Tomorrow? Soon? It's Dina's turn to speak: "We don't know if we will have time to receive you. You will need a new authorisation." But we've got it! Lana insists. Nikolai has already left with his trolley. He almost flees into the corridor. It is 8:00 in the evening. We have abused their patience quite enough.

BERLIN, 30 MAY 1946

Operation "Myth" was under threat. The vast counter-inquiry into Hitler's death faced a considerable obstacle: the Ministry of State Security of the USSR (MGB), under Viktor Abakumov. Abakumov's representative in Germany, Lieutenant General Zelenin, ordered his staff to oppose head-on the men sent to Berlin by the Ministry of Internal Affairs (MVD). The investigators had not expected such hostility. They had to face up to the facts: their minister, Sergei Kruglov, carried little weight in the face of Stalin's right-hand man, the dangerous Abakumov. More than five months of investigations and muscular interrogation to end here ... When the discovery of two fragments of skull outside Hitler's bunker had promised so much.

The Nazi prisoners who had witnessed the Führer's final moments also felt that something strange was happening. Seven of them had been transferred from their Moscow cell to Berlin. Among them, the usual trio of SS men from Hitler's inner circle: Heinz Linge, the valet, Hans Baur, the pilot, and Otto Günsche, the aide-de-camp. The only one missing from this line-up was SS General Rattenhuber. And for the good reason that he was in the hands of the MGB. Suspecting that the men from the Ministry of State Security would reply in the negative, the men from the Ministry of Internal Affairs had not even requested his transfer to Berlin. So it was without Rattenhuber that the last witnesses of Hitler's death were sent to the German capital. This was on 26 April 1946. They had been dragged from the Butyrka prison and thrown on a special train bound for the city of Brest, formerly Brest-Litovsk, in the far west of the USSR, near the Polish border. From there, they had joined another equally secret railway convoy to Berlin. Their journey lasted over a week. To avoid any contact between them, each inmate was placed in isolation in a wagon, unaware of the presence of the others. Years later, after his release from Soviet camps in 1955, Linge would describe that uncomfortable journey: "About a year after the end of the war I was thrust into a barred railway wagon and transported like some wild animal back to Berlin."* Hans Baur was concerned about the quality of the food: "We travelled for nine days, and during that time our daily rations consisted of some brownish water from the locomotive, half a salt herring and about a pound of bread. We arrived – in Berlin! – half starved."†

In the German capital they were immediately locked up in the former women's prison in Lichtenberg. Hans Baur: "We thought that we knew a thing or two about bad prison conditions, but Berlin-Lichtenberg prison under the Russians beat the lot. The warders were sadists who took pleasure in beating up their prisoners. One day my cell door was wrenched open and I was beaten up and left half-unconscious on the floor – vaguely I heard through a mist of pain that it was because I had been sitting on the edge of my bed."‡ It was no coincidence that the blows and the humiliations were resumed worse than ever during the former SS men's stay in Berlin. The Russian officers had been ordered to maintain total pressure so as to break any possible psychological resistance. The prisoners were to be made to cooperate unconditionally, because if they were here it was to resolve one of the last mysteries of the end of the war: the identification of the Führer's body. A Soviet officer asked Baur to stay prepared: "He told me that the bodies of Hitler and his wife had not been burnt at all, but preserved, and that I had been brought to Berlin to identify them."§ But nothing happened as

---

*Heinz Linge, *With Hitler to the End*, op. cit., p. 213.
†Hans Baur, *I was Hitler's Pilot*, op. cit., p. 221.
‡Ibid.
§Ibid., p. 207.

planned. At the last moment, everything was cancelled. "Actually I was never called upon to inspect any body," Hitler's personal pilot notes. And for good reason: Abakumov, the Minister of State Security, was opposed to the idea.

What was to be done? Was the group from the Ministry of Internal Affairs to return to Moscow and confess to Stalin that they had been unable to fulfil their mission? Kruglov, and through him Beria, would never recover. They had to get around the "wall" erected by Abakumov and pursue the investigations. For want of access to the body, the team from operation "Myth" took out their fury on the prisoners they had brought from Moscow. The investigators knew they were playing their final cards. In a few days they would have to write their definitive report and pass it on to the highest level of the Kremlin. Their careers were now at stake. Without waiting, they organised new interrogations and confrontations between the key witnesses as well as reconstructions in the bunker. They called them in one by one. In emergency situations such as this, records were written down directly in German and by hand. As usual, the austere and soldierly Günsche refused to be intimidated. As a field-based SS man used to combat, Hitler's former aide-de-camp barely unclenched his teeth.

> **Question:** During previous interrogations you gave a set of contradictory and imprecise statements about Hitler's supposed suicide. Once again, the judge requires accurate and authentic witness statements from you, in which you undertake to tell the truth.
> **Answer:** I wish the whole truth about Hitler's suicide to be made public, and I have no reason to tell the judge of any inexactitude or lie. My previous declarations correspond to the truth. I gave them in good faith.

To the same question, Linge, the valet, replied like Günsche:

Answer: I declare that my statements made in Moscow in February and March of this year correspond to the reality of the facts. I declare that Hitler is dead and that he died in circumstances that I have already described: on 30 April 1945, Hitler committed suicide in the bunker which is underneath the garden of the Reich Chancellery [Reichskanzlei] by firing a bullet from a revolver into his head, I assume through his right temple.

When his turn came, air force general Hans Baur, apparently more tense than the others, was much more forthcoming:

Question: Your declarations concerning the fate of Hitler in February and March this year are contradictory and untruthful. We are waiting for sincere statements from you about this question.
Answer: I have told only the truth. I declare that Hitler committed suicide along with Eva Braun in his bunker beneath the Chancellery on 30 April 1945. It happened in the following circumstances: two hours after my farewells to Hitler, I went back to the Führer's bunker. The bunker was full of cigarette smoke, which surprised me because smoking was forbidden anywhere near Hitler. Dr. Goebbels, Reichsleiter Bormann, Lieutenant General Rattenhuber and about 15 to 20 SS men were talking nervously. I immediately went towards Dr. Goebbels, Rattenhuber and Bormann, who were standing together, and I asked if it was all over. Answer: Absolutely (*Jawohl*). "Where are the remains?" "They are already up there burning." I heard the voice of an SS man adding: "He's already burnt to ashes." I asked General Rattenhuber how Hitler had killed himself. Answer: With a 0.8 pistol.

The investigators knew that they wouldn't be able to interview Rattenhuber, Abakumov's men would never accept it. Luckily, Baur was frail and a physically unwell man. He had never recovered from the loss of his right leg after his attempted escape from the bunker in early May 1945. His mental state was hardly any better. The Soviet informers who shared his cell systematically gave an account of the airman's mental decline. For the Russian officers, Baur was easy prey. If there was any secret surrounding the dictator's death, it would be hard for him to conceal it from them. To make him confess, the Soviets would tell a lie to get at the truth.

> **Question:** We have documents attesting that in late April 1945, Hitler was no longer in Berlin. That's why we see your statements as a refusal to tell the truth, and we demand the truth.
> **Answer:** That is a lie pure and simple. I said my personal farewells immediately before his death. That was on 30 April 1945 between 6 and 7 in the evening [Baur is the only one to give this time between 6:00 and 7:00 pm. According to Linge and Günsche, Hitler committed suicide at about 3:00 pm]. I was summoned to the Führer at the same time as Colonel Betz [Hitler's second personal pilot, he would be killed by the Soviets in early May 1945 while trying to flee the bunker]. It was completely out of the question that I could have talked to anyone but the real Hitler. Besides, I knew Hitler too well to be fobbed off with someone who looked like him.

Although he didn't know it, Baur had just put his finger on one of the main doubts of the Russian investigators: the theory of a lookalike! After the fall of Berlin on 2 May 1945, rumours of a "fake Hitler" rapidly circulated around the world. Like any good dictator, would the master of Nazi Germany not have had lookalikes at his disposal to take his place if there was a risk of an assassination attempt? Other dictators often resorted to that strategy. Including Stalin, with his famous "doubles."

But Baur denied the existence of another "Hitler." He had never heard of one, he swore. The investigators would take pleasure in destroying what remained of the pilot's confidence. Hans Höfbeck was a simple Untersturmführer SS, and one of the seven key witnesses transferred from Moscow to Berlin. He too was in the

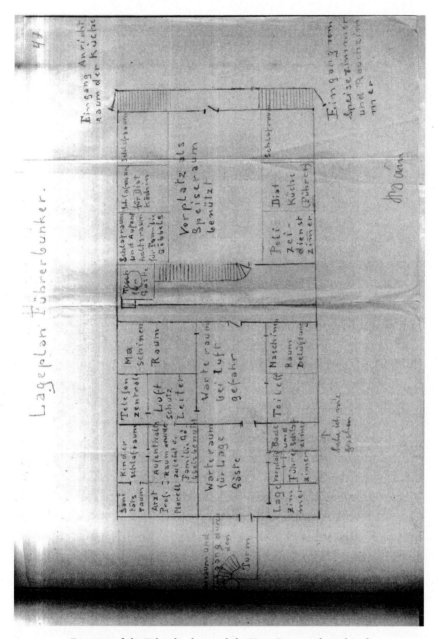

Drawing of the Führerbunker made by Hans Baur on the order of Soviet investigators. At the bottom on the right he states that he never went to the Führer's personal bedroom (GARF Archives).

bunker on 30 April 1945, as a member of Hitler's personal guard. He had been appointed head of the protection service of the Führer's shelters. What Baur didn't know was that this NCO had revealed the existence of a double of Hitler in the bunker. A confrontation between Höfbeck and Baur was organised.

Question to Höfbeck: Repeat the statements you have previously made concerning the existence of an individual in the Reich Chancellery who bore a strong resemblance to Hitler.
Answer: In the Chancellery there was a man employed as a porter by the Reich Minister, Dr. Lammers. He bore the following distinguishing features: he wore his hair combed back at a slight angle on the temple, he had a black moustache and pointed nose. But he was a little shorter and thinner. He wore a brown jacket, his office uniform, which was the same colour as the Party uniform. As he bore a resemblance to Adolf Hitler, sometimes partly as a joke, his comrades called him "Führer."

I have personally seen this man. From a distance he looked like Hitler. According to statements that Lieutenant General Rattenhuber has made in my presence, there is a man who looks like Hitler in Breslau. Rattenhuber told me that 10 or 12 years ago. But I have not seen this man personally.

Checking that the Nazis did not organise a fake death of Hitler by burning a lookalike: it was all that the Russians could think about. Baur's denials were not enough to convince them otherwise. To rule on the authenticity of the body found in May 1945 in the garden of the Führerbunker, they tried to recover as many of Hitler's physical details as possible. Identifying the corpse of Josef Goebbels had not been a problem. With his easily recognisable physical deformity (his right leg was several centimetres shorter than his left as the result of osteomyelitis in childhood), no controversy was possible. For the Führer, nothing so simple. In May 1946, no known deformation had been proven. But you never know. Perhaps his entourage was aware of a detail that would change everything? Hans Baur was interrogated along those lines:

Question: Are you aware of any physical defect or distinguishing feature in Hitler?
Answer: I am not aware of any kind of physical defect in Hitler. What I am aware of is that during the Great War Hitler was the victim of a gas attack. As to any wounds, not that I am aware of. Apparently following his gas poisoning he was obliged to follow a special diet, and became strictly vegetarian. Hitler also wore dentures.

Günsche gave the Soviet officers the same answer: he had no idea of any physical peculiarity:

By his own account, Hitler had suffered from a nervous ailment since the middle of 1944, which was also apparent in trembling in his left arm. I am not aware of any other physical deformities. I know that Hitler had accrued two wounds during the World War of 1914–1918, including asphyxiation by gas. I know of no other injury.
Question: Do you know Hitler's blood group?
Answer: No, I do not know Hitler's blood group.

While Baur and Günsche were subjected to torrents of questions in secret rooms, a special treatment was reserved for Linge. Since he had been the first to discover Hitler's lifeless body in his antechamber, he was asked to go into great detail about what he had seen on 30 April 1945. But this time he would tell the story on the exact spot, inside the bunker. That way the slightest incoherence could be unmasked. He was led to the ruins of the New Reich Chancellery where a large number of Russian officers awaited him, including Marshal Sokolovsky, the commander-in-chief of the Soviet-occupied zone in Germany.

We have brought you here today to the shelters beneath the Reich Chancellery, in the rooms occupied by Hitler. Are the rooms that you have seen identical in furnishing and decoration to those from the days when Hitler was present?

Linge: Yes. In the rooms occupied by Hitler in the shelters located beneath the Reich Chancellery, the furniture shown to me today on the spot is the same as the one used by Hitler. The items of furniture include in particular those that I have seen in Hitler's old bedroom: a simple wardrobe in light-coloured wood and an open fire-proof safe, and in his old study a sofa and a desk of the same wood as the wardrobe. The sofa is covered with light blue fabric with a floral pattern. The sofa and the desk are exactly in the same place as they were when Hitler lived in the shelters, which is to say that the sofa is against the wall facing the entrance and the desk against the opposite wall to the right of that door.

To make his account clearer, Linge was invited to draw a plan of Hitler's apartments. The valet carefully obliged.

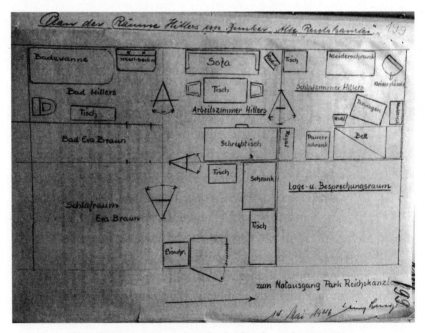

Plan of Hitler's apartments in his bunker drawn by Heinz Linge
on the request of the Soviet investigators (GARF archives).

After Linge's visit, Hitler's office was attacked by Soviet criminal investigators. They were looking for clues and particularly for blood. Among them, one man particularly took his time. His name was Piotr Sergeyevich Semenovsky. This sixty-four-year-old doctor was something of a celebrity in the USSR. A graduate of the prestigious university of Tartu in present-day Estonia, perfectly bilingual in Russian and German, he enjoyed considerable prestige in his country. His reputation must have gone beyond the borders of Russia, as he was elected an honorary member of the International Institute of Anthropology in Paris. Brilliant, efficient, and well known for the strength of his character, he invented a method of classification of fingerprints. His work was greatly appreciated by the Soviet regime, which was keen to keep the best possible records of its own citizens. When the Ministry of Internal Affairs summoned him on a secret mission, Semenovsky did not hesitate for a second. Looking for Hitler was a mission that was a match for his talent. A year had passed between the date of Hitler's alleged suicide and Semenovsky's inspection in 1946. Dozens, perhaps even hundreds, of soldiers and other Soviet officials had already contaminated the scene of the crime. A disaster for any decent criminal investigator. In the bunker itself, Semenovsky tore his hair out. Of course, he had suspected the difficulty of his mission and the conditions in which he would be working. But was he in a position to complain? Even he, the gold standard of scientific policing in Stalin's regime, did not have the right to make a mistake without paying the price immediately. Obey and succeed. Meticulously, the old doctor paced the room. The antechamber measured only a few square metres, barely ten or so. His eyes became accustomed to the poor lighting. He was given the records of Linge's interrogations. Not all of them. Only the ones that might help him understand. The place where Hitler had been on the sofa, the position in which his body was lying, where the shot had been fired ... blood, he had to find blood. The forensic expert looked. If there had been suicide by bullet, there would have to be blood. The sofa had not been stolen or destroyed. A stroke of luck.

Semenovsky ordered the head-rests to be removed. Dark trickles were perfectly visible. He thought he could spot bloodstains on the walls as well. These were not splashes caused by the bullet to the head, but traces left when the body was being moved. The expert mentally reconstructed the scene. The dictator's body, still warm and bleeding copiously. Yes, it was wrapped in a blanket, but that was quickly drenched in blood. The blood dripped onto the floor and against the walls. Semenovsky left the antechamber, pushing aside the soldiers on either side of him. He could no longer see them, absorbed as he was by the past. He almost closed his eyes to concentrate better. It was 30 April 1945, when the last of the Führer's loyal followers carried the body to the garden. Semenovsky did find some blood, further off in the corridors, but not only there. There was some in Hitler's antechamber, at the top of the stairs leading to the exit.

Photograph of the spurts of blood found on the walls along the stairs of the bunker during the counter-investigation of May 1946 (GARF archives).

The forensic examiner reread the records of the interrogations of those involved in removing Hitler's inert body on 30 April 1945.

Günsche: I went straight to the conference room in the bunker to tell the people there about the death of Hitler. They had come with me to the antechamber where the two corpses lay, those of the Führer and his wife. We rolled them up in blankets. Then they were transported through the conference room and then the central room to the stairs to reach the exit of the bunker.

Linge: Hitler's body was wrapped in a blanket, and then Bormann and I transported it. I held it by the legs and he by the head.

These witness statements agree with the traces taken in the bunker. The result of analyses would confirm that they were indeed traces of blood.

After the blood, the other fundamental index of the counter-inquiry: the two pieces of skull recovered outside the exit from Hitler's bunker. They were in the same place where the two alleged bodies of Hitler and his wife had been discovered a year before. These new bones were hidden at a depth of sixty centimetres. Semenovsky analysed them and concluded that they were fragments of the same cranial arch. He assembled them to form no more than a piece. According to him, this bone belonged to an adult male. Obviously the hole that pierced the top did not escape his vigilance. He immediately imagined a bullet from a revolver. The exit angle of the bullet suggested to him that the shot had been fired from bottom to top, from right to left, towards the back. Very certainly in the mouth or under the chin. And not in the temple as Linge claimed. Had Hitler's valet lied on that point? The Russian investigators expressed serious doubts concerning the reliability of his answers. They had already made him crack on his version of the Führer's suicide, particularly about the shot fired by Hitler. That was during an interrogation on 28 February 1946:

Question: In your previous declarations, you have indicated that you were outside Hitler's apartments on 30 April, at about 4:00 pm, and that you heard a shot and smelt gunpowder. Do you remember how many shots you heard, one or two?

Linge: I must admit that the statements I gave you before on this matter were not precisely accurate. I didn't hear a shot. I just smelled powder. It was after that smell that I went and told Bormann that the suicide had taken place.

In late February 1946, Linge was a wreck. He had lost about ten kilos, and his skin was eaten away by vermin. He had hardly slept for several weeks. That was exactly what the Soviet wanted. It was not without reason that the interrogation sessions were held at irregular intervals between 10:00 pm and 5:00 in the morning. Hitler's proud valet had lost his arrogance. He smelt so bad that his own odour was unbearable to him. This special treatment was intended to make him crack. It worked. After more sleepless nights spent answering the questions of Russian officers and enduring their death threats, the former SS man requested some mercy. His eyes were the colour of a battlefield, his mouth twisted into an uncontrollable rictus. He wanted rid of his secret. That secret that weighed so heavily. The one that questioned the theory of Hitler's double suicide: poison, then revolver. The investigators couldn't get over it. Was this another trick on the part of this ill-omened Nazi? The questions came flying:

How can you explain that you didn't hear the shot, even though you were so close to the room? Particularly if it was fired by a Walther [German pistol much used by the Nazis], as you yourself stated?

Linge: The shot must have been fired when I left my position to go into the corridor. When I came back after a few minutes, I smelled gunpowder and I immediately went to the meeting room where Bormann was waiting. I told him it was over.

But on 30 April 1945, at about 4:00 pm, Linge also swore to the last occupants of the bunker that he had heard that famous shot. At least that was the version that Günsche gave to the Soviet investigators:

Question: Who was the first to learn of Hitler's suicide?
Answer: Linge. He was outside the door of Hitler's apartments, not far from the antechamber. At about 4:00 he heard a shot.
[. . .]
Question: How did Hitler commit suicide?
Answer: According to Linge, Hitler fired a bullet into his temple.

And yet Linge had lied to everyone. He had just admitted as much. It remained to be seen whether he had only lied about the shot ... Was it really possible to smell the gunpowder from a firearm after only one shot, through doors designed to resist a chemical attack?
Linge's interrogation continued:

Question: Did Hitler's apartments have good ventilation?
Answer: Yes. All the rooms in Hitler's apartments were equipped with it because he hated the smell of cigarettes. And in any case he was very sensitive to smells.
Question: What doors were there between you and him and were they closed?
Answer: There were the doors of the two rooms. They were all double doors, and at the moment of the suicide they were closed.
Question: How could you smell the gunpowder of a shot from a revolver through several doors, with good ventilation, bearing in mind that those doors were double and closed?
Answer: I can confirm the smell of gunpowder. How that smell reached me I don't know.

The valet's answers seemed to be becoming more and more confused. Their incoherence did not escape the investigators:

Question: Why in the course of previous interrogations did you state several times that you heard the shot coming from Hitler's antechamber and immediately informed Bormann of the suicide?
Linge: I said that because my witness statement concerning Hitler's suicide might seem frail because of those shadowy areas. And you would become suspicious. That was why I claimed to have been outside Hitler's apartments all the time, and to have heard that gunshot.

That essential lie was only discovered three months before the counter-inquiry in Berlin. Semenovsky, the forensics expert, took it into account in his report. And he had no hesitation in distancing himself from Linge's version as regards the bullet to the temple. On the other hand, he did follow the former valet's version concerning the fact that the individual on the sofa had received a shot to the head:

Taking into account the large number of blood spatters and trickles on the sofa, we may conclude that that wound was accompanied by copious bleeding. When wounded, the victim was sitting in the right-hand corner of the sofa, beside the armrest. [. . .] The distribution of spatters and trickles of blood on the sofa as well as their characteristic appearance testify that the wound was localised to the head and not the torso or the abdomen. [. . .]

The lesion to the head was caused by a gunshot and not by a blow administered by a heavy object. The proof is the absence of blood spatters on the back, the sofa and on the frame of the back of the sofa. Following the wound to the head, the wounded man lost consciousness and remained inanimate for a certain time with his head leaning against the side of the right arm of the sofa.

With this statement, Semenovsky could reduce to nothing the inquiry in June 1945 led by SMERSH. Except that there was no proof that the blood belonged to Hitler. The blood tests carried out on the trickles on the arm of the sofa would reveal that the blood was Group A. Like Hitler's, according to the statements of his personal doctor, Dr. Morell. But also like millions of Germans. And given that he was unable to examine the corpse held by the Ministry of State Security, Semenovsky's work remained incomplete. Mad with rage, the old criminologist went so far as to vent his fury at Viktor Abakumov in person. His report leaves no room for nuance:

> Because the first autopsy was carried out carelessly – no investigation into the changes to the bones of the aorta, no dissection of the vital organs to reveal traces of potassium cyanide – and because the corpses were not made available to another more detailed autopsy, the first report established in May 1945 can only be considered as preliminary. In consequence, the present Commission estimates that it is not possible to draw definitive conclusions on this file.

The political system of the USSR was not used to seeing the flaws of its rulers being exposed to the light of day. The results of the Berlin mission risked being explosive. Particularly in late spring 1946. Moscow was undergoing a new series of purges. As always, Stalin acted on his own, and with brutality. He ruined some, promoted others, and fed grudges among his accomplices the better to control them. Heads rolled, even the biggest, particularly the biggest. Generals, but also eminent members of the intelligentsia. Among them was the very popular Marshal Zhukov. On 3 June 1946, the man who had won so many battles against the Nazis was stripped of his functions as commander in chief of the land army and deputy Defence Minister of the USSR. In particular, he was accused of "having lost all modesty and being carried away by personal ambition." A perfect dialectic that could have applied to Stalin himself. Only one man emerged stronger from this wave of dismissals – Abakumov.

When he received the report from Dr. Semenovsky, Kruglov, the Minister of Internal Affairs, didn't know what to do with it. Essentially, the conclusions hardly came as a surprise, and in a political system as unusual as the Soviet one, he considered it satisfactory. His ministry had worked hard to establish historical truth. But he also knew from experience that to attack one of Stalin's protégés was to run the risk of disappearing for good. He didn't want to end up like his colleague, the Minister of the Aeronautics Industry, Alexey Ivanovich Shakhurin, who was fired and then sentenced on 11 May 1946 to seven years in the gulag. His crime was to have disappointed Stalin in the quality of aeroplane manufacture for the air force.

After thinking long and hard, Kruglov opted for prudence. The old pathologist would have worked in vain. His work would be kept carefully at the bottom of a drawer, far from the eyes of the Soviet tyrant.

On 18 June the Nazi prisoners were sent back to the Soviet Union. Operation "Myth" came to an end. The mystery about Hitler's death would remain unsolved for decades.

SUMMER 2017

It's raining in Moscow. Late June. More than two months have passed since our disastrous stay in the Russian capital. Two months during which we tried to persuade Alexander Orlov, our contact at the Ministry of Foreign Affairs, the MID, to obtain authorisation for us to analyse Hitler's teeth. But Alexander has vanished. We can't get through to him, either by phone or mail. We are stuck. Is this how our investigation will end? A year and a half of persistence to reach this impasse? Many times, our contacts had given us commitments, made promises. "Yes, of course, we are in favour of these forensic studies. The skull? The teeth? You want them? Come on, we're waiting for you!" The mysterious acronyms (GARF, MID, TsA FSB ...), the administrative subtleties, the grim hierarchical decorum, we thought we had tamed them one after the other. We had endured internal quarrels and put up with inflated egos. Even the sudden disappearance of some of our contacts. Disappearances both literal and figurative, since one of our helpers at GARF died of a heart attack during winter 2017. Almost systematically, we quickly found that when one door opened another closed. But that didn't matter because we had no choice. Hitler's last human remains, or the remains alleged to be Hitler's, are in Russia, and nowhere else. This indisputable premise grants enormous power to the Russian authorities. The power to decide who can examine them. Who and when.

A reality that has lasted since 5 May 1945, since the discovery in the garden of the Chancellery of the Third Reich of the alleged corpse of Hitler by the Red Army. We imagine that in just over seventy years we are not the first to have tried to persuade Moscow. Lana calls this seduction exercise the "belly dance." As in the famous piece of oriental choreography, we have to keep on smiling in spite of the cavalier and disobliging attitudes of our contacts. Like the almost obligatory lack of respect at meetings, the authorisations cancelled at the last minute … Keeping calm and seducing them into letting us close to those pieces of historical evidence. The game is a biased one because we are the supplicants. Others have run the same gauntlets. People more illustrious than ourselves. Starting with the Allies in 1945.

★   ★   ★

At the time, the Anglo-American-French staffs tried to charm their Soviet "colleagues" to obtain information about Hitler. They generously offered confidential documents, in the hope of receiving something reciprocal:

MILITARY ADMINISTRATION IN GERMANY (USA)
Head of the intelligence service
APO [Army Post Office] 742
8 January 1946
Dear General!
I have the pleasure of sending you photographs of the following documents:
    letter from Martin Bormann to Admiral Dönitz;
    Hitler and Eva Braun's wedding certificate;
    Hitler's personal and political testaments.
Our document experts have declared that they are authentic, without any doubt. I am sure that these documents will be interesting to you and your collaborators.
Best wishes,
Yours sincerely,
T.J. Koenig
Colonel, Director of General Staff, interim head of the intelligence service

To Major General A. SIDNEV,
General Command, 58 Luisenstrasse, Berlin

The particularly friendly tone of this letter between the heads of
secret services is very much at odds with the reality of the time. In
Berlin, relations between the Allies and the Soviets had already dete-
riorated in early 1946. The Russians refused to share their data on the
Hitler file and the definitive point of rupture was inexorably on the
way. The American Colonel Koenig couldn't ignore it. His letter looks
like a last attempt at reconciliation, a friendly hand.

Reconciliation that the strict Alexey Sidnev spurned. The thirty-
nine-year-old Russian general and representative of SMERSH in
Berlin, and then of the NKVD, was already partly familiar with the
documents sent by the Americans. Particularly Hitler's testaments.
The British had sent them to him the previous week. An initiative that
the British had clearly taken without telling their American friends.

General staff,
Regulatory commission for Germany
British sector
Intelligence group
31-12-1945
Berlin
For the attention of Major General SIDNEV
Head of the intelligence service
Red Army headquarters
Berlin.
Contents: Hitler's testament
Please find enclosed the testament of Hitler which has been found.
It was communicated to the British press on 30 December 1945.
Signature: Captain VOLIS

These "presents" from the Allies would soon stop. On 5 March 1946,
Winston Churchill delivered a speech at Westminster College in
Fulton, Missouri, in the presence of the American President Harry

Truman. Churchill was no longer Prime Minister of the United Kingdom, since his defeat in the general election in July 1945, but he remained a political heavyweight at the international level. He was the first to be officially worried about the aggressive policies of the Soviet Union.

A shadow has fallen upon the scenes so lately lighted by the Allied victory. Nobody knows what Soviet Russia and its Communist international organization intends to do in the immediate future, or what are the limits, if any, to their expansive and proselytizing tendencies. [. . .] From Stettin in the Baltic to Trieste in the Adriatic, an iron curtain has descended across the Continent. [. . .] If now the Soviet Government tries, by separate action, to build up a pro-Communist Germany in their areas, this will cause new serious difficulties in the British and American zones, and will give the defeated Germans the power of putting themselves up to auction between the Soviets and the Western Democracies. Whatever conclusions may be drawn from these facts – and facts they are – this is certainly not the Liberated Europe we fought to build up. Nor is it one which contains the essentials of permanent peace.*

Stalin immediately seized the opportunity to confirm the rupture with the Western camp. In an interview granted to the Soviet daily newspaper *Pravda* on 14 March 1946, he demonstrated an unprecedented violence towards his former allies:

Question from journalist: Can it be considered that Mr. Churchill's speech is prejudicial to the cause of peace and security?
Stalin: Yes, unquestionably. As a matter of fact, Mr. Churchill now takes the stand of the warmongers, and in this Mr. Churchill

*Winston Churchill, *The Sinews of Peace*, North Atlantic Treaty Organization (NATO), 5 March 1946.

is not alone. He has friends not only in Britain but in the United States of America as well. A point to be noted is that in this respect Mr. Churchill and his friends bear a striking resemblance to Hitler and his friends. [. . .] There can be no doubt that Mr. Churchill's position is a war position, a call for war on the USSR.*

The Anglo-Americans compared to Hitler? Stalin had followed what we now call Godwin's law with disconcerting swiftness, and established a point of no-return between the two camps. From then on, all contact between the Western and Soviet secret services was severed. The famous "Iron Curtain" also fell on the Hitler file. However, investigations into the circumstances of the Führer's death continued. Each camp used the information in their possession to the greatest advantage. In this little game, the Soviets where a length ahead. In April–May 1945, they were the first to arrive in Berlin. They didn't wait for the Anglo-Americans before laying their hands on thousands of documents and taking a large part of Hitler's innermost circle prisoner. The Allies had also captured a number of witnesses in the western part of Germany, and discovered some highly valuable documents. Particularly Hitler's doctors, his medical file, and even x-rays of his face. Information that is accessible today because it has been unclassified. An opportunity that we wouldn't pass up. There is a sequence of five x-rays of Hitler's face in the American archives. In these pictures dating from 1944, one can clearly make out the Führer's jaws and teeth. Thanks to this historical source, we should be able to confirm the identification of the teeth that the FSB allowed us to observe in December 2016. But above all, we need to know where these x-rays come from and check that they are authentic.

Hugo Johannes Blaschke was Hitler's personal dentist between 1934 and 20 April 1945. This Prussian was a man of great refinement, perfectly bilingual in English and German. And a convinced

*New York Times, 14 March 1946.

Nazi. A graduate of Philadelphia Dental School at the University of Pennsylvania, he returned to his country and served as a "field doctor" in the First World War. In 1931 he joined the NSDAP, and became a major in the SS in 1935. On Göring's recommendation he became dentist to the Nazi elite. His patients included Himmler, Göring, Goebbels, Bormann, Speer, and above all Hitler and Eva Braun. As a reward for his good and loyal service he was awarded an honorary professorship and the rank of ober-führer (brigadier general) of the Waffen-SS. He would be inter-rogated in November and December of the same year. The inten-tion was to obtain as many details as possible about Hitler's dentures, in order to be able to identify his corpse if the situation presented itself.

The dentist had no x-rays or access to his patient's file, but his memory was perfect. He provided extremely important informa-tion for our investigation, particularly concerning the fact that Hitler suffered from severe dental problems. He had had extensive caries on many occasions. He was also subject to gingivitis and suffered from halitosis (bad breath). Many bridges had been designed to preserve his teeth. In spite of this treatment, his poor dental condition did not abate. "Towards the end of September 1944 I was called to the headquarters," Blaschke relates. "Hitler complained about slight tenderness of the gingiva of the upper left jaw. He was bedridden. He was, as Professor Morell told me, suffering from an inflammation of the naso-pharyngial area."* In January 1945 Hitler, who still complained about his teeth, asked his dentist to move to the Chancellery, near his bunker. The Führer consulted him only once, in February, for a superficial examination.

Faced with Soviet troops coming dangerously close to Berlin, Blaschke obtained permission to flee on the night of 19–20 April

*US National Archives, noo1 FIR 31, in Reidar F. Sognnaes and Ferdinand Ström, "The Odontological Identifications of Adolf Hitler: Definitive Documentation by X-Ray, Interrogations and Autopsy Finding," *Acta Odontology Scandinavica*, 31 (1973), pp. 43–69, here p. 57.

1945. All of his medical files, including Hitler's, would be lost with the aeroplane carrying them to Salzburg. The dentist, who was travelling on another flight, reached Bavaria safe and sound.

Luckily the Americans soon discovered other medical files on Hitler. Notable among these were x-rays of his face taken after the attempted assassination of Hitler on 20 July 1944. Three of these were taken on 19 September 1944 by Dr. Giesing at the military hospital in Rastenburg, in East Prussia. Erwan Giesing was Hitler's personal ENT doctor. The x-rays show the frontal sinus (position nose-forehead), the sphenoidal sinus (position mouth-chin), and the maxillary, ethmoidal, and frontal sinuses (position chin-nose).

Two other x-rays dated 21 October 1944 were also found among the documents of Hitler's personal physician, Dr. Morell. He declared to the Americans that he could not remember under what circumstances they had been taken. These views show the maxillary, ethmoidal, and frontal sinuses (position chin-nose). To check that the two series of pictures showed the same person, the investigators compared the shape of the frontal sinuses. The examination was positive. Hitler's sinuses were very large, and showed indications of frequent sinusitis.

★   ★   ★

For twenty-three years, this information served no purpose. The Soviets never allowed the Americans to approach the alleged bodies of Hitler and Eva Braun that they had in their possession. Besides, how could they have granted them this privilege, when officially they did not have the bodies? This version of events would be questioned by the publication of a sensational book in 1968. Lev Bezymenski, a former army translator and now a journalist, brought out a book in West Germany, entitled *The Death of Adolf Hitler*. For the first time since the fall of Berlin in May 1945, the secret of the bodies discovered by the Soviets was revealed with photographic evidence. This included photographs of the teeth attributed to Hitler: a maxillary bridge of nine teeth and a lower jaw of fifteen teeth. Thanks to this book, Blaschke's testimony and the x-rays finally served a purpose.

In 1972, two Norwegian scientists, Reidar F. Sognnaes, Dean of Harvard School of Dental Medicine in Boston (United States), and Ferdinand Ström, pioneer of forensic odontology (the use of teeth to identify corpses), decided to carry out the first thorough examination of Hitler's teeth.

An examination was performed under conditions that were less than optimal given that the two scientists had no physical access to the teeth, since these were still classified as military secrets in Moscow. The Norwegian dentists could work only from documents. On the one hand, they had the material from the American secret services: the records of interrogations of Hitler's dentist and the five x-rays. On the other, they had the photographs published in the book by the former Red Army interpreter. At the time it was impossible to check Bezymenski's reliability. In principle it remained questionable. But no matter. Sognnaes and Ström estimated that they had enough information to launch their investigation. They were sure that they could put an end to the most insane scenarios about the escape of Hitler and his survival of the fall of the Third Reich. Their work occurred in a special context. In fact, at the start of the 1970s, the Nazis were back in the news, thanks to the work of "SS hunters" like the Klarsfelds, but also the Israeli secret service, Mossad. The wider public thus became aware that former senior figures in the Hitler regime were living peacefully in the authoritarian republics of Latin America. Some would be arrested, like Eichmann and Barbie. Others, including Mengele, known as the "Angel of Death" for his sadistic medical experiments on prisoners, would escape judgement. If those men were able to flee Germany in 1945 and find refuge, why not the Führer? It was in this atmosphere of rumours and mystery that the dentists Sognnaes and Ström intervened.

[. . .] It is evident that most of the large posterior teeth on the right side are missing. [. . .] On the left side of the lower jaw, the diagram indicates absences and replacement of the first premolar by a porcelain-faced gold pontic and of the first and second molars by solid metal. [. . .]

In the lower jaw, one can very clearly see on the left side three roots carrying a long bridge replacement. [. . .] It became clear that Hitler had only four remaining teeth which were not involved in either bridging a gap or supporting a bridge between adjacent teeth. [. . .]

Where the material at hand permitted definitive conclusions, it will be noticed that there exists a remarkable conformity between the individual tooth identifications established through the analysis of the American and Soviet data. In addition to the individual teeth which were present, absent, restored or replaced, as the case may be, we have also noted a few other special areas, namely, the unique lingual bar serving as a fixed bridge bypass between the lower right canine and second premolar, and also the alveolar bone resorption around the roots of the incisor teeth.

From this overall comparison of odontological evidence we conclude that the individual identified by means of the 1945 Hitler files located in the US National Archives in 1972, is the same person as that whose 1945 autopsy report was published on the basis of the previously unknown documents from Soviet Archives of 1945.*

For the first time since the end of the war, a non-Soviet scientific report lent credit to the theory of Hitler's death. The story caused a storm at the time. But for want of direct access to the human remains, doubt persisted. Forty-five years after the work of Sognnaes and Ström, Philippe Charlier was able to provide an analysis of these teeth. Like the two Norwegian specialists, he hadn't

*Reidar F. Sognnaes and Ferdinand Ström, "The Odontological Identification of Adolf Hitler," *Acta Ondotologica Scandinavica*, Vol. 31 No. 1 (1973), pp. 43–79.

seen them. But he had at his disposal the photographs and videos that we had taken in December 2016. In this way he was able to compare them with the x-rays of Hitler's face. The results were conclusive, morphological comparison of the dental prostheses left no doubt:

> Morphological comparison between the dental prostheses and bony elements, and the photographs presented as being of Adolf Hitler *intra vitam*.
>
> The dental and bony elements show lesions of carbonisation, of cutting, of fragmentation, wear and an upper and lower apparatus entirely compatible with the photographs presented (x-rays of face and details). In the present state of observation of the anatomical pieces it is not possible to determine the sex and age of the subject (except that the subject is an adult). [. . .]
>
> Summary: perfect agreement between the x-rays presented as being of Adolf Hitler *intra vitam* and the dental elements presented. [. . .]

Dr. Charlier's report confirms the conclusions of his illustrious predecessors. These are indeed Hitler's teeth. Our inquiry could stop there. We could stop harassing Alexander Orlov, and give up all hope of returning to the FSB offices with Philippe Charlier so that he could examine the pieces of jaw hidden away so carefully since 1945. It would be so simple.

★   ★   ★

12 July 2017. Summer obstinately refused to come for the Muscovites. The sky merges with the grey of the pavements to form a horizon of impenetrable sadness. Pelting rain clears the streets of the few passers-by. We are with Philippe Charlier in Putin's city. With a small suitcase. It contains a state-of-the-art binocular microscope. The Lubyanka, its heavy door, ID check, the

suspicious expression on the guard's face ... We act out the same film as we did last December. Alevander Orlov likes springing surprises on us. Two weeks previously, he had told us the FSB's reply. "You can come back. With Dr. Charlier. Your request has been confirmed. We should inform you that after you there will be no further examinations. We will refuse them." Why this change of mind? We won't ask that question. We don't want to give them an excuse to change their minds again.

Inside the Lubyanka (FSB archives), in the security door, a youngish man with a light-coloured beard is waiting behind the military guard at reception. His name is Denis, and he is replacing Dmitri, the FSB officer who escorted us in December. Only first names, never surnames. Are those even their real first names? They both start with the same letter, a "d." Probably a coincidence. Denis smiles complicitly at the guard, who checks our passports. We are in order. The same lift, the same floor. The third. The same little room, office 344, on the right of a window-less corridor. Nothing in the office has changed. Only the little Christmas tree has disappeared. Otherwise, there are still as many FSB officials keeping an eye on us. Including that tall blonde young woman who treated us with such suspicion. This time she is wearing a floral nylon dress short enough to reveal solid knees. Her taut face is at odds with the brightness of her outfit. Our smiles leave her cold. Did she have better things to do than waste her afternoon with some foreigners? Probably. Lana introduces Philippe Charlier to the five men and the young woman who will be standing next to us throughout the whole examination. They are intrigued by the small case. They want to check the forensic examiner's equipment. The agreement made with Alexander stipulated that nothing was to be removed. The examination would be entirely visual. That requirement was mandatory. To respect the Russian imperatives, Philippe decided to bring a binocular microscope. The equipment does not damage the object under examination, and allows the user to study it by zooming up to thirty-five times. It can also take films and photographs with an integrated digital camera.

Lana lists the technical specifications of the microscope for her compatriots. Denis asks if there is a light on the machine. "A light? Yes a small one ..." We don't have time to finish the phrase before a flurry of "niets" echoes around the room. Everyone becomes agitated. They are worried by the light. "Niet laser, niet!" I hurry over to Lana and ask her to reassure them. It's only a little built-in lamp, not a laser. Translate, quickly and clearly. Lana does so. The apparatus is on the table. It is turned on. The light is activated. Not a laser! It's not a laser! We all insist. Denis leans over the machine before stepping back and confirming this to his colleagues. It's fine! Philippe Charlier gives Lana and me a quizzical look. It's 2:00 pm, and after an eighteen-month wait we have been given permission to study the remains attributed to Hitler.

In spite of the orders from FSB head office, the young woman in her summer dress can't help balking at the idea of our being allowed to handle the teeth. She picks up the little cigarillo-box in which they are stored. She moves it away from Philippe. He intervenes gently and calmly. He asks Lana to translate. "Please tell her that I am only going to handle the teeth with sterile gloves. My gloves. Look, they're new, I'll put them on in front of you ..." He picks up a medical plastic bag, tears it open and takes out the gloves. Very carefully, he puts them on, looking the young woman from the FSB in the eye. "Now I'm equipped, the best thing would be for her to arrange the pieces of jaw, one by one, on the sterile paper that I have arranged in front of me. That way nothing will be contaminated." Philippe Charlier speaks slowly. His voice emanates a sense of professionalism that finally convinces the young woman. Against all expectation she complies.

The silence is total. The only sound is the rustle of the paper on which the first teeth have been laid out. The scientist handles them carefully, turning them around on their axis. First of all, the examination must allow him to check the authenticity of the teeth. Reassure himself that they aren't fake. The FSB team are perfectly capable of making a copy on the basis of the x-rays and Hitler's dental files. Lana and I share Philippe Charlier's tendency to doubt everything. We are at the heart of one of the most powerful and controversial secret services on the planet. Manipulation is always possible. Not to admit that fact would be a professional shortcoming. So we need to check for traces of wear and patina, clues proving the age and authenticity of the teeth. "It's really interesting," Charlier says, zooming in. "Deposits of tartar are particularly visible on this prosthesis. I can see some organic remains, a bit of gum, perhaps some mucous membrane and partially carbonised soft tissue. The yellow metal of the prosthesis is marked with small stripes. That corresponds to the past presence of small crystals in foodstuffs. As far as I'm concerned there is no doubt, these dental prostheses are authentic. They have been worn long enough for tartar deposits to form. Their age seems compatible with the Second World War. I can state with confidence that they are not fake!"

The teeth have not been recreated by the KGB or its successor, the FSB. They are real, and the same ones as those seen in the x-rays of Hitler's face. Their shape, the prostheses – there is no doubt about it. These are the teeth of the Nazi dictator. At last we're making some progress. We can confirm that Hitler died in Berlin on 30 April 1945. Not in Brazil at the age of ninety-five, or in Japan, or in the Argentinean Andes. The proof is scientific, not ideological. Coldly scientific.

"His dental health was very poor," Charlier observes. "This individual suffered from parodontopathy [a resorption of the mucous membrane to the level of the root of the teeth], resulting in tooth loss." This coincides with the statements of his dentist, Dr. Blaschke. He told the Americans that Hitler had developed chronic gingivitis. There are multiple causes of this well-known illness," Charlier goes on, "tobacco-smoking, poor nutrition, drug-taking, chronic infections of the mouth and vegetarianism." Hitler didn't smoke, he didn't lack nutrition either in terms of quality or quantity, but he was a vegetarian. In those days decay caused by vegetarianism had not been identified, and a vegetarian diet was not backed up by nutritional supplements.

The pieces of the puzzle are coming together perfectly. But we need to go still further. Understand how he died.

"Don't film me! No photographs!" The threatening tone is decidedly at odds with the floral pattern on her dress. The FSB official didn't like me taking a photograph with her in my field of vision. Lara intervenes, as ever, to calm everyone down. Let's not forget where we are. Or the fact that it could be stopped with a click of the fingers. Or a rustle of an acrylic dress. My deepest apologies seem to satisfy everyone present. The examination continues.

Looking for traces of acid or gunpowder from a firearm. According to the different versions, Hitler committed suicide with cyanide and/or a pistol shot to the head. If the gun was fired into the mouth, remains of gunpowder, antimony, lead and/or barium, to be precise, might still be present. The different fragments of jaw pass one by one before the Frenchman's eagle eye. They all bear marks of carbonisation. "We may have information on exposure to fire," Charlier explains. "The intense black traces at the level of bone and mucous membrane," as well as the roots of the teeth, demonstrate a high degree of carbonisation. The fire must have been intense, since it managed to split part of the roots, exposing the dentine [also called the ivory of the tooth]." According to the statements of Linge and Günsche, Hitler was burnt using two hundred litres of petrol. The fire was intense, violent but relatively short. This scenario accords with Charlier's observations. He establishes, for example, that traces of gum and muscle are perfectly apparent. This means that the body was not burnt completely. On 30 April 1945 the incessant Russian bombardment of the Reich Chancellery prevented the total cremation of Hitler. No one in the Führerbunker wanted to take the risk of staying in the gardens to keep alive the fire burning the corpses of the dictator and his wife.

"I think I've found something ..." Philippe Charlier zooms in as far as possible on one of the dental prostheses. The image appears on the laptop computer connected to the binocular microscope. A vague mass slowly takes shape. "Look at this: the metal alloy of the prosthesis has undergone an astonishing alteration. One can distinguish the enamel of the tooth underneath it." Sure enough, there is a hole in the gilded metal plaque and the white of the tooth can be seen underneath it. "We're looking at the premolar," he goes on. "What could have caused this?" Several hypotheses are possible. A manufacturing defect? A poor-quality prosthesis? Unlikely. Hitler was tended to by a famous dentist. He wouldn't have risked giving him mediocre treatment. "So it might be due to acid, an oxidation of the metal." Cyanide? On a premolar? Does that make sense? Hitler was said to have crushed his poison capsule with his back teeth, so his molars or premolars. Other teeth show the same traces of oxidation. In the course of the only autopsy performed on the alleged body of Hitler, the Soviets indicated that "fragments of glass and fine pieces of the ends of the medical ampoule were found in the mouth." More than seventy years later, is it possible to find these fragments of glass?

The binocular microscope works miracles. It shows you things invisible to the naked eye. Philippe Charlier has never been so satisfied with his equipment. While he goes on inspecting the tartar deposits, he happens upon crystals that he immediately identifies. "They are grains of silica. They're there, wedged between the dentine and the cement [the tissue that covers the dentine at the level of the root]. Was Hitler buried in sand?" Silica is a metalloid chemical element found in sand and cement, but also in the manufacture of laboratory glassware. It has the quality of being resistant to many acids including cyanide. But let's come back to Dr. Charlier's question. Was Hitler buried in a sandy area? It's a hard one to answer. Not a priori. His body was found in the garden of the Chancellery. On the other hand, there could be traces of cement since the bunker was very close by and it had been damaged by the bombs. And most importantly, silica is a mineral present everywhere in earth. As to its use in laboratory glassware, its microscopic form is totally different from naturally occurring silica. The silica found on these teeth does not resemble the silica of laboratory glassware. For Philippe Charlier, that trail is closed. On the other hand, he is much less circumspect about blue traces. "On the surface of this tooth there is a surprising bluish deposit that I have difficulty explaining. Was there an interaction with an external element at the moment of death? Or at the moment of burial?" The blue is intense, almost a "Klein blue," like a paint stain. The trace is small and could go unnoticed by the naked eye. The tooth in question is one of Hitler's few remaining natural teeth. "You can see growth rings on it, the surface, the enamel, fibrous remains, dental tartar … There was an interaction between something and this tooth, but I don't know with what. It is not dental tartar, I'm sure of that." Charlier reflects. He has never seen this before. "There is no reason why cyanide would interact directly with enamel to create bluish coloration like this. Physically, chemically, there is no particular reason." And yet this blue trace exists. "I will have to consult the forensic literature, particularly in the field of toxicology, because I'm at a loss."

The French doctor now turns his attention to other tooth fragments. "Look! You can also see this blue in the crevices of the other teeth. It also appears on the surface of these prostheses." More tiny deposits of the same appear. They are partially covered by deposits of sediment. At first Philippe Charlier thought they might be tartar. And that consequently these blue marks dated from several weeks or even months before Hitler's death. The forensic pathologist quickly corrected his mistake. They are sediments, which could date from the burial of the bodies in the earth. Do these blue stains give us a clue to Hitler's poisoning. At this stage, and since it is impossible to take even a tiny sample. Charlier is unable to reply.

The examination is coming to an end. All the teeth have been carefully analysed. For some minutes I have heard Lana talking to

Denis in a low voice at the back of the room. I gesture to her to say that we've finished. Two hours was enough. The rest of the forensic study will now take place in Paris, with the examination of the images recorded by the binocular microscope. Lana isn't listening to me. She's very excited. "They're going to show us Eva Braun's teeth. This is a first!" A fragment of the teeth of the Führer's wife! Philippe Charlier is still hunched over his machine. He asks simply: "Can I examine them too?" Lana has joined the group of FSB officials to

Teeth attributed to Hitler kept in the FSB archives

thank them. So we've got Eva Braun's teeth. Alleged teeth, to be precise. Because, unlike the situation with Hitler, we have no x-rays to confirm their identification. As a precaution, Philippe Charlier changes his sterile gloves and takes another sheet of paper, also sterile. Once he is ready he gestures to the young woman. She opens a box. It is much smaller than the one holding Hitler's teeth, but just as "eccentric." It looks like the box for a pair of earrings. Inside, resting on cotton wool, are three teeth, molars and a premolar, connected by a yellow metal prosthesis. *"Spasiba"* (Thank you) Charlier says, picking them up. He puts them delicately down in the middle of the microscope and adjusts the focus.

The first observation comes quickly: "We see the same bluish deposits on the surface of the teeth!" Cautiously, he adds: "On these teeth, which are presented to us as being those of Eva Braun." Some clues corroborate the hypothesis that these remains have undergone the same post-mortem treatment as those of Hitler. Namely a cremation and a burial in a similar natural environment. "They have been carbonised in the same way. They are artificial teeth with a deposit of tartar on the prosthesis as well as grains of silica, exactly the same as on the previous teeth. We can

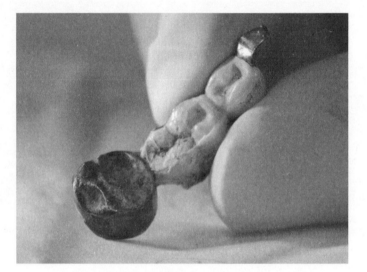

Fragments of teeth attributed to Eva Braun by the Russian authorities and stored in the archives of FSB in Moscow.

clearly see the patina of wear on the metal of the prosthesis. I can confirm that these teeth have really been worn. And they cannot belong to the same individual as the one just now, because they are from an identical anatomic area." So no trickery on the part of the Russians.

Eva Braun was thirty-three when she died. She had been the Führer's official spouse for only a day. According to Soviet and Anglo-American investigations, she committed suicide by swallowing cyanide. "I'm going to have to analyse all this from scratch,"

Philippe says, still zooming in on the little blue traces, "It's really very strange …" He takes more photographs with the digital camera built into the binocular microscope. These photographs will allow him to re-examine the teeth in his Paris laboratory and perhaps close the file on Hitler's death.

PARIS, SEPTEMBER 2017

They're barely discernible to the naked eye. How many are there? Two, maybe three. Pieces – crumbs, rather – dark as dust. Philippe Charlier is holding up in front of his eyes a plastic phial sealed with a red cork. A label is attached to it, bearing the words "dental plaque A.H." How did these fragments from Hitler's teeth make their way to Paris? An accident, a concatenation of circumstances. After the test that he carried out at FSB headquarters in Moscow in July 2018, Dr. Charlier carefully put away the materials he had been working with. In this instance, two pairs of latex gloves and two sheets of paper on which the teeth had been arranged. Meticulous as ever, he didn't mix them together: the paper and the gloves used for Hitler's remains on one side, the ones for the teeth attributed to Eva Braun on the other. When he returned to Paris, before throwing everything away, he realised that some tiny pieces of tartar from Hitler's teeth had come away during the examination. He automatically recovered them and stored them in a phial.

What was to be done? Alexander, our contact at the Russian Ministry of Foreign Affairs, and the officers of the FSB had always opposed any samples being taken from the teeth. We were familiar with that condition. And besides, how could we have escaped the close vigilance of the FSB officials during the microscope analysis? Inside the Lubyanka itself? Even Lana, always ready to attempt the impossible, wouldn't have dreamed of it. Now we're in Paris, far from Moscow. The Russian secret services can no longer intervene to prevent us from exploiting these fragments. Nonetheless, acting without their consent is out of the question. For two quite simple reasons: out of moral principle and out of professionalism. Two ideas on which Philippe Charlier is particularly keen. All the more so since, without the green light of the Russian authorities, it will be impossible to treat the analysis of these pieces of tartar in any official way. We would then find ourselves in the same situation as the American team from the History Channel that made the American documentary that was broadcast in 2009. Because they had no agreement with the Russian archives (GARF, in this instance), their revelations about the fragment of skull allegedly belonging to Hitler remain tainted with suspicion. In their case, several questions linger. How were those pieces of skull collected and by whom? The mystery surrounding the work of the American team means that their results cannot be exploited scientifically. Not without reason has Dr. Nick Bellantoni never published his work in a scientific journal, which means that it has never been validated. We aren't going to make the same mistake.

Lana jumped with joy. "Some pieces came away? That's incredible! What a stroke of luck ..." Her enthusiasm barely surprises me any more, and neither does her boundless energy. As usual, obstacles seem to melt away as if by magic when she's around. My fears and doubts become deluded neuroses. But I still take the time to set out my point of view: the potential wrath of our Russian contacts, their possible refusal, coercive reprisals (particularly for Lana who has the good fortune to have a Russian passport and to live mostly in Moscow). My imagination amuses her. She laughs at it. I can distinctly hear her doing so down the telephone. Is it an exaggeration to imagine that the FSB could, quite freely, harm in some way or another a Russian citizen who had put them in an awkward position?

"Don't worry about me; quite the contrary, they will be delighted to learn that we have some pieces of the teeth." Her logic makes me feel like a child learning a lesson.

"What was our agreement?"

"To make a purely visual examination."

"Were we under constant surveillance during the analysis?"

"There were at least five of them watching us."

So far, Lana is not mistaken. All we did was play the game by the rules they imposed.

"Is Philippe Charlier going to call into question the authenticity of the teeth?" Lana already knows the answer. She is practising a form of Socratic method on me. She is pulling me in the wake of her thought, and she insists that I reply. "No, he's not going to claim that they aren't Hitler's teeth. On the contrary, he is categorical."

So? I can hear the smile in Lana's voice. "So, it's all fine, Jean-Christophe. They will accept it. Trust me."

The Laboratoire de Physique des Solides (Laboratory of Solid State Physics, LPS) of Paris-Sud University is under scaffolding. Some workmen are busy from dawn till dusk around the central building. They're hammering, pounding, drilling. The quiet forest and the affluent detached houses of the little town of Orsay, south-west of Paris, barely pay the slightest attention to these regular disruptions. Philippe Charlier has come to terms with it as well. The essential thing is that he can carry out the analyses of the samples carefully stored in his little phial. In his forensic investigations, Charlier is able to rely on a cluster of experts. One of the very best is Raphaël Weil. This engineer at the LPS specialises in the scanning electron microscope. Equipment indispensable for the analysis of the morphology and chemical composition of samples, without damaging them. Thanks to this machine and to Raphaël Weil's gifts, the "crumbs" of dental tartar from the teeth stored at the TsA FSB will yield up all their secrets. It's a huge project: a search for vegetable and meat fibres (since the Führer had been a vegetarian for years, the slightest fibre of meat would destroy our hypotheses), and traces of the components of gunpowder (from firearm ammunition). The chief goal is to know whether Hitler really fired a bullet into his mouth. Not forgetting, of course, the bluish traces found on the surface of the prostheses. "You can no longer do without the scanning microscope when performing a historical anthropological study," Charlier insists. "I hope that the chemical analysis will allow us to discover the elements that go to make up the prosthesis," he adds. "And thus understand what could have caused that blue deposit. Is it an inter-action with the cyanide …?"

For once, the FSB has reacted promptly. It's Dmitri, the first one who replied to Lana. Dmitri, the agent of the Russian secret service who escorted us on our first visit to the Lubyanka. "Of course. No problem. Niet problème!" Lana was right. As she had imagined, a simple letter from Philippe Charlier should be enough to reassure the Russian authorities. Concise, clear, and precise, the report from the French forensic pathologist was swiftly dispatched. He repeated that he had no doubt about the identity of the teeth. They were Hitler's. Normally, within a day or two we would receive the official letter from the FSB or the Ministry of Foreign Affairs, the agree-ment, the green light, a positive sign, however vague, however brief.

Nothing. Two weeks.

Then a month.

Then almost two months.

Nothing!

The same absurd and Kafkaesque routine. Lana told me over and over that her contacts had confirmed once again on the phone that we could carry out analyses. I insisted on having a written record. "Ah, a written record …?" Lana said with surprise, having suddenly fallen victim to amnesia. "I get it, I'll send them a reminder." And again we wait. For days.

Then, when all seemed lost, the answer came. My email. It was Alexander Orlov, our dear Alexander from the Ministry of Foreign Affairs of Mother Russia, sending me an email in French. Here, in English translation, is an extract: "It seems to me that if you analyse the particles from Hitler's jaw that adhered to your gloves and your conclusions are not in conflict with the official position of the Russian side, we will have no right to."

It is 7 November 2017, the leaves are turning yellow on the trees, the silent birds are saving their strength for bracing temperatures to come. I catch myself smiling. Is it exhaustion, nerves, or a lack of lucidity?

Alexander's email appears in front of me. And I smile at it. Everything's there. Or almost everything. "We will have no right to." A word is missing and everything collapses. Over two months waiting for this message. Dozens of calls to Russia, reminder letters, supplications ... And for what? To receive an incomplete and unusable phrase. Is it out of malice? A perverse desire to play with our resilience? Or simply a highly developed form of Muscovite administrative procrastination?

Clearly Philippe Charlier isn't satisfied with Alexander's message. "We will have no right to." No right to WHAT?!!!

Dear Alexander,

Many thanks for your permission to allow us to exploit this analysis of the fragments from Hitler's jaw.

Late afternoon: 7 November 2017. I decide to send a reminder to Alexander.

Not to annoy him. Not to vex him. Choosing my words tactfully.

"I notice the care that you have taken to reply to me in French. Nonetheless ..."

Think.

"Nonetheless, a word is missing from your reply. You say: 'We will not have the right to ...' I imagine you mean 'the right to prevent you' or 'to forbid you'. Could you please just confirm?"

Lana? Nothing"! Lana is no longer in contact with the FSB, or with Alexander. The situation in Russia is becoming increasingly tense. Accusations are being made about Russian interference in the last presidential elections. No end is in sight for Syria and its military-humanitarian-religious nightmare either. The Putin regime is increasingly adopting a hard line of aggressive isolationism. Everything that comes out of the Kremlin smells of sulphur, as it did in the good old days at the height of Stalinism. And here we are benefiting from the goodwill of the Russian power that frightens so many people.

Seven days. It took Alexander seven days to pick out the right word, the most correct one, the one closest to his thoughts and send it to me. He even found several. He writes them in capital letters as if screaming them in my face: "WE WILL NOT ACCUSE (INCRIMINATE, INCULPATE) YOU."

Now we can carry out the analyses. As far as we know, these are the first ever performed with a scanning electron microscope.

A world first.

And the hope of resolving the mystery of Hitler's death.

"With current scientific techniques, we have the means to go much further than we could in 1945 or 1970," Dr. Charlier says enthusiastically. "We have the means to acquire a toxicological, chemical vision of this tartar. All kinds of advantages encouraging the revelation of the truth."

"You've done them all. St Louis, Richard the Lionheart, Charlemagne, Mary Magdalene ... So who's this one?"

Raphaël Weil knows Philippe Charlier very well. He's been working with him for about ten years. He suspects that this time, yet again, the object of study for the day is a leading historical figure.

"So, which era?"

"World War Two," the pathologist replies evasively. "The subject is a German," he goes on. "An important historical figure, very important, even."

Raphaël Weil looks down at the phial and sees the label with the initials "A.H." He asks no further questions. "I've only got the morning," is all he says, in a serious voice. "So let's get going." Of the three pieces collected, only two will be examined. The two larger ones. The less small, to be precise. The first is, at the most, 2.5 mm long by 1.3 mm thick. The second one is even thinner. But size doesn't matter. The microscope is so powerful that it can see things on the scale of a micron. Most importantly, it will tell us the chemical composition of these tiny samples. "The idea is to have confirmation of the composition of this tartar, what was the individual's diet, do we find only vegetable fibres, or also meat fibres? And then, last of all, I would like you to look for traces of poison."

Not having been able to take a sample of the blue traces, Philippe Charlier hopes to collect convincing information from the tartar.

Not least concerning the nature of the prostheses. "I wasn't able to examine those prostheses at an elemental level," he explains to Raphaël Weil. As in detective novels, the slightest detail can turn out to be the determining factor that resolves an investigation. Charlier is all too aware of this. That's why he warns his partner: "Those prostheses were quite badly damaged, and they didn't seem to me to be of very good quality. What I'd like you to do is to find their elemental signature. That's essential for an understanding of a possible interaction between them and the cyanide." In plain words, could the blue traces have been caused by a reaction between the cyanide and the metal of the prostheses? Did Hitler commit suicide by poisoning, as the Soviet investigators claimed in May 1945?

★   ★   ★

Is cyanide an effective poison? Is it painful? Hitler must have asked those questions to the doctors surrounding him in his bunker. We know that he checked its deadly effects on his dog Blondi, the Alsatian dog that he loved so much. As described earlier, he forced it to swallow a capsule. Many witnesses have described the scene. It was on 29 April 1945, in the middle of the night. Hitler no longer had any illusions about the outcome of the battle of Berlin. The Red Army was only a few streets away from his lair. In his eyes suicide was becoming the only imaginable end. But Himmler had just betrayed him by trying to negotiate directly with the Anglo-Americans; the same man who had supplied the cyanide capsules. And what if that "traitor to the Reich" had altered its composition? In a new fit of paranoia, Hitler decided to test the poison on his dog. Professor Haase, who was in charge of the hospital in the bunker, performed the macabre task with the help of the bunker's dog handler. The animal died. The versions of this episode vary according to the witnesses. Rattenhuber, the head of the Führer's personal guard, would later tell the Russians who took him prisoner that the dog suffered, cried out in agony and finally died after long convulsions. Hitler was profoundly shocked by the effects of the poison. Linge, Günsche, and Traudl Junge, one of Hitler's private secretaries, agreed on a different version: after Blondi's death, which he did not in fact witness, the Führer just acknowledged the effectiveness of the poison, showing no emotion. What is certain, on the other hand, is that the capsule worked perfectly. Was Hitler reassured? Yes, if we are to believe his entourage. He boasted of the merits of the poison to those around him. Traudl Junge reveals: "Hitler told us that death by poison was completely painless. Your nervous and respiratory systems were paralysed, and you died in a few seconds."* Was he lying to his devoted followers, or did he really not know the secondary effects of cyanide? All his life Hitler was suspicious about doctors and any treatment they prescribed. He must have known the terrible truth: poisoning of that kind is fatal, but absolutely not painless.

Depending on the dose of cyanide and the weight of the individual, their age, their state of health, and whether they have just eaten or not (it has been proven that cyanide acts more quickly on an empty stomach), death is more or less swift. But it always follows intense suffering. The first pains are manifested at the neurological and cardiovascular levels. Severe migraines appear very quickly. Then dizziness, confusion, a sense of inebriation ... After that comes the sense of being unable to breathe. Like a prolonged fit of apnoea. Anxiety is added to pain. The individual is seized by general convulsions and then loses consciousness. A few minutes later death comes by cardiac arrest. How long does it take to lose consciousness? It is all a matter of dosage, the type of cyanide, and the mode of its administration. Himmler would have taken fifteen minutes to die after taking his cyanide capsule. That detail was reported by British soldiers who had just arrested him by the Danish border and impotently witnessed his suicide on 23 May 1945. However, the death of the head of the SS also remains surrounded by shadowy areas. Himmler's autopsy, like the official report of his death, is not declassified even today. Both remain classified as "military secrets" in the British archives. They should not

*Traudl Junge, *Until the Final Hour*, op. cit., p. 177.

be accessible until 2045, or a hundred years after his death.

It is often noticed that a strong smell of bitter almonds is given off after the use of cyanide. In the episode with the dog Blondi, the witnesses are united in remembering this typical odour hanging in the air. That tenacious smell can linger for a long time. In the case of Hitler and Eva Braun, the Soviet forensic team noticed it during the autopsy. But the bodies had been carbonised and buried for several days: "[. . .] upon opening of the corpse a marked bitter almond smell was perceived. The conclusion reached is therefore that the death [. . .] was cause by poisoning with a cyanide compound."* Is it possible that the smell could have persisted for such a long time after the suicide? And particularly that it could have resisted intense carbonisation? Did the Soviet forensic team not exaggerate this theory of bitter almonds in order to confirm the cyanide theory? A theory, as we were able to establish in the Russian Archives, which Stalin preferred because, in his eyes, suicide by poison was a contemptible act for a warlord.

Some eyewitnesses to Hitler's death mention that famous smell of almonds. Others do not. That incoherence is easily explained. Today we know that the smell is not perceptible to everyone. It is accepted that between 20 and 40 per cent of people are insensitive to the smell. So should we still accept the hypothesis of cyanide in Hitler's suicide? Might the smell of bitter almonds reported by the witnesses to the suicide not have been caused solely by the death of Eva Braun? In her case, the use of cyanide has never been called into question. Linge remembers seeing traces of pain characteristic of this kind of poisoning on the young woman's face. In his memoirs, Hitler's valet adds that he found a small box on the table by the sofa where the two corpses were lying. It was in that box, according to him, that the Führer's wife's capsule had been stored. But it is important to note that this box "no longer exists" in the reports on the Soviet interrogations of Linge.

The night of 26–7 February 1946:

---

*Lev Bezymenski, *The Death of Adolf Hitler*, op. cit., p. 89.

Russian investigator: Did you find, on the sofa or somewhere nearby, on the floor, an ampoule or a box of poison that Eva Braun might have been able to use?

Linge: No. There was no trace of poison: no ampoule or box of poison has been discovered by me, even when I came back after cremating the corpses of Hitler and his wife to attend to their personal effects.

More contradictions, more doubts. Was Linge lying when he gave his answers to the officers of the Soviet secret services? Or when he wrote his memoirs? These changes to his story, the constant alteration of details, encouraged conspiracy theories, according to which Hitler might not have died in his bunker and might have been able to escape.

The Soviet investigators also had their doubts. They very quickly identified a flaw in Linge's scenario. That of establishing the deaths of Hitler and his wife:

Investigators: Which doctor confirmed the death of Hitler and his wife?

Linge: Bormann and I did not call any doctors because it was clear to us that Hitler and his wife were dead.

Investigators: Do you or Bormann have a degree in medicine?

Linge: No. Neither Bormann nor I have a degree in medicine.

Investigators: How in that case were you able to conclude that Hitler was indeed dead? Did you check his pulse, listen to his heartbeat?

Linge: No. We did none of any of that. We just reached the conclusion that he was dead by looking at him.

Investigators: How did you deduce that Hitler's wife, Eva Braun, was dead?

Linge: We concluded that she was dead only by her appearance. She remained inert. We thought she had poisoned herself.

[. . .]

Investigators: Were there doctors in the bunker of the Reich Chancellery?

293

Linge: Yes. There was Hitler's personal physician, Standartenführer Stumpfegger, and Hitler's former personal physician, Professor Haase.
Investigators: Why did you not summon those doctors to establish whether they were dead or not?
Linge: I cannot explain why we did not call doctors to confirm the deaths of Hitler and his wife.

Joël Poupon is very familiar with the effects of cyanide. Unlike Linge, he has no shortage of degrees. He is a specialist in mineral analysis in the laboratory of biological toxicology at the Saint-Louis-Lariboisière Hospital in Paris. Philippe Charlier immediately thought of him as the one to help him resolve the mystery of the blue stains found on Hitler and Eva Braun's teeth. Dr. Poupon's first reaction to the pictures of those stains was to say "that's incredible!" in an open manner quite unfamiliar in this rather reserved scientist. Perhaps it was the clarity and depth of that blue that left him anything but indifferent. A thick, almost sombre blue like ... Prussian blue. That is the name of this singular colour. A colour created chemically by mixing iron sulphate and potassium ferrocyanide. The blue owes its name to the fact that it was discovered by a German chemist in Berlin in the early eighteenth century. Its shade corresponds to many of the traces left on the teeth stored in the FSB archives. Dark blue – *kuanos* in ancient Greek – which gave us the word "cyanide."

As the quotation attributed to the Swiss doctor and philosopher Paracelsus has it, "Everything is a poison and nothing exists without toxicity; it is only the dose that makes a thing not a poison." For cyanide this is very much the case. If, in everyday language, cyanide is widely associated with a poison that causes sudden death, often used in the shady worlds connected with espionage, in reality this chemical compound is part of our everyday life. Without necessarily putting us in danger. Thus we find cyanide, hydrogen cyanide (HCN), in cherry and apricot stones, and indeed in apple pips. If it is quite rare to eat those stones, we do eat bitter almonds. And they contain a fair amount of cyanide. Luckily, unless we eat them in enormous quantities, our body has no difficulty resisting this natural cyanide.

This compound can also be extracted by chemical methods and produced in different forms: gaseous (used by the Nazis in the gas chambers), liquid, but also in soluble salts. In this last case we talk about potassium cyanide, ammonia cyanide, or calcium cyanide. Was this the case with these teeth? To check, you need only to lay hands on one of these capsules. Not just any capsule: one of those dedicated to senior Nazi dignitaries, the ones that were distributed in the Führerbunker. After a great deal of research in all the museums and archives of Europe, we learned that one of those capsules was kept in the pharmaceutical museum in Heidelberg, Germany. Sadly that information was correct but out of date. When we contacted them, the museum told us that they hadn't kept the capsule! A photograph, just a photograph, would have allowed us to check whether the cyanide was in liquid or salt form. No photograph! The staff of the museum hadn't kept anything. No photograph, even in black and white, even blurry. Nothing.

And a report? Some data, an analysis, anything ...? "Nein!" A "nein" not much different from the "niets" that we received so often in Moscow.

No capsules in Germany, nothing in Russia and nothing in France. Which left the British and the Americans.

A video dated 4 June 1945 gave us hope. This was a British news story soberly titled "The Last of Europe's Butchers." The "butcher" in question was none other than Himmler. In these pictures, you can see the house where he is supposed to have committed suicide, as well as his corpse. But most importantly it shows a cyanide capsule. The quivering, nasal voice of the journalist of the time explains that this is a capsule identical to the one used by Himmler. By freezing the image we can tell without risk of error that the cyanide is in the form of a colourless liquid, not powder. Only one of the ends of the capsule, thinner than the other, presents an opaque and coloured appearance.

In all likelihood, the cyanide used by Himmler must have been hydrogen cyanide, better known as Prussic acid. Prussic, because it was discovered in the late eighteenth century by a Swedish chemist, Carl Wilhelm Scheele, on the basis of Prussian blue. Furthermore, in German, Prussic acid is called *Blausäure*, or "blue acid." This form of cyanide is probably the most dangerous of the lot. Fatal from a dose of 50 milligrams. Hitler and his wife very probably received the same type of cyanide.

It remains to be seen if the dictator used this poison to kill himself. Günsche didn't think so!

He swore as much in a court in his country, in Germany. That was in 1945. The former SS man had just been freed from the Soviet camps after ten years of detention. He came back on 28 April 1956. He then discovered that Germany had been divided into two states in 1949. In the west, the three occupied zones under American, British, and French control formed the BRD (the Federal Republic of Germany). He learned, most importantly, that after being sentenced (in 1950) and condemned to twenty-five years in prison by a Soviet court (he would be freed six years later after an intervention by Konrad Adenauer, the Chancellor of the BRD), he also had some questions to answer in a German court. Not on his own behalf, but to bring a legal end to Hitler's fate. Ten years after the fall of the Nazi regime, it was time to rule once and for all on the death of the dictator. Günsche was not the only person close to Hitler to return to German soil. In 1944, Adenauer negotiated with the Soviets for the repatriation of the last German prisoners, those convicted of war crimes. Among them we find the three major witnesses of the last hours of Hitler, Günsche as well as Linge and Baur. Günsche and Linge's statements were recorded by the court in Berchtesgaden. They were made separately and over several days between 10 February and 19 June 1956.

Until 2010, these audio tapes slumbered on shelves in the State Archives in Munich. For technical reasons it was impossible to play them. Carefully restored, they are now accessible once again. In the recordings, the two men testify before a judge and representatives of the Bavarian police, including the head of the criminology service and an expert doctor. Once again, Linge and Günsche were interrogated about the last moments of Hitler in his bunker on 30 April 1945. The two men were exhausted by years of detention in Soviet jails, and particularly by the unstinting interrogation sessions conducted by the Russian secret services. For ten long years they were asked to repeat the same facts over and over again. Could they even remember with any precision what really happened on 30 April 1945? Had their memories not been erased by being repeatedly summoned and called into question?

Before judges in their country, the two men replied again, almost mechanically. Günsche declared: "As I have already said, I carried the body of Eva Braun – which was not covered – in my arms, and I noticed an extraordinarily strong smell of almonds. I did not notice that smell on Hitler. Particularly when his corpse was set down on the ground in the garden. When Bormann pulled away the blanket [covering Hitler], I brought myself quite close to it, and noticed nothing of the sort."*

Was the Führer's former aide-de-camp telling the truth? Unlike the Soviets, who stressed the theory of suicide by poisoning, an act which they thought was tainted with cowardice, did Günsche not want to present his boss as a man capable of killing himself with a bullet to the head? With all the warlike symbolism attached to the gesture in his eyes? The witness statement that Günsche gave to the German court, while rich in details, partially contradicts the one given by Linge. And it does so on certain important points. This is what Günsche has to say about discovering the corpse of Hitler and his wife in their antechamber:

Bormann and Linge prepared to enter Hitler's office. I followed them, and the following image presented itself to me: Hitler

---

*Audio archives of the interrogation of Otto Günsche, 1956, Munich State Archives (Staatsarchiv München), CD/DVD 71 à 74.

THE DEATH OF HITLER

was sitting in an armchair, almost facing the door, with his gaze directed towards the door to the left, his head leaning towards the right shoulder which rested against the arm of the chair, his hand dangling. [. . .] Eva Braun was lying on the sofa facing the door at the end of the room, her head turned towards Hitler, lying on her back, her legs slightly bent and drawn up towards the body; the shoes – light women's shoes – were on the sofa.*

The German investigators took note, but were surprised. They wanted details. Günsche obliged:

Hitler was sitting – I would say slightly sagging, but that wasn't very remarkable – on the armchair, leaning slightly towards the right, his right hand dangling over the right arm, his head leaning slightly to the right over his right shoulder. As far as I remember, his mouth was slightly open, his chin slightly slack, but I can't confirm that …

So Hitler had killed himself in an armchair and not on a sofa with Eva Braun. The aide-de-camp's version contradicted the one that Linge gave the German investigators:

When I entered the room, Hitler was sitting on the left – seen from my point of view – Hitler on the left, more precisely in the left corner of the sofa.

Investigator: So on the left from your point of view, on the right-hand side of the sofa?

Linge: Yes, right in the corner.†

Who is telling the truth? Is it possible to make a mistake like that? If we keep to the arrangement of the furniture in the room where the two suicides took place, the answer is no! The German investigators

*Ibid.
†Ibid.

returned repeatedly to the arrangement of the room. And they asked Linge to confirm it.

> **Investigator:** The room had a surface of about 8m2, it was more or less square, it had a door that opened from the central corridor, we may imagine that the corridor also served as a meeting place for the people from the entourage when waiting, you could also sleep there, there was a sofa.
> **Linge:** Only on the last day …
> **Investigator:** [. . .] The room had two other exits, on the right towards Adolf Hitler's bedroom, and on the left towards the bathroom. In terms of furniture, there was a sofa that was about 2 metres long, a normal sofa with arms. In front of that sofa, a table, not very large …
> **Linge:** A small table …
> **Investigator:** On either side of that table, you mentioned the presence of an armchair on each side. The sofa was against the wall facing the door, there was a table in front of it, and again to the right of this entrance a large desk with a chair in front of it. Herr Linge said that it was so cramped that one could barely pass between the table and the desk when there were chairs in the room. Then the painting of Frederick the Great – which is not of any great importance for us – above the desk, a painting that Hitler was particularly fond of.
> **Linge:** The painting was by Menzel.
> **Investigator:** So much for the site.*

It's hard to be more precise.

Unlike the written reports of the Soviets, for the first time Linge's and Günsche's statements are given here in oral form. The intonations of their voices, the tone and the phrasing, are additional information that helps us spot flaws in their answers.

Linge and Günsche seem very sure of their memories in these

*Ibid.

recordings. Neither of them has to search for words, neither is hesitant. And yet, for Linge, Hitler was facing the entrance on a sofa, beside Eva Braun. For Günsche, he was in front of the sofa, in an armchair.

This was a serious dilemma. Who were they to believe? Which version would they accept? Who was lying? Or who was mistaken?

Was Günsche telling the truth when he stated that Hitler hadn't taken poison?

This episode is a perfect illustration of the near impossibility of trusting statements by witnesses to Hitler's last moments. To get round this factual lacuna, there is, however, a solution: science.

★　　★　　★

Hence the presence of Philippe Charlier in the Laboratory of Solid State Physics in the Paris suburbs.

They have already spent over two hours going over the two fragments of tartar, micron by micron. Raphaël Weil works patiently and methodically. Nothing must escape him. In a few moments he will know everything about the chemical composition of these two pieces of evidence from the FSB archives. And perhaps he will find information about the composition of the prostheses. He is looking in particular for mercury, lead, arsenic, copper and, of course, iron. Because cyanide is impossible to reveal. Its traces disappear within twenty-four hours after its ingestion. And even faster if the corpse is burnt or kept at temperatures higher than 20° C. The clock shows 12:30pm. Raphaël Weil has gone on working for longer than planned. He has forgotten to be hungry. His concentration is at its peak, errors of interpretation are out of the question. Philippe Charlier is getting impatient. He awkwardly apologises to his fellow investigator. "Take your time," he repeats to conceal his excitement, before asking again: "So ... Is there any?" Calmly, after each calculation by the machine, the technician lists the chemical elements that have been revealed: calcium, potassium, phosphorus ... but no iron, or so little that it is impossible to determine whether it comes from the fragments or the "chamber" of the microscope in which the pieces of tartar were arranged. Philippe Charlier will find out no more than that. His disappointment is total.

In fact it isn't. Or not entirely.

Raphaël Weil turns towards the forensic scientist. Admittedly there is no information about the prostheses, but he has something better. He has absolute scientific proof of the authenticity of the tartar.

On the screen of the scanning electron microscope, a black-and-white image appears. It is blurred. It looks like a NASA command post from the time of the moon landings. Pebbly ground like that of a meteorite appears very gradually. The top of the screen comes into focus at last. "We're getting there, you have to be patient," Raphaël Weil says, without looking at me. Small bubbles form and fill the whole screen. Philippe Charlier recognises them immediately. "We have a classic view of dental tartar with these round shapes, like globules. This testifies to the phenomenon of calcification of dental plaque into dental tartar." The engineer confirms: "All these globules are really the signature of the tartar."

But the analysis doesn't stop there. Very quickly, a vegetable fibre appears. Then another one. On the other hand, no meaty fibre is revealed. A simple piece of meat of even a micron would have been enough to call into question the attribution of these teeth to Hitler. At the moment of his suicide, the dictator had been a vegetarian for several years. The pathologist is reassured by the absence of any elements of meat.

Can he go even further with these two fragments of tartar? Can he tell if the Führer fired a bullet into his mouth? Antimony, atomic number 51, barium, atomic number 56, lead, atomic number 82. That is what Raphaël Weil is looking for. After quickly checking the periodic table, the engineer precisely calibrates his electronic microscope. Philippe Charlier has chosen to concentrate on those three minerals with a very precise goal in mind. If a gun was fired into

Hitler's mouth, traces of those three chemical elements would inevitably be found in his dental tartar.

The theory of Hitler's suicide by firearm in the mouth was first presented by the British in November 1945.

Not even the best investigator would dare to inquire into the death of an individual without having access to the body, and without the opportunity to question eyewitnesses. But that was the situation of the Allied forces when they learned of Hitler's suicide, in early May 1945. As we have already described the Anglo-American staffs could not agree on confirming the Soviet version. The one which claims that the Führer had very probably escaped. Then they tried the impossible. To bring together the greatest possible number of witness statements with their few Nazi prisoners who had been in the Führerbunker. The British delivered their report to the occupying forces in Germany (the Americans, the Russians, and the French) on 1 November 1945. With pragmatism and realism, the report begins with a confession in the form of resignation: "The only conclusive evidence that Hitler is dead would be in the discovery, and certain identification, of the body. In the absence of this evidence, the only positive evidence consists in the circumstantial accounts of certain witnesses who were either familiar with his intentions or eye-witnesses of his fate." The British inquiry relied on a man who was close to Hitler. His name was Erich Kempka. He was thirty-five years old, and the dictator's personal chauffeur. But he had only found out about the Führer's death through Otto Günsche, Hitler's aide-de-camp. Kempka gives an account of that scene with Günsche in his memoirs, published in 1951: "It was a dreadful shock. 'How could that happen, Otto? I was speaking to him only yesterday! He was healthy and calm!' Günsche was still so overcome that he could not speak. He merely raised his right arm, imitated holding a pistol grip with his fist and pointed to his mouth."* Kempka presented this episode in the same way to British investigators in 1945. It was partly because of Kempka that the inquiry report by the British on 1 November 1945 states in black and white:

*Erich Kempka, *I was Hitler's Chauffeur*, op. cit., p. 77.

On 30 April at 2:30, Hitler and Eva Braun last appeared alive. They walked around the bunker and said goodbye to their direct entourage, the secretaries and the assistants, then withdrew to their apartments where they both committed suicide. Hitler by firing a bullet into his mouth and Eva Braun (although she had been given a revolver) by swallowing one of the capsules of poison distributed to everyone in the bunker.

Did the author of this report, the English historian Hugh Trevor-Roper, suspect that the Soviets hadn't told the whole truth about Hitler's death? During the official presentation of his inquiry to the officers of the occupying forces in Germany, Trevor-Roper attentively observed the attitude of the Russian representatives. A Red Army general was invited to react to the work of the British. Would the officer with the red star finally reveal something? Trevor-Roper would never forget his reply: "When invited to comment, [he] replied laconically and in a toneless voice: 'Very interesting.'"*

More than seventy years after this episode, we may be about to find out if Trevor-Roper was right. And if Kempka wasn't lying. Had Hitler fired a bullet into his mouth?

"Antimony?" Charlier asks.

"No," Raphaël Weil replies.

"Lead?"

Raphaël says: "No, and no barium."

This exchange of short phrases goes on for many minutes. Until the result of the last analysis.

"And?"

Charlier turns towards me. He had almost forgotten that I was there. My question surprises me. His "nothing" sounds like everything.

"Nothing!"

On the other hand, he is able to announce with certainty the end of the Hitler mystery.

*Hugh Trevor-Roper, *The Last Days of Hitler*, London, Pan Books, 1947, p. 6.

THE DEATH OF HITLER

★   ★   ★

Winter is about to fall like a languorous veil over Paris. Nearly two years of investigation are coming to an end.

Lana has stayed in Moscow. She is waiting.

I go to the Paris suburbs. Towards the west, just past Versailles, to Philippe Charlier's medical anthropology and forensic laboratory at the university of Versailles-Saint-Quentin.

A grimacing face and bulging eyes that leave no doubt about his mood; the welcome is far from warm. All around us, other equally malevolent expressions, some of them sticking out their tongues as if summoning us to a sacrificial rite.

"So, this one comes from Oceania. The other one is from West Africa ..." Philippe Charlier no longer knows where to put his masks and other totemic figures. His office looks more like the store-room of an imaginary museum of primitive art than the office of a forensic research scientist. Is it to help us remember that he is also an anthropologist?

A certain tension fills the office. Is it the doctor's white coat or the worrying assemblage of indigenous tutelary figures around us? Unless it's simply the exhaustion of those months of battles over a historical and political inquiry.

Philippe Charlier is sitting down, using the serious voice of those who are aware of the importance of the moment.

He begins: "Quite often the death of a historical figure is surrounded by mystery: people always imagine that the person isn't dead, that they have escaped. People don't like a classic death; it's too simple, too ordinary. Forensic work seeks to separate the true from the false, and supply definitive conclusions in line with scientific developments. I apply the same seriousness and the same objectivity to a case pleaded in a courtroom and an archaeological case."

A giant portrait of Henry IV rests on the floor, against the wall. It is a reconstruction made in 3D by Philippe Charlier's team. The old French king seems to be listening impatiently.

"And?" I ask, just to bring his circumlocutions to an end. "The human remains stored in Moscow: are they Hitler's or not?"

Not a sound. Then: "The skull, I don't know."

The visual examination carried out by Philippe Charlier, limited by the uncooperative attitude of the GARF teams, did not allow him to reach a conclusion: it was impossible to determine the age of that fragment of skull. Contrary to the declarations of Nicholas Bellantoni, the retired American archaeologist at the University of Connecticut, the extent of the sutures is not an indication of whether that piece of skull belonged to a young person. Philippe Charlier is categorical. The x-rays of Hitler's face made in the autumn of 1944 allowed him to contest the analysis of his American colleague. "In those x-rays, you can see the sutures at the top of Hitler's skull," he explains. "These sutures are quite wide apart. That is the proof that you can't claim that because sutures are open they belong to a young individual. It's an argument that doesn't hold water." As you may remember, Nick Bellantoni explained in 2009 that: "The bone seemed to be very thin," the American archaeologist says. "Male bone tends to be more robust, and the sutures where the skull plates come together seem to correspond to someone under forty."[*]

Philippe Charlier insists: "The skull belongs to an adult. Full stop. On the other hand. I do know about the teeth. They're Hitler's!"

I go on: "Are you a hundred per cent certain?"

"In forensic science, we don't like to give figures for our results, but we are certain that this isn't a historical forgery. And we are certain that there is an anatomical match between the x-rays, the descriptions of the autopsies, the accounts of the witnesses, mainly those who made and manufactured those dental prostheses, and the reality that we have held in our hands. All of these analyses taken together confirm to us that the remains examined are those of Adolf Hitler, who died in Berlin in 1945. And all of this destroys the theories of his possible survival."

[*]https://www.youtube.com/watch?v=ZqrrjzfnsVY

And the bullet in the mouth? And the cyanide?

Did the bits of dental tartar allow him to answer those two questions? Was the British theory in 1945 about Hitler's death erroneous? Was Trevor-Roper mistaken?"

"The chemical analysis of the surface of dental tartar has enabled us to look for traces of metals that are found when a shot has been fired into the mouth. Normally there are combustion gases, gunpowder, incandescence deposited in the oral cavity, the tongue, the mucous membrane … and therefore in the tartar. But we have found nothing."

So Hitler didn't fire a bullet into his mouth!

Kempka lied when he said that Günsche, the aide-de-camp, had mimed the gesture of a pistol being fired into his mouth. Even Günsche stated in 1956, when questioned by the German court, that Kempka had made everything up. Here is his deposition:

I rule out the possibility that Hitler fired a bullet into his mouth. I would also like to insist that I have never spoken to anyone in the bunker about the way that Hitler fired a bullet into his head and under what circumstances. I only told certain people present that Hitler had shot himself and that his body had been burned.*

We had to wait for over half a century to prove Günsche right, and confirm that Hitler did not shoot himself in the mouth. And right beyond any possible doubt. Science triumphs over all the witness statements taken together, over emotion, over attempts at manipulation. And it confirms the version repeated several times by the man who first discovered the bodies of Hitler and Eva Braun: Heinz Linge, the dictator's loyal valet. During the interrogations carried out by the Soviets, in the interviews given to the newspapers, to the radio stations and television channels, in his memoirs published after his death in 1980, it's always the same scenario: "When I came

*Munich State Archives (Staatsarchiv München), op. cit.

in, on my left, I saw Hitler. He was in the right-hand corner of the sofa … Hitler's head was tilted slightly forward. On his right temple there was a hole the size of a ten-cent coin."*

And the cyanide?

And the blue traces on the teeth?

Philippe Charlier has to admit his helplessness. Those blue traces are surprising, startling, and most importantly, disconcerting.

But the scientist can't go any further without taking a sample of the teeth kept in Moscow. Alexander Orlov claims it's impossible. For his part, Dmitri confirmed to Lana that she had to move on to something else.

Switch to a new inquiry.

"They told me that no analysis will be carried out." Lana herself told me that we could hope for nothing else for now. "They just wanted proof that the teeth belonged to Hitler. Now that it's done they're closing everything up again."

But what if we had concluded that they weren't his?

My question, rhetorical though it was, made Lana freeze: "That would have been a big problem for Russia."

*Ibid.

EPILOGUE

Paris, London, Moscow, New York, Beijing ... May 2018

"A scientific study is debunking conspiracy theories about Hitler escaping to South America." "A new study of Hitler's teeth confirms that he did indeed die in 1945."

In English, French, Chinese, German, Vietnamese – the information was relayed by the press all over the world. Thanks to a famous internet search engine, I am able to consult the headlines on my computer screen. They confirm, if confirmation is needed, that Hitler remains an inescapable historical figure. And that in a way the question of his death and the precise conditions under which it occurred still excites the public.

More than two years have passed since my first visit to Moscow, in the rather inhospitable offices of GARF. Two years after my meeting with the archivists Dina Nikolaevna Nokhotovich and Nikolai Vladimirsev. I am thinking about them. We assured them that we wouldn't make the same mistake as Nick Bellantoni with his team of American journalists, namely asserting scientific facts without validating them in a renowned scientific publication. We didn't want to lay ourselves open to criticism and create suspicion and doubts about our work. Rumours about Hitler's survival after the fall of Berlin in early May 1945 would only have been reinvigorated. Philippe Charlier was aware of the obligation to publish his results, which were oh so vital to Lana and me. The French pathologist never doubted. That's what he kept telling us throughout our investigation. In fact, to be frank, Philippe Charlier did doubt. Just as we did. In silence.

Particularly when the officials at GARF, our dear Dina and Nikolai, denied him the right to analyse the fragment of skull. On the other hand, after the examination of the teeth and particularly the agreement by the Russian authorities to exploit those small pieces of tartar with a scanning electron microscope, hope was reborn. The scientific conclusions of the investigation were drawn up by Philippe Charlier and us, working together with extreme caution, reread several times and then submitted to an international scientific journal, the *European Journal of Internal Medicine* (EJIM). This journal practices what is called "peer review," meaning that the work put forward by researchers has been checked and validated (or not) by other researchers. The EJIM is the official journal of the European Federation of Internal Medicine (EFIM), but also of the associations of several European countries such as Iceland, Norway, and Sweden.

On 18 May 2018, Philippe Charlier sent me a cryptic text: "It's coming out today!" So the article had been validated, and the results of the investigation – our investigation – were recognised by the international scientific community. As we expected, its impact would soon go beyond the strict contours of the scientific world. The website of *Le Monde*, the famous French daily newspaper, almost immediately picked up the information and set out Dr Charlier's analysis point by point. It underlined the main pillars of our work, particularly the absence of gunpowder in the tartar (which rules out the theory of suicide by bullet in the mouth), but even more so the authentication of the teeth. And *Le Monde*'s headline left no room for doubt: "Some teeth preserved in Moscow are indeed those of Adolf Hitler, who died in 1945." Over the days that followed, the world's press relayed the news. All the way to Russia, of course. To the FSB and the Kremlin. Lana knew, and called me to tell me. "They've read it, they've seen it ..." she begins nervously on the telephone. I try to ask her who she's talking about, but I know her too well to hope to stop her halting flow of words. She isn't listening to me. Too excited, she goes on, her voice a few tones too high: "Alexander, Denis, Dmitri, they've all seen ..." And Dina

Nokhotovich? Does Dina, the keeper of the skull, the faithful archivist of GARF regret preventing the analysis of that key piece of bone from the Hitler mystery? "Ah, Dina ...!" Lana sighs. "She's not at GARF any more!" Dina, not at GARF?! My imagination goes into overdrive. Has she been fired? Exiled somewhere beyond the Arctic Circle, to Siberia, synonymous with the supreme punishment for opponents of the regime? Lana is amused by my fears. "No, she retired." After forty-three years of good and loyal service, Dina decided to leave that bit of skull and those hundreds of historical documents devoted to Hitler's death to a new generation of archivists. All through her life she has protected those shades of history from prying eyes. The world was not to know, her superiors told her. But that was another time, the time of the Soviet Union in the 1970s. Today I think of her and of all those Soviet officials (whether they were members of the secret services or the state archives) who, without always knowing why, helped to create the legend of Hitler's survival. All because Stalin wanted to keep the death of the German dictator secret. I think of them.

PHOTO ADDENDUM

Photo 1: The two main pieces from the Hitler file kept at GARF (State Archives of the Russian Federation) in Moscow. According to the Russians, on the left are parts of the sofa on which Hitler committed suicide and on the right, in a computer diskette box, is a piece of Hitler's skull.

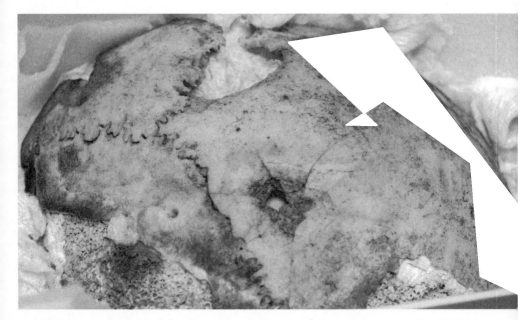

Photo 2: A close-up of the fragment of the top of the cranium stored at GARF in Moscow. It is said to have been discovered outside the emergency exit of the Führerbunker in Berlin in May 1946 during the Soviet counter-inquiry into Hitler's death. The impact of the bullet as well as signs of cremation and traces of earth are perfectly visible.

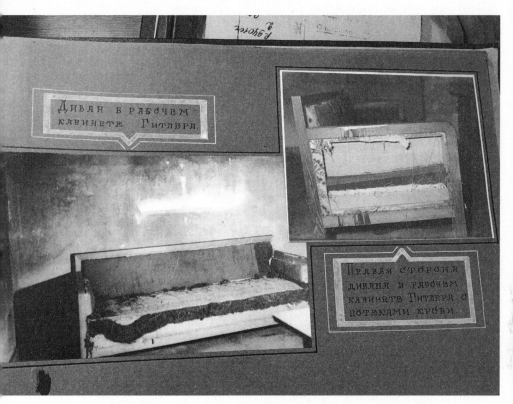

Photo 3: These photographs were taken by the Soviet investigators in May 1946 in the Führerbunker in Berlin. It is said to be the sofa on which Hitler committed suicide. On the right side of the headrests are dark trickles – could this be the dictator's blood?

Photo 4: Detail of the pieces of the sofa kept at GARF in Moscow. The traces of dark trickles (just beside the piece of fabric) remain visible seventy years later.

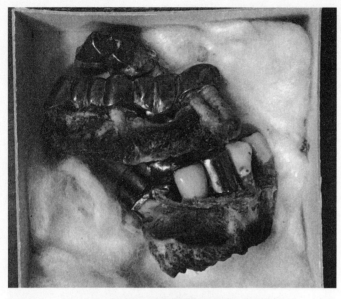

Photo 5: Pieces of Hitler's jaw stored at the archives of the Russian secrets services (TsA FSB). The Soviet investigators were said to have removed them from the corpse discovered on 4 May 1945 in the gardens of the Reich Chancellery in Berlin.

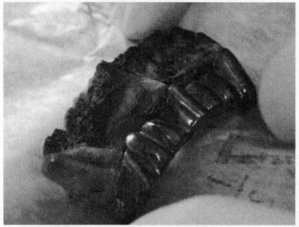

Photo 6: Detail of part of Hitler's teeth. The traces of carbonisation on the remains of the jaw prove that cremation was intense, but not prolonged enough to damage either teeth or prostheses.

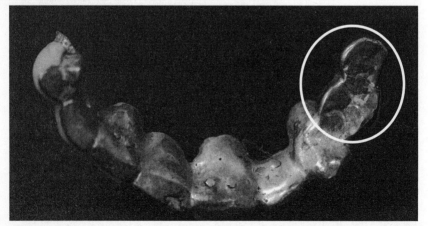

Photo 7: Blue stains that appear on one side of the jaw (in white circle) are a surprisingly bright blue and raised the question if it was possibly a trace left by cyanide.

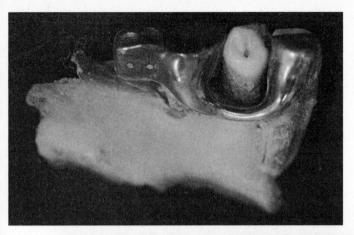

Photo 8: At the end of his life, Hitler only had four good teeth with no prostheses. In order to save one of those he asked his dentist to make this prosthesis in the shape of a gutter. Its unique and recognisable shape made it easier to identify these as his teeth.

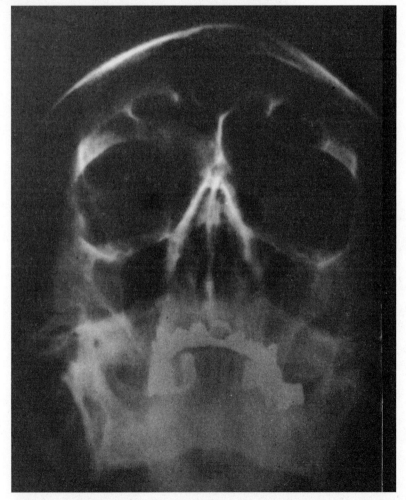

Photo 9: An x-ray taken of Hitler's face in Autumn 1944 (stored in the U.S. National Archives in College Park, Maryland, No. 27500765). The metallic prostheses of the teeth appear in the form of white patches, particularly the one with the gutter, bottom left.

NOTES ON THE ARCHIVES

The FSB officials didn't allow us to record the inventory numbers of the documents made available to us. So we are presenting the documents from the FSB archives and cited in this work under the term 'TsA FSB." TsA means Tsentral'nyi arkhiv, or Central Archives.

For the Russian State Military Archives (RGVA, Rossiiskii Gosudarstvenni Voennyi Arkhiv) the documents cited are taken from the individual files of the Nazi prisoners judged to be war criminals. We present them under the term "RGVA."

The GARF archives are referenced according to the number listed on the file in question, along with the folio.

p. 39 : GARF 9401/2/552, f.8-9.
p. 40 : GARF 9401/2/551, f.225.
p. 42 : GARF 9401/2/552, f.191-193.
p. 43-44 : GARF 9401/2/552, f.280-284.
p. 83 : GARF 9401/2/552, f.83.
p. 85 : GARF 9401/2/552, f. 84.
p. 96-97 : GARF 9401/2/552, f. 93.
p. 107 : GARF 9401/2/550, f.68-69.
p. 126-127 : GARF 9401/2/556, f.175.
p. 127-128 : GARF 9401/2/556, f.177.
p. 136 : TsA FSB.
p. 145-146 : TsA FSB.
p. 153 : GARF 9401/2/556, f.178.
p. 156-158 et 189 : GARF 9401/2/556, f.179.
p. 159-160 : GARF 9401/2/556, f.182.

p. 169-173 : RGVA.

p. 174-178 : GARF 9401/2/551, f.49-61.

p. 193 : GARF 9401/2/552, f.113.

p. 194-195 : GARF 9401/2/552, f.2.

p. 195 : GARF 9401/2/552, f.2, 1.

p. 196 : GARF 9401/2/552, f.1 pour la photo, f.4 pour le texte.

p. 197-198 : GARF 9401/2/552, f.5.

p. 198-199 : GARF 9401/2/552, f. 12-13.

p. 205-206 : GARF 9401/2/553, f.97 et f.103.

p. 207 & 210 : GARF 9401/2/550, f.71.

p. 210 : GARF 9401/2/550, f.72.

p. 213 : GARF 9401/2/553, f.97.

p. 218 : GARF 9401/2/553, f.98 et 99.

p. 215 : GARF 9401/2/553, f.100.

p. 216 : GARF 9401/2/553, f.103.

p. 216 : GARF 9401/2/550, f.76.

p. 217 : GARF 9401/2/551, f.32.

p. 231-232 : GARF 9401/2/551, f.134-139.

p. 235 : GARF 9401/2/551, f.136.

p. 235 : GARF 9401/2/551, f.59.

p. 236-237 : GARF 9401/2/551, f.30.

p. 238-239 : TsA FSB.

p. 240 : GARF 9401/2/550, f.26.

p. 240-241 : TsA FSB.

p. 241-242 : TsA FSB.

p. 250-251 : GARF 9401/2/552, f.275, f.574 et f.363.

p. 252 : GARF 9401/2/552, f.263.

p. 253 : GARF 9401/2/551, f.47.

p. 254 : GARF 9401/2/552, f.268.

p. 255 : GARF 9401/2/552, f.276.

p. 255 : GARF 9401/2/552, f.276.

p. 255-256 : GARF 9401/2/552, f.197.

p. 256 (photo) : GARF 9401/2/552, f.199.

p. 259 : GARF 9401/2/551, f.55 et 138.

p. 260 : GARF 9401/2/552, f.140.

p. 260 : GARF 9401/2/552, f.58.

p. 261-262 : GARF 9401/2/552, f.140.

p. 262 : GARF 9401/2/552, f.141.

p. 263 : GARF 9401/2/552, f.207.

p. 266 : GARF 9401/2/556, f.197.

p. 267 : GARF 9401/2/552, f.198.

p. 293 : GARF 9401/2/551, f.137.

p. 303 : GARF 9401/2/552, f.114.

p. 303 : GARF 9401/2/552, f.116.

ACKNOWLEDGEMENTS

To the various authorities of the Russian archives:
  Larisa Alexandrovna Rogovaya, GARF, State Archive of the
    Russian Federation
  Vladimir Ivanovich Korotaev (RGVA, Russian State Military
    Archives)
  Oleg Konstantinovich Matveev (COS, Press relations centre, FSB)

To the scientists who have brought us their skills and illumination
  throughout the investigation:
  Raphaël Weil, Joël Poupon, Patrick Rainsard.

To Philippe Charlier and his constant enthusiasm, without whom
  we couldn't have taken to its conclusion the scientific inquiry
  into the teeth attributed to Hitler.

Special thanks to :
  Olivier Wlodarczyk and the whole Ego team who have always
    believed in this crazy investigation
  Alexander Orlov (of Russian Ministry of Foreign Affairs) for his
    valuable support.

To our inexhaustible translators:
  Tatiana Shutova for Russian and Ulrike Zander and Aymeric Le
    Delliou for German.

Thanks from Lana Parshina:
  To Lyudmila Vasilievna Dvoynikh and Natalia Petrovna Parshina.

Thanks from Jean-Christophe Brisard:
  To Céline Lison for her pertinent rereadings.
  To Claude Quétel who, thanks to his memories, made me want
    to throw myself into this adventure.

INDEX